To Richard,
A little gift that you have wanted for a while,
I hope you enjoy reading every page from front to back! Then
I can try and learn about it!!!

with all my heart
Amanda (Sunday 19th Aug 2001)
x x♡xx

The Concise
Encyclopedia of
FORMULA
ONE

The Concise
Encyclopedia of
FORMULA
ONE

by David Tremayne and Mark Hughes

p

This is a Parragon Book
This edition published in 2000
Parragon
Queen Street House
4 Queen Street
Bath BAI IHE, UK

Copyright © Parragon 1998

ISBN : 0-75254-220-6 Hardback
ISBN : 0-75224-464-0 Paperback
Printed in Indonesia

Edited, designed and produced by
Haldane Mason, London

Acknowledgements

Art Director: Ron Samuels
Editorial Director: Sydney Francis
Managing Editor: Charles Dixon-Spain
Editors: Ian Penburthy, Conan Nicholas
Design: Janet James
Index: David Tremayne
Illustrator: Richard Burgess
Picture Research: Charles Dixon-Spain

Picture Acknowledgements:

All pictures by LAT, except the following:

Behram Kapadia: 1, 21 top, 25 top,
36 bttm, 37, 39 top, 40, 42 bttm, 43, 49,
50 top, 51 bttm, 53 top, 54 bttm, 55,
top, 57 bttm, 60 bttm left, 61 bttm left,
94 bttm centre & right, 100 top, 102 bttm,
103, 122 bttm, 127 top, 161 bttm left &
right, 198, 199, 204 bttm, 214 top, 215,
223 bttm, 226 top, 228, 229, 230, 231, 239,
240 bttm, 241 bttm,

Sporting Pictures: 194 top & middle

CONTENTS

Introduction

Formula One Grand Prix motor racing is one of the world's most exciting sporting activities, blending leading-edge technology with human strengths and frailties and the feral appeal of raw speed.

Half a century ago, the current concept of a primary post-war racing formula was created when the Fédération Internationale de l'Automobile (FIA) in Paris tasked its sporting subsidiary, the Commission Sportive Internationale (CSI), with identifying the way forward after the

hiatus of World War Two. That led to the introduction of the 1.5-litre supercharged/4.5-litre normally aspirated formula that formed the basis for the inauguration of an official World Championship for Drivers in 1950, and thus proved the foundation for today's globally popular series.

Over the years, the formula has often changed. When entries subsided in 1951, the years 1952–53 saw F1

run to the current Formula Two regulations for 2-litre normally aspirated cars. From 1954 until 1960, the years during which the seeds of the current British domination of the sport were sown, it catered for 2.5-litre normally aspirated and 750cc supercharged cars. Between 1961 and

Below: James Hunt drives the McLaren which would take him to his crown in 1976.

Opposite: The crowds cheer on as another GP ends with the victorious on the podium.

Right: *Glamour at the 1998 Australian GP.*

Opposite above: *Frentzen battles to remain in touch with Hakkinen, who once again beats him to the podium and champagne (Opposite below).*

1965, this was superseded by the 1.5-litre normally aspirated formula which, in turn, gave way to 3-litre engines, unsupercharged, from 1966 to 1987. At the same time, this 'Return to Power' formula made allowance for 1.5-litre supercharged engines, a route that nobody travelled until Renault returned to F1 in 1977. Within five years, everybody had to have a turbocharged engine to stay competitive, and such was the imbalance between turbos and 'atmos' that, in 1987, 3.5-litre normally aspirated engines were allowed.

The next change came for 1989, when only 3.5-litre non-supercharged engines were permitted, which subsequently was amended to 3 litres at the end of the traumatic 1994 season. This is the formula that exists today, when the cars, although less powerful than some of their forerunners, continue to lap ever faster.

This relentless acquisition of speed, of course, is one of the primary appeals of a sport that never stands still. Development is everything, whether it concerns the cars and engines themselves, or merely the politics that are an inherent part of everyday paddock life. F1 is in a continuous state of change, generating fresh news and interest by the week.

Formula One's story has been compelling, right from the moment when Dr Giuseppe Farina triumphed in the British Grand Prix at Silverstone on May 13 1950 in his red Alfa Romeo, to usher in the era of the World Championship. Since then, some have questioned whether the championship really is a measure of true greatness, or merely an overblown adjunct that can obscure the truth and simply get in the way of individual performances. In the main, however, it is a reasonable indication of ability and a means of grading drivers, although when the likes of Stirling Moss and Gilles Villeneuve went uncrowned, one could sympathize with the viewpoint of its detractors.

Therein lies another appeal. Within these pages, you will find profiles of drivers, and selections of the best races, the best cars and the best tracks that have featured in F1 during the past half-century. You may disagree with some of the choices, for we all have personal favourites and differing criteria for selecting and judging these things. If nothing else, what you read here may evoke powerful argument for or against the views expressed. Which can only be a good thing.

David Tremayne
London, 1999

1

THE DRIVERS

CHAPTER 1

The World Champions

THE GREATEST DRIVERS OF F1

It is given to few men to stand at the very top of their profession. Since the World Championship was officially inaugurated in 1950 only 26 men have been crowned as the world's champion driver, though some of them have achieved the feat on more than one occasion.

Giuseppe Farina

1950

Born in Turin in 1906, Giuseppe Farina was the son of the eldest of the Farina brothers, who would go on to form the famous styling house of Pininfarina. Although he raced from an early age, it wasn't until the mid-1930s, after he'd gained a doctorate in political studies, that he began to establish an international reputation. Prior to the intervention of World War Two, he had looked set to become one of the top Grand Prix drivers.

As it was, Farina was already 40 years old when he resumed his career post-war, and 44 by the time the World Championship was inaugurated in 1950. As a driver with the crack Alfa Romeo squad, however, he was well placed to achieve success in this new contest. With the rival Ferrari team not yet fully competitive, Farina's Alfa team-mate, Fangio, was the only real opposition.

Although Fangio was generally faster, Farina enjoyed better reliability. On the way to Monza for the sixth and final round of the series, Farina had won the British and Swiss Grands Prix, while Fangio had won in Monaco, Belgium and France, and was marginally ahead on points. In the Italian race, though, Fangio suffered a series of mechanical problems, giving Farina an easy win and the title of the first-ever World Champion.

Farina remained in Grand Prix racing until his retirement in 1955, only to perish in a road accident in 1966. Fangio, for one, always suspected that was how he might go.

Left: *Head back, arms straight, Giuseppe Farina introduced a new style to driving that was swiftly emulated by newcomers such as Stirling Moss.*

Above: *Fangio was never happy with Ferrari, and the Lancia-derived contender of 1956 was frequently a handful. Nevertheless, the great Argentinian took his fourth title that season.*

Juan Manuel Fangio

1951 · 1954 · 1955 · 1956 · 1957

Although Juan Manuel Fangio was born in 1911 in Balcarce, Argentina, his house-painter father was an Italian immigrant. Given such a humble background, Fangio's early racing exploits in his home country were with a series of modified road cars, financed with the help of people from his home town. Victory in a post-war Argentinian race against top European drivers led to him being funded by the national automobile club to race a Maserati in Europe. Once there, his sensationally fast driving brought him to the attention of Alfa Romeo, who quickly signed him up for 1950.

After losing out to team-mate Farina in the first year of the championship, Fangio took his first title for Alfa in 1951. He'd driven his Alfetta to victory in two of the first three races – Switzerland and France – but by mid-season Ferrari's new car had gained the upper hand. Therefore the second half of the season required him to mount a strong rearguard defence, but Fangio retained the serene calm that was always a trade mark and clinched the title with a beautifully judged win in the final event of the season in Spain.

A neck-breaking accident early in 1952 kept him out of racing for most of that season, and it was late 1953 before he won again – in a Maserati. This association continued into the early part of 1954 when, using the team's new 250F model, he took wins in the opening two Grands Prix of the season. His contract for that year, however, was with Mercedes-Benz, returning to Grand Prix racing for the first time since the war. He gave its new W196 model a victorious début in France, and a further three wins gave him his second World Championship.

There was more of the same in 1955, Fangio winning four of the six races that comprised that year's championship and a third title. Mercedes then withdrew from racing, and Fangio signed with Ferrari, the team that he had always considered to be 'the competition'. It was an uneasy alliance, and although he took yet another championship, it was an accomplishment that required the help of team-mate Peter Collins who, in the Italian Grand Prix, gallantly gave up his car after Fangio's had broken down, thereby relinquishing his own title hopes.

Fangio was relieved to return to Maserati for 1957 when, 46 years old, he enjoyed what was probably his finest season. His fifth championship – a feat that remains unequalled to this day – was clinched with a staggering drive at the German Grand Prix, where he fought back to win after a slow pit stop had put him behind the two leading Ferraris. It was his final, and greatest, victory.

Fangio retired part way through the following year, by which time the Maserati was no longer competitive, and returned to Argentina, where he continued to be revered and built up a highly successful Mercedes dealership. He died in 1995 and is remembered by many as the greatest of them all.

Left: *Already 38 years old when he arrived in Europe, one of the greatest of Fangio's many assets was his incredible stamina.*

Left: *Classic motor racing. At Monaco in 1957 Fangio's poise in the elegant Maserati 250F epitomized everything about an era that was soon to change radically.*

Right: *The son of inter-war Alfa Romeo ace Antonio Ascari, Alberto proved an even stronger force, one of the few capable of resisting – and overcoming – Fangio.*

Below: *The wet road at Spa in 1952 held no fears for Ascari. That year, and again in 1953, he and the 2-litre Ferrari 500 were an utterly dominant combination.*

Alberto Ascari

1952 · 1953

The son of pre-war Alfa Romeo Grand Prix ace Antonio Ascari, Alberto was 6 years old when his father was killed in an accident in the 1925 French Grand Prix. Nevertheless Ascari Jnr wanted only to race and, after beginning his career on motor cycles, entered his first car race in 1940, courtesy of Enzo Ferrari, a former friend and team-mate of Antonio's. Ascari impressed with his speed before having to retire the car, and he managed to fit in a couple more races with a Maserati before World War Two brought racing to a halt. He immediately resumed his career post-war with Scuderia Ambrosio, where his team-mate, the older Luigi Villoresi, adopted him as a protégé. His abundant promise led to Ferrari offering both drivers a place

on his Grand Prix team for 1949. They were to stay there for the next five years.

It was midway through 1951 before Ferrari had a car with which to beat the previously dominant Alfa Romeos, but once the breakthrough had been made, Ascari won both the German and Italian Grands Prix, and was runner-up to Fangio in the World Championship. The following two seasons saw complete domination by Ascari and Ferrari. Armed with the fastest car in the field, he was unbeatable and won every single championship Grand Prix he contested in 1952, a feat that has never been repeated. With one world title under his belt, he quickly added another, taking five further wins in 1953, despite the increasing potency of the Fangio/Maserati combination.

Ascari then left Ferrari for Lancia, where he showed all of his familiar blistering speed, although results were restricted because of poor reliability. In the 1955 Monaco Grand Prix, he crashed into the harbour. However, he was only slightly injured and while recuperating visited Monza, where the Ferrari team was testing a sports car. He asked if he could try a few laps, and during one of these he crashed fatally, a result of suspected tyre failure. The only man who could match Fangio's speed was gone.

Mike Hawthorn

▶ 1958

Britain's first World Champion, Mike Hawthorn retired after attaining the feat, but by cruel irony was killed a few months later in a road accident.

Along with Stirling Moss, Hawthorn represented a new generation of world-class British drivers. His progress through British club racing and on to the international stage was meteoric, but aided by the adoption of Formula 2 as the World Championship category for 1952. This meant that Hawthorn's strong performances in an F2 Cooper-Bristol prepared by his father – a keen motor cycle racer pre-war – got him noticed. To such an extent, in fact, that Hawthorn drove for Ferrari from 1953. He won his first Grand Prix that year in France, in a sensational duel with Fangio.

After a short break driving for British teams, Hawthorn went back to Ferrari for a year in 1958, the year of his title win. His hopes were pinned

on the new V6 powered Dino 246. It was a strong tool, both powerful and reliable, and he had his close friend Peter Collins and Italian Luigi Musso as team-mates. Chief competition came from the streamlined Vanwalls of Stirling Moss and Tony Brooks.

Although the Vanwalls were frequently faster, Hawthorn and the reliable Dino Ferrari invariably scored well. Furthermore, following the deaths of both Musso (in France) and Collins (in Germany), Hawthorn was very much team leader, whereas Moss and Brooks tended to score off each other. Hawthorn's sole win of the year was in the French Grand Prix, yet he entered the final round four points ahead of Moss, who had already won three times. Moss made it four in Morocco, but Hawthorn tailed him home and took the title by a single point.

Mike Hawthorn retired to run the family garage business, but in January 1959 fatally crashed his Jaguar road car.

Above: Hawthorn and his close friend and team-mate Peter Collins were on the receiving end of Fangio's driving lesson in the 1957 German GP at the Nürburgring.

Left: But for Stirling Moss's intervention, Hawthorn might well have been penalized out of the 1958 Portuguese GP at Oporto. Instead, he went on to beat Moss by a mere point to become Britain's first-ever champion.

Jack Brabham
1959 · 1960 · 1966

A dirt-track racer in his native Australia, Jack Brabham's early European successes came in partnership with the Cooper Car Company. After winning two World Championships, in 1959 and 1960, he set up on his own as a racing car constructor, becoming the first – and so far the only – man to win a world title in a car bearing his own name.

In 1957, Brabham had shown indecently well against faster opposition in the rear-engined 'bob-tail' Cooper in sports car races. So well, in fact, that the Cooper family decided to base an F1 car around the same concept. It was to cause a revolution in race car design, and Brabham was the first beneficiary.

In 1959, Brabham and the Coopers faced a predominantly front-engined field and, aside from his own team-

Right: Heralding the arrival of the new era and a new champion, Jack Brabham and his hump-backed rear-engine Cooper at the Monaco GP in 1959.

mate, Bruce McLaren, the main competition proved to be the privately entered Cooper of Stirling Moss. Although Moss was invariably faster, his Rob Walker-owned car was fitted with a Colotti gearbox, which

let him down with unfailing regularity, leaving the way clear for Brabham. He won both the Monaco and British Grands Prix of that year to take his and Cooper's first World Championship.

There was a rush to copy the Cooper recipe in 1960, notably by Lotus which produced its first rear-engined F1 car. Worse still, Moss was driving one of them. Cooper responded with a lower car and better suspension. The season looked to be shaping up in Moss' favour until he suffered a serious accident in practice for the Belgian Grand Prix, which put him out for most of the remainder. With his major rival sidelined, Brabham swept all before him, winning five Grands Prix in succession to take a second title.

Phil Hill

1961

The United States' first Formula One World Champion, Phil Hill was the son of a postmaster in California and made a name for himself in the post-war road racing boom that took place there.

As the stature of the events in which Hill competed grew, he came to the attention of America's Ferrari importer, Luigi Chinetti. No doubt motivated by commercial considerations, Chinetti encouraged Enzo Ferrari to give Hill a try-out in Europe.

Thereafter Cooper rather fell behind in the design game, and Brabham left at the end of 1961 to set up with his old friend Ron Tauranac as designer. The Brabham cars soon became competitive, although the early successes were not gained with Brabham behind the wheel, but Dan Gurney. Brabham didn't win, in fact, until 1966. But once he started, there was no stopping him.

A new 3-litre formula doubled the engine capacity of F1 cars and took effect from 1966. Most teams were not prepared for the change, but Brabham had shrewdly opted for the simple engineering of the Repco V8 motor. It wasn't the most powerful engine, but it was the most reliable, and his wins in France, Britain, Holland and Germany enabled him to canter to a third world title at 40 years of age.

He continued for another four years and was still winning, or leading races, in his final season. Perhaps the quietest champion, he has since helped guide his three sons in racing careers.

Ferrari used Hill primarily in sports car events for a couple of years, and it wasn't until 1958 that he made the breakthrough to the Ferrari Grand Prix team, following the successive deaths of Luigi Musso and Peter Collins. It was unfortunate that the team was in a period of decline at this point, and outdated front-engined cars limited his success through the following two seasons.

For 1961 though, it was all change. Ferrari had at last produced a rear-engined F1 car and, furthermore, was the only manufacturer properly prepared for the new 1.5-litre formula.

Top: One year on, and Brabham's Cooper was just as dominant, winning him the championship with five successive Grands Prix.

Above: In 1966, Jack Brabham made history as the only man ever to win the World Championship in a car of his own design and manufacture.

Its cars were by far the most potent and, despite the heroic efforts of Stirling Moss in an underpowered Lotus, the championship battle boiled down to a tussle between Hill and his team-mate, Count Wolfgang von Trips. Entering the penultimate round of the year, von Trips was marginally ahead on points, but tangled early in the race with the Lotus of Jim Clark, sending the Ferrari into the crowd. Fifteen spectators – and the unfortunate Trips – were killed. Hill went on to win the race and, in the most tragic of circumstances, his World Championship.

He never again found himself in a properly competitive FI car, his last full

Above: *Phil Hill on the banking at Monza, in the fabulous shark-nose Ferrari during his championship year.*

season being in 1964. Thereafter there were sports car successes before he retired completely after winning the BOAC 805-km (500-mile) endurance race at Brands Hatch for Chaparral. A true fan of the automobile, he set up a classic car restoration shop in Santa Monica, and still regularly visits FI races.

Right: *In the mid-1960s Graham Hill's familiar dark-blue helmet with white rowing stripes was an intrinsic part of BRM's make-up.*

Graham Hill
1962 · 1968

A man who hadn't even learned to drive until he was 24, then drove in his first race a year later and was a Grand Prix driver four years after that, Graham Hill's rise to prominence had a fairy-tale ring to it. That impression was confirmed by his two World Championships and five wins at Monte Carlo.

Brands Hatch Racing School was the very beginning of the story, but Hill's serious career began with Lotus,

where he had talked his way into becoming a mechanic and subsequently an F2 driver. By the time Lotus made the graduation to FI in 1958, Hill was one of the drivers, but the team's front-engined cars were no match for the rear-engined Coopers, so for 1960 Hill accepted an offer to drive the new rear-engined BRM.

He had another couple of quiet seasons in cars that were outclassed, apart from spinning away the lead of the British GP (a race he would never win), but for 1962 the team

had a secret weapon ready: a new V8 engine. Suddenly Hill had a competitive car, which he used to win the Dutch, German, Italian and South African Grands Prix, edging out Lotus's Jim Clark for the world title in the very last race.

During the following years, Hill and the BRM remained highly competitive and regular race winners, but generally gave best to Clark and Lotus. For 1967, he became Clark's partner after deciding to rejoin the team he'd left seven years earlier. In the new Ford DFV powered Lotus 49s, they were a formidable combination and looked set to dominate 1968. Then Clark was killed. Hill pulled the devastated team together magnificently and, after winning in Spain, Monaco and Mexico, snatched his second world crown.

Graham Hill remained an F1 driver until well past his peak, retiring in mid-1975, but he retained his popularity. He'd formed his own team and was returning from a test session in

France, in the winter of 1975, when his light aircraft struck trees in bad weather. Hill and all on board, including the devastatingly talented driver Tony Brise and designer Andy Smallman, were killed. The racing world mourned the loss of its greatest ambassador.

Above: In 1962 Hill fulfilled all his promise when he took his first world title driving for BRM.

Below: Six years later, Hill dragged Lotus from the depths after Jim Clark's death, to take his second World Championship, winning in Spain and Monaco, and here in Mexico.

Jim Clark

1963 · 1965

A Scottish border farmer who came to be recognized as the greatest racing driver of his era, Jim Clark will be forever remembered as half of the most magical partnership motor racing has ever seen. Clark and Lotus boss Colin Chapman represented a symbiotic relationship between the respective masters of F1 driving and design. Once their time had arrived, if they didn't win together, it was invariably due to some mechanical oversight, and it was virtually unheard of for Clark genuinely to be beaten into second place.

After early days spent racing sports cars in Scotland, Clark came to Chapman's attention when he tested a Lotus as a potential customer. He soon became a Lotus junior driver and, within a matter of months, made his F1 début. During the next couple of years, Clark learned the ropes and built up his uncanny rapport with Chapman. When the latter produced the first monocoque F1 car, the Lotus 25, for the 1962 season, the Clark era had begun.

Only mechanical failures allowed the 1962 championship to go elsewhere – Clark was fastest in seven of the nine races and led the final until retirement – it was resolved then that these failures would be corrected for 1963. His record seven victories in that year much more accurately reflected the general run of play. Each of those wins was dominant, apparently effortless, and the three remaining races were accounted for by a faulty clutch, a misfire and a battery failure.

Right: The incomparable Jim Clark was synonymous with Lotus. And though he hated Spa (where he is seen in 1963), the Belgian circuit was one of his happiest hunting grounds.

Nineteen-sixty-four was a repeat of 1962, with Clark and Lotus clearly the fastest combination, but losing out in the final race, within sight of victory, through a pitifully minor problem. But 1965 was a repeat of 1963, the partnership's results once more matching its speed. Clark won six of the nine races he contested; he missed one race because he was away winning the Indianapolis 500! Even in his three non-finishes, he had again proved to be the fastest.

In his remaining two full seasons, Clark retained his status as F1's pacesetter, but no titles followed. In 1966, Lotus was without a suitable engine for the new 3-litre formula (although he was the only man ever to win with BRM's highly complex H16 engine), and 1967 saw the first days of the Cosworth DFV, which was fast, but at that time not completely reliable. He was favourite for the 1968 title, particularly after recording his 25th Grand Prix win in South Africa, but before he could achieve this he was killed in an F2 race at Hockenheim. The sport was devastated to lose the man everyone acknowledged to be the best.

John Surtees

▶️ 1964

Several drivers have arrived in Grand Prix racing from motor cycle competition, but only John Surtees has won World Championships in both disciplines.

Although he proved instantly competitive when he made the transition to four wheels at the highest level, it wasn't until Surtees finally accepted a repeated offer from Ferrari, in 1963, that his career really took off. Enzo Ferrari – who in the distant past had run his own motor cycle team and who had achieved much of his early success in cars with such legendary ex-motor cycle racers as Tazio Nuvolari and Achille Varzi – had a soft spot for such men.

After helping to re-establish Ferrari as a competitive force in 1963, Surtees went into 1964 with high hopes. A new V8 engine had been developed to replace the V6, and Surtees' skills as a test driver had helped produce a chassis with good handling. In the first half of the season, however, it appeared that his hopes had been misplaced, the car proving less than reliable, while rivals Clark and Hill pulled ever further clear in the points battle. The turning point came mid-season at the Nürburgring for the German Grand Prix, where Surtees won in commanding fashion after an early dice with Clark ended with the Lotus's retirement.

That Ferrari had improved its car's reliability was underlined at the next race, the Austrian Grand Prix on the car-breaking Zeltweg circuit. Surtees' team-mate, Lorenzo Bandini, won after all the regular front runners suffered suspension or driveshaft failures. Although Surtees didn't score, neither did the two title favourites, Clark and Hill. With three races remaining, in theory Surtees could still claw his way to the front. This looked a much more realistic

prospect after a second Surtees victory, this time at the Italian Grand Prix in front of a hysterically happy home crowd. Even better for his chances, Clark and Hill had failed to finish again.

Although Hill won in the USA, Surtees was a solid second, while Clark retired once more. All of which meant that Surtees needed to finish only second in the final round, in Mexico, if Clark won, but that he would be beaten to the crown if Hill won. If Surtees won, he would take the crown unless Hill finished second. In the event, Clark retired while in the lead right at the end, Surtees' team-mate, Bandini, clashed with Hill, putting the latter out of the reckoning, then moved aside to allow Surtees to take second place behind

Dan Gurney. The crown belonged to Surtees.

He was never to come close again, as Ferrari lost the pace of development in 1965 prior to an acrimonious split with Surtees in 1966. He went on to win races for Cooper and Honda before easing into retirement from driving and forming his own Grand Prix team, which he ran until 1978.

Left: *The only man ever to win World Championships on two wheels and four, John Surtees was a fearless fighter whose true promise nevertheless went unfulfilled.*

Above: *The closest his FI team ever came to Grand Prix victory was in South Africa in 1972, as fellow motorcycle champion Mike Hailwood dominated until his Surtees TS9B broke.*

Denny Hulme

The plan hadn't been for Denny Hulme to win the 1967 title at all. He was supposed to be there with the reliable Brabham, while team leader Jack Brabham formed the cutting edge with a more highly developed machine. Reliability proved the key, however, and Hulme became New Zealand's first, and so far only, World Champion.

Hulme had won a New Zealand 'Driver to Europe' scheme after considerable success at home with a Cooper in 1959 and 1960. He worked at Brabham's garage to support his racing and, when Brabham established his own race car company, was able to build up his own Brabham for Formula Junior races. Eventually he became a works Brabham F2 driver and, when Dan Gurney left the F1 team, was brought in as his replacement in 1966. Hulme proved solid, intelligent and

measured, rather than blisteringly quick. This was exactly what was required in the early years of the 3-litre formula, when the machinery tended to be fragile. He won the second Grand Prix of the year, at Monaco, and followed with regular runs into the points in the next few races. At the Nürburgring in Germany, he gave the sort of performance that said everything about his approach. In the leading group from the start, he was elevated to second place when

Left: Stewart's partnership with Ken Tyrrell was one of the legends of the sport, yet needed nothing more to seal it than a handshake.

Clark retired his Lotus. Ahead of him was Dan Gurney's Eagle, but with half of the race still to go, Hulme elected not to sit in the leader's slipstream, but rather to ease off and save his engine. Two laps from the end, Gurney retired and Hulme was an easy winner.

There followed a few more forays into the points, which was all that was required in a season when the front runners could not put a sequence of results together, and Hulme took the crown.

He almost did it again in 1968, this time more aggressively with McLaren, and until his retirement in 1974, he was always a possible threat, but never again did he mount a serious title challenge. When well into his retirement, he took up racing Touring Cars in Australia and New Zealand, and it was during the 1992 Bathurst Touring Car race that he suffered a heart attack and died at the wheel. A tough, gruff old bear with a heart of gold, Denny was much missed by his friends.

Right: Stewart's brilliance was never more evident than at the foggy Nürburgring in 1968, where he won by four minutes.

Left: Occasionally grumpy but usually wonderful company, the late Denny Hulme, fending off Stewart at Monaco in 1967, was New Zealand's only champion.

Jackie Stewart

1969 · 1971 · 1973

Between the death of his friend and countryman, Jim Clark, in 1968 and his own retirement in 1973, Jackie Stewart was the standard by which others were judged. No one facet of his skill stands out because all were at the same high level: he was fast, calculating, shrewd and methodical.

He also had a core of steel. It was an overwhelming combination.

After drives in sports cars for locally based teams, Stewart was noticed by F3 team owner Ken Tyrrell, who gave him a test in one of his Coopers in early 1964. When he proved faster than Cooper's F1 driver, Bruce McLaren, he was signed. Then when he steamrollered the opposition in F3, the F1 offers came

flooding in. He chose to go with BRM, as team-mate to Graham Hill, and in his first season won the Italian Grand Prix, taking third place in the championship. Two relatively quiet seasons followed as BRM struggled to produce competitive equipment for the new 3-litre formula, and for 1968 he joined forces with Tyrrell once more.

Tyrrell had managed to persuade Matra, which was entering F1 with its own cars, to allow him to run a separate team of the cars powered, not by Matra's own V12, but by the new Ford Cosworth DFV, which had already established itself as by far the best engine in F1. It was a dynamic combination with Stewart winning three Grands Prix and only just losing out in the championship, despite missing races because of a wrist injury.

For 1969, with a season's experience behind it, the team was unstoppable. Stewart dominated in a way that hadn't been seen since Clark, and waltzed to his first World Championship. Matra, though, had decided not to renew the agreement to run the Ford-engined cars for political reasons. Both Stewart and Tyrrell were adamant that they needed a DFV for success, so Tyrrell began to make plans to construct his own car. In the meantime, he bought a March, with which Stewart won the 1970 Spanish Grand Prix, but little else. By the end of the year, however, the new Tyrrell car had made its first appearance.

It was with this machine that Stewart enjoyed an even more dominant season in 1971 than he had in 1969. Each of his six victories was

Left: *Stewart in the Tyrrell he drove for the 1971 season, pitting during practice at Zandvoort.*

Below: *Stewart in the 006/2 which won him the 1973 championship at the Dutch GP.*

taken in masterful style and gave him almost double the points score of his nearest rival. It was the era of the 'kit car', when most of the field were using the DFV engine. Stewart and Tyrrell were simply adding the other parts of the equation better than anyone else.

The momentum was checked slightly in 1972 by a stomach ulcer, which afflicted Stewart, and the new-found maturity of Emerson Fittipaldi at Lotus. But for 1973, Stewart and Tyrrell wanted their title back. Secretly Stewart already knew that this would be his final season and wanted to go

out on a high. It was no rerun of 1971, because of the speed of the Lotus in the hands of both Fittipaldi and Peterson, but Stewart's five impeccable wins gave him that final crown. Statistically they also made him the most successful driver there had ever been at that time, with a total of 27 Grand Prix victories.

Jackie Stewart's relationship with Ford continued after he'd hung up his helmet, and in 1997 the partnership entered a new era with Stewart Grand Prix, powered by Ford, making him an F1 team owner. A highly popular one, too.

Jochen Rindt

 1970

A fantastically gifted driver who could bend a car to his will, Jochen Rindt has gone down in history as the only man to win the World Championship posthumously.

Born in Germany, but raised in Austria after his parents were killed in an air raid, Rindt used his inherited wealth to make his way through the junior ranks of racing. Right from the start, he displayed a startling talent

and, determined to make an international impression, he sold the spice mill that had been the source of his parents' wealth and entered F2 racing. In his third race in the formula, at Crystal Palace in 1964, he sensationally beat Graham Hill. His reputation secured, he made his F1 début later the same year in Austria.

Rindt drove for the Cooper team from 1965 to 1967, in cars that were overweight and underpowered. For 1968, he left Cooper and joined Brabham, whose cars were more

Above: *Few wins were as dramatic as Jochen Rindt's at Monaco in 1970, the last for the ageing Lotus 49C, and one that did not augur well for the opposition anticipating the Lotus 72.*

Opposite: *Though Jochen Rindt reckoned a monkey could have won the 1970 German GP in his Lotus 72, the Austrian's brilliance was a key factor.*

competitive, but unreliable. A blistering sequence of qualifying performances in the Brabham completely overshadowed team boss

Jack Brabham and maintained his burgeoning reputation.

For 1969, Rindt accepted an offer to join Lotus, alongside World Champion Graham Hill. He proved the only man capable of taking on Jackie Stewart and the Matra that year, but while Stewart posted victory after victory, Rindt's races invariably ended in retirement through mechanical failures. It wasn't until the end of the season, in the US Grand Prix, that he finally won an F1 race.

His relationship with Lotus boss Colin Chapman was frequently a bitter one, but he chose to stay into 1970 on the promise of Chapman's latest creation, the superb Lotus 72. This instantly rendered rival cars obsolete visually, although its early unreliability led to a shaky start to the season. Rindt was forced to use the older 49 model in that year's Monaco Grand Prix, but pulled off one of the greatest victories of all time in a fantastic display that saw him set a new lap

record almost a second quicker than anyone had managed in qualifying. Once the 72 was properly ready, there was no stopping Rindt as he reeled off a sequence of four consecutive victories.

In qualifying for the Italian Grand Prix, a mechanical failure caused the Lotus to crash violently, and Rindt did not survive the impact. His seasonal points total was not overhauled, however, even though four races remained, and his memory, rather than the man himself, was crowned.

Emerson Fittipaldi
1972 · 1974

The youngest ever World Champion, Emerson Fittipaldi enjoyed a glittering career, which didn't end until 1996, even though he last drove in FI in 1980.

The son of a Brazilian motor sport journalist, Fittipaldi and his elder brother, Wilson, were immersed in the sport from an early age and, after winning karting championships, progressed to Brazilian GT and saloon car racing. Emerson then took the step of emigrating to Britain, blazing the trail for countless numbers of South American drivers who have since followed. After winning instantly in both Formula Ford and F3 in 1969, he was picked up by Colin Chapman for the Lotus F2 team in 1970.

Above and below: After getting his big FI chance with Colin Chapman's Lotus team in 1970, Fittipaldi went on to become the youngest-ever champion in the John Player Special Lotus 72. He won his second title with McLaren in 1974.

Within months, Fittipaldi had made his F1 début with Lotus and, following the death of Jochen Rindt, he was promoted to team leader before the year was out. In fairy-tale fashion, he won his first race in this role, the US Grand Prix, which helped seal Rindt's posthumous world title. After such a sensational start, the following season was relatively barren, compromized by a road crash and by Lotus's tyre supplier falling behind the competition. In 1972 though, aided by the health problem of reigning champion Jackie Stewart, Fittipaldi rattled off a superb sequence of wins in the John Player Special Lotus 72. His victory in the Italian Grand Prix clinched his first world crown at the age of 25, a record that still stands.

There were more wins in 1973, although his outside chance of retaining the title disappeared when Chapman refused to instruct his team-mate, Ronnie Peterson, to move aside in the Italian Grand Prix. This seemed indicative of the team swinging behind Peterson, who had proved the quicker of the two, so Fittipaldi moved on to McLaren for 1974.

That year was the first post-Stewart season, and the competition

Above: *Fittipaldi stayed with McLaren for two years, before the disastrous switch to his own team.*

to establish a new order was intense. After winning his home Grand Prix for a second time, Fittipaldi took further victories in Belgium and Canada. Entering the last round, he was in contention for the title with Ferrari's Clay Regazzoni and Tyrrell's Jody Scheckter. Fittipaldi's undramatic run to fourth place displayed his usual coolness and was enough to collect title number two.

Incredibly he left McLaren at the end of 1975 to join the team that his brother, Wilson, had founded. For the next five years as a driver, and a further two years after that, Fittipaldi struggled to make this dream work, but to no avail. After a brief retirement, he resumed his career in Indycars in 1984, with more remarkable results. He finally retired after taking as 'a message from God' a neck-breaking accident in 1996, by which time he'd added an Indycar title and the Indianapolis 500 to his tally of victories.

Niki Lauda

1975 · 1977 · 1984

So much of what Niki Lauda achieved is remarkable, and he stands out as being a little bit different, even among a collection of World Champions.

It was remarkable that he took the huge gamble of taking out a bank loan – apparently using his wealthy Austrian family's good standing as collateral – to fund his initial racing

career. Remarkable that after only sporadic promise, he developed into a seriously quick Grand Prix driver. Remarkable that he helped turn the Ferrari team from an 'also ran' to the best in the business. Remarkable that he came back to racing just 33 days after being given the last rites following a fiery crash. Remarkable that he'd lost none of his touch when he did return. Remarkable that he retired for two years, then took a

third World Championship in his come-back campaign.

In company with team manager Luca di Montezemolo and designer Mauro Forghieri, Lauda had made the 1974 Ferrari 312B3 the fastest in the business, and only his inexperience had cost him the title. The response to that failure was devastating. Forghieri designed a new transverse-gearbox car, the 312T, which handled wonderfully well, and Lauda used it to good effect. The winning sequence began in Monaco and was followed in quick succession by victories in Belgium and Sweden. In Holland, he gave best to an inspired James Hunt, but scored a fourth victory in France. He clinched the title with an easy run to third at the Italian Grand Prix, the perfect place to take Ferrari's first title for 11 years, and followed it with another win at the end-of-season US Grand Prix.

Above: *In 1975 Lauda was unbeatable in Ferrari's 312T, winning the title easily.*

Right: *1977 was tougher but even more satisfying, after recovery from his dramatic accident in 1976.*

He looked well on his way to a second successive title before his near-fatal Nürburgring crash, and lost out to Hunt by a solitary point. Ferrari had been against his return and gave him little support, feeling that he would never be the same driver again. Thus he took great delight in winning a second title with the team in 1977 and leaving the instant he had achieved that goal, even though the season was not over.

He spent two years with Brabham before walking out half-way through a practice session and retiring, feeling that he'd lost motivation.

His return in 1982, with McLaren, was partly motivated by money, but there were no half-measures, as he won within three races of the start of this second career. When McLaren formed an allegiance with Porsche to obtain turbo engines in 1984, Lauda was ready to do battle for the title once more, his only real competition coming from team-mate Alain Prost. In a see-sawing season between them, Lauda emerged on top by a scant half-point.

He won one more race, in Austria in 1985, shortly after announcing his retirement at the end of that year, this time for good.

Below: *Where Lauda's previous titles had come through speed, his third, in 1984, came more by stealth and cunning. Unable to match team-mate Alain Prost's pace, he settled for consistency and won the title for McLaren by a mere half point.*

James Hunt

1976

A man of his time, James Hunt brought an individualistic indolence to F1. It was an image that hid an obsessively competitive edge and a keen intelligence, which made him a formidable force when behind the wheel of a good car.

After working his way through British club racing, Hunt was a washed-up F3 driver by the time he joined forces with eccentric aristocrat Lord Alexander Hesketh. Within a short space of time, they had graduated to F1 together and made a big impression, Hunt ending his début season of 1973 with a strong second place. The partnership enjoyed its day of 'Boys' Own' glory when Hunt and the Hesketh defeated the Ferrari team fair and square at the 1975 Dutch Grand Prix. But Grand Prix racing is expensive, even for a Lord, and

Hesketh pulled the plug at the end of the season.

Fortuitously a vacancy had arisen with one of the top teams, through Emerson Fittipaldi's shock decision to leave McLaren and join his brother's outfit instead. Such was the rapidity of Hunt's move that he had not even

Above: Was any season more controversial than 1976, when against the odds James Hunt came through to triumph?

Below: Together with rivals Lauda, Peterson (hidden) and Jarier, and Max Mosley, Hunt awaits the Japanese GP in 1976. This was the race which would win him his crown.

tested the McLaren before he took pole position with it at the 1976 season opener in Brazil. Although he took his first McLaren win in Spain, it was surrounded by controversy, as the car was slightly over the width limit. Initially he was disqualified, but was reinstated on appeal. But even this, combined with a second win in France, left him a long way behind Ferrari's Niki Lauda as the season reached its half-way point in Britain.

There Hunt took a magnificent win after a straight fight with Lauda, but subsequently he was disqualified – and this time it stood – over a hazy regulation concerning the race restart procedure. Then came Lauda's near-fatal crash, and Hunt notched up two more wins before the Austrian returned. But still he was a long way behind and needed victories, nothing less, in the races that followed. Remarkably, under the most intense pressure, that is what he achieved, taking consecutive wins in Canada and America so that he went to the season finale, in Japan, within striking distance of the Ferrari driver. After Lauda pulled out early in that race, his Nürburgring injuries preventing him from seeing properly in the blinding spray, Hunt's run to third place was enough to clinch one of the most dramatic title battles in the sport's history.

He won three more Grands Prix with McLaren, but as the team declined so Hunt's interest waned. He tried a switch of team to Wolf, but when that was found to be no more competitive, he retired part way through 1979 and established a new career as a pithy television commentator. Hunt died suddenly from a heart attack in 1993, just as his turbulent life was settling down.

Right: In appalling conditions in Japan Hunt brought his McLaren home third, which was enough to beat Lauda by a single point.

Above: Andretti revelled in the elegant Lotus 78, F1's first true ground-effect car, but the 79 would play an even greater role in making him America's second World Champion.

Mario Andretti

 1978

It rankles Mario Andretti that he achieved his world title in a car that was demonstrably superior to the rest. The evidence of his achievements outside of that season suggests, in the strongest possible terms, that he was among the absolute élite of drivers for a very long time.

Andretti was born in Italy, but his family moved to the USA as post-war refugees. Together with his twin, Aldo, Mario made a name for himself in dirt-track racing during the early

1960s. His prowess led to a chance in Indycars and, remarkably, he took the national championship in his first full season, 1965. This was when Colin Chapman was making his successful raid on the Indycar scene with Jim Clark, and the Lotus boss was impressed.

In 1968, Andretti accepted a one-off drive for Lotus at the US Grand Prix. He qualified on pole position, one of only three men in the history of the World Championship to do so on their début. He would continue to run occasional F1 races for both Lotus and Ferrari, as and when his Indycar programme allowed.

However, although he took victory in the 1971 South African Grand Prix for Ferrari, racing in the two programmes didn't really allow him to show his true F1 potential.

After many years of trying, Chapman finally got Andretti to agree to a full season in 1976, and he helped turn the team around. From struggling at the back of the grid, Lotus became a winner again in the final Grand Prix of the year. For 1977, Chapman had the first ground-effect F1 car, the Lotus 78. It was the fastest in the business, and only poor engine reliability kept Andretti from the title.

With a further development of the ground-effect principle, the Lotus 79 was in a class of its own in 1978. This time, Andretti demolished the opposition, winning the Argentinian, Belgian, Spanish, French, German and Dutch Grands Prix. His closest rival, team-mate Ronnie Peterson, had been neutralized by agreeing to a supporting role in Andretti's title campaign. Therefore it was all the more poignant and ironic that Andretti clinched the title at Monza, the scene of Peterson's fatal accident.

Chapman failed to keep pace with the imitators his design had spawned, and Andretti was not given competitive equipment in his remaining two seasons with Lotus. A move to Alfa Romeo in 1981 proved little better, and he returned to the States to round off his career back in Indycars. He gave one last demonstration of his F1 prowess when called by Ferrari as a stand-in for the 1982 Italian Grand Prix, qualifying on pole. There were many more Indycar race wins before Andretti finally retired in 1994, a racer to the very end of his active career.

Right: A calmer man by the time he joined Ferrari in 1979, Jody Scheckter was ready to win the World Championship.

Jody Scheckter
1979

When Jody Scheckter entered F1, it was as a hot-headed wild boy who relied solely on his car control and reflexes. By the time he achieved his World Championship, he was a mature, smooth elder statesman of a driver.

The South African Scheckter burst on to the British racing scene on a sponsored 'Driver to Europe' campaign. He won immediately in Formula Ford and F3, and was taken on by McLaren as a driver for its F2 team. It gave him a token run in the final Grand Prix of 1972, where he impressed with his raw speed. In 1973, McLaren ran him in an occasional third car alongside the senior drivers, and in France, his third Grand Prix, he led. Then he caused the biggest pile-up in F1 history, going off on the first lap at Silverstone and taking 13 cars with him.

Despite Scheckter's wayward reputation, Ken Tyrrell took him on in 1974, and after winning two Grands Prix, he was a close third in the championship. Only occasional wins followed in his two subsequent Tyrrell seasons, however, and in 1977 he joined the newly created Wolf team, making history by winning first time out. He won a couple more times and again was third in the championship. After a lacklustre second season with Wolf, he joined Ferrari.

Although he signed as outright number-one driver, Scheckter was teamed with the mystically fast Gilles Villeneuve, then just embarking on his second full season with the team. Initially it was Villeneuve who did all the winning in Ferrari's new 312T4, Scheckter being the runner-up. Ferrari responded by giving Scheckter until the Monaco Grand Prix to stamp his authority on the team; if he did not, it would put its efforts into gaining the

title for Villeneuve. Fortunately Scheckter took a win in Belgium and a dominant victory in Monaco to retrieve the situation.

By the time the season reached Monza for the Italian Grand Prix, only Scheckter or Villeneuve could take the title. When the cars settled down into the two leading positions of the race,

team orders were issued, and Villeneuve was instructed to hold station behind Scheckter. True to his word, that is exactly what he did, conceding Scheckter the world crown.

Jody took in one more season, but the 1980 Ferrari was hopelessly off the pace and he called it a day at the season's end. After walking away from

the sport to establish a very successful arms business, today he supervises the racing careers of his two sons.

Below: Ferrari decreed that whichever of its drivers finished ahead at Monaco would be favoured for the title. Scheckter, seen here heading team-mate Villeneuve, won the race and went on to take the championship crown.

Alan Jones

The man who began the Williams championship winning streak that continues to this day, Alan Jones, was considered a competent FI driver when he first hooked up with Frank Williams and Patrick Head. When he left for a short-lived retirement, four years later, he was a legend.

The son of noted Australian racer Stan Jones, Alan had earned a solid reputation in British F3 and F5000 in the mid-1970s. He broke into FI in 1975 with a 'rent-a-drive' Hesketh and, later, a number-two seat with Graham Hill's nascent team. He did enough to attract John Surtees' attention, for whom he drove in 1976. These were not top-line drives, however; neither was his 1977 berth

Below: Alan Jones's unique blend of speed and aggression came together with Williams' emergent status at just the right time. In 1979, 1980 and 1981 they were the class of FI.

with the Shadow team, gained when its lead driver, Tom Pryce, was killed in the South African Grand Prix. Yet in Austria that year, in wet slippery conditions, Jones shocked the F1 world by winning. It wasn't enough for the top teams to beat a path to his door, but Williams and Head – about to embark on their first season with their own car – took him on. The Williams FW06 turned out to be an excellent car, and together Jones and Williams gave the establishment several frights.

With the ground-effect FW07 in 1979, Williams and Jones really came of age, winning four Grands Prix together and proving the fastest combination in the season's second half. For 1980, the idea was to string a whole season together in similar winning vein. They began on the right note with a win in Argentina, but by the time the second win came, in France, it was clear that they had a formidable opponent in Nelson Piquet's Brabham, a car of similar configuration and power to the

Williams, operated by a similarly slick team and a similarly quick driver.

Jones took a straight win over Piquet in the British Grand Prix, and by the time the series arrived in Holland, he looked comfortably clear, 11 points up with only four races to go. But then he damaged his car's under-body when leading the first lap, necessitating a pit stop, and Piquet won, coming within two points of the series lead. In Italy, Piquet won again, although Jones at least contained the damage by finishing second. Now though, Piquet was a point ahead, with two races to go.

The two of them headed into the first corner at Montreal, disputing the lead, and Jones, with his customary aggression, took up his line to intimidate Piquet into submission. But Piquet didn't back off, and a multi-car shunt was triggered, causing the race to be stopped. On the restart, Jones again led away, but Piquet almost immediately passed him on the straight, only for his engine to blow some laps later. Jones was left to cruise home an easy winner, safe in the knowledge that the title was his on account of Piquet's dropped scores. He even followed it up with victory in the final race in America.

Jones and Williams were regular winners again in 1981, but this time he faced competition from team-mate Carlos Reutemann, and Piquet won the title. Jones retired after winning the final race of the year. He came back a couple of years later, with Arrows, and again in 1985 with the new Beatrice team, but neither had race-winning cars, and he went back to Australia where he still races Touring Cars.

Left: *Frank Williams and Patrick Head still remember with great fondness their racing days with the laconic Australian.*

Right: *Fast, aggressive and smart, Nelson Piquet was always a fearsome competitor. Brabham's BT52 gave him his second title in 1983.*

Nelson Piquet

The son of a Brazilian diplomat, Nelson Piquet was well connected and talented. It was a combination that made for a relatively painless rise to F1 and, once there, he had the fortune to happen upon the Brabham team at exactly the right time. Piquet and the Gordon Murray Brabhams became an irresistible team.

After dominating the 1978 British F3 series, Piquet started with Bernie Ecclestone's Brabham team at the end of that season. He did enough to be retained for 1979, alongside Niki Lauda. When Lauda retired, Piquet became team leader. Once free of the bulky Alfa Romeo engines that Ecclestone had shackled the team to for commercial reasons, Murray was able to design the beautiful, compact and effective BT49 with Cosworth DFV power. It almost took Piquet to a world title in 1980.

For 1981, the sport's governing body had introduced a 60mm (2.36in) minimum ride height requirement, in an effort to limit the effectiveness of the latest generation of ground-effect cars. Murray was the first designer to find a way around this, and by the third race of the season, Piquet's BT49 was fitted with a hydraulic system that kept the car at the regulation height when stationary, but lowered it to the ground when on the track, making a seal to gain maximum ground-effect suction. It put the Brabhams in a different league from the rest, and Piquet took a ridiculously easy win in the Argentinian Grand Prix, followed immediately by another at Imola.

Rival teams soon copied the idea though, and Piquet went through a barren patch mid-season, becoming caught up in a simmering row with his rival Alan Jones and crashing out of several races. Williams' Carlos Reutemann edged comfortably clear of him at the top of the championship table. A solid win in Germany formed the foundation of a fight back, but even so, Piquet entered the final round at Las Vegas two points adrift of his rival. Ligier's Jacques Laffite was also in with an outside chance of the title if he won the race. In the event, it was Jones who won. Reutemann, after qualifying comfortably on pole, quickly fell down the order, and Piquet – although only semi-conscious through heat exhaustion – passed the Williams on his way to fifth place, enough to give him the title by one point.

Although the BMW turbocharged Brabhams of 1982 were fast, they were unreliable, and Piquet had to wait until 1983 for another realistic shot at the title. By three-quarters of the way through the season, Renault's Alain Prost looked comfortably on course for the honours, having taken four victories to Piquet's one. But

then BMW and Brabham retaliated.
Irritated that Renault had been
allowed to keep its exhaust-enhanced
aerodynamics, they came up with a
special fuel that boosted the BMW's
power considerably, and Piquet took
dominant victories in Italy and at
Brands Hatch. He was similarly
masterful in South Africa for the final
race and, with Prost's retirement,
became champion for a second time.

Although he stayed with Brabham
for two more seasons, Piquet felt that
his chances of success were being
compromized by Ecclestone's
contract with Pirelli tyres, and also
that he wasn't being paid as highly as
some of his rivals. Reluctantly he left
and joined Williams for the 1986 and
1987 seasons. Thanks to rivalry with
his team-mate, Nigel Mansell, Piquet
allowed the 1986 title to be snatched

Left: *Matched against Nigel Mansell at Williams, Piquet never felt comfortable, but took his third title in 1987.*

Below left: *In his days at Brabham he had always been the clear number one, a situation he far preferred.*

Right: *Jones' successor at Williams in 1982, Keke Rosberg mirrored the Australian's speed and feistiness.*

from his grasp at the last race by Prost. But for 1987, the Williams-Hondas were even more dominant, and Mansell was the only real threat. Although the Briton was frequently quicker, Piquet used guile and cunning in a campaign that took wins in Germany, Hungary and Italy. When Mansell injured his back during the penultimate round and could take no further part, Piquet's third crown was secure.

His remaining days in FI were patchy: he was frequently unmotivated and unimpressive in his two years at Lotus and occasionally a real contender again in his final two seasons with Benetton. In 1992, he badly injured his legs when practising for the Indianapolis 500. Since then, he's made a low-key come-back in GT racing with BMW.

Keke Rosberg

 1982

A spectacular attacking driver, Keke Rosberg was a worthy replacement at Williams when Alan Jones retired, something that he proved by instantly winning the world title. He was seen to best effect when the circumstances called for improvisation.

The first Finn to make a serious effort in international motor racing, as opposed to rallying, Rosberg had an uphill struggle in his formative career, and it took quite some time for him to arrive on the brink of FI. He entered in 1978 with the Theodore team, and although its car was hopelessly uncompetitive, he caused a sensation by using it to win the non-

Above: *Though the Swiss GP at Dijon in 1982 was Rosberg's sole win of the season, he did enough elsewhere to snatch a worthy title.*

championship International Trophy in the teeming rain at Silverstone. Even so, in the four seasons that followed, he raced a succession of uncompetitive cars – ATS, Wolf and Fittipaldi. His career seemed to have stalled, but then came a lifeline: Alan Jones had informed Williams, at very short notice, that he would not be continuing into 1982. With all the top names already signed up, Williams opted for Rosberg.

He immediately showed the top teams what they had been missing, proving superbly fast and aggressive. When team-mate Carlos Reutemann retired, just two races into the season, Rosberg was promoted to team leader. He took seconds in Brazil, the USA, Belgium and Austria,

but that elusive first win was taking an agonisingly long time. It finally happened at the 'Swiss' Grand Prix (held at Dijon in France). Prost's Renault was leading going into the closing stages, but had lost fourth gear; Rosberg was catching him hand over fist. But this was France, and Williams' team manager, Peter Collins, noticed that the official with the chequered flag was about to hang it out one lap too early – which would have given Prost the race. Collins pointed out this 'error', and in the final lap Rosberg overtook to win. An easy run to fifth place in the season's finale, at Las Vegas, clinched the crown.

Unfortunately for Rosberg, the next three years proved to be a transitory period for Williams as it struggled

with its early turbo cars. Nevertheless he managed the odd inspirational victory. For 1986, he signed with McLaren as team-mate to Prost, around whose driving style the car was designed. Rosberg found it didn't lend itself to his very different technique, and there were no wins. He led in Australia, however, which was his final race before retirement. He came back later to race sports cars and Touring Cars, but has since hung up his helmet for good. Today he runs a Touring Car team in Germany for Nissan, and manages Mika Hakkinen's career.

Alain Prost

1985 · 1986 · 1989 · 1993

The 'winningest' F1 driver of all time, with 51 Grand Prix victories to his credit, Alain Prost drove with a lack of drama, but this hid a stunning talent.

After rising through the ranks of French racing via the classic Elf-sponsored route, Prost won the 1979 European F3 championship. He graduated straight to F1 with McLaren in 1980, after comfortably out-performing several other young hopefuls in a test session. Although the car was not a race winner, Prost caused an immediate stir by consistently overshadowing his supposed team leader, John Watson.

Such form saw him recruited by Renault to drive its turbo car in 1981. Grand Prix wins followed immediately, but it was not until 1983 that the Renaults were sufficiently consistent and reliable to form a championship threat. Nevertheless, Prost lost out in the final race to Piquet and was immediately sacked by the French team. He returned to McLaren, now a much more potent

force than when he'd last driven for the team. He and team-mate Niki Lauda fought tooth and nail for the 1984 title, but again he lost out in the final round.

In 1985, Prost's opposition seemed to crumble around him. Team-mate Lauda suffered an appalling reliability record; Michele Alboreto started strongly, but his Ferrari became less competitive and desperately unreliable as the season progressed; it took most of the year for the Williams-Hondas to come good; and the Lotus-Renaults were not as

Above and below: Prost's early years with McLaren were characterized by blinding speed and back-to-back titles in 1985 and 1986.

aerodynamically or fuel efficient as Prost's McLaren-Porsche. So with five victories, Prost sailed to his first title.

By the end of the season, the Williams-Hondas had become the pace-setters, a trend that continued throughout 1986. Yet as Williams' team-mates Nelson Piquet and Nigel Mansell battled between themselves, splitting their success, Prost picked up wins wherever they faltered and entered the final round in Australia with an outside chance of retaining his title. In the event, one of Mansell's tyres exploded, Piquet had to make a precautionary stop as a result, and Prost won both the race and the championship.

Left: *Prost's fourth title came smoothly with the Williams FW15 in 1993, the season's dominant machine.*

Although the Williams duo blitzed all before them in 1987, leaving Prost only three wins, he looked in good shape for 1988, as Honda had switched its allegiance to McLaren. But with the Hondas came a team-mate whose intensity and commitment were beyond even the reach of Prost, Ayrton Senna. Between them, Prost and Senna won all but one race, although it was the Brazilian who took the title.

In 1989, they were pitched together again and their relationship became more acrimonious, but it was Prost who emerged ahead. The campaign was decided in Japan where, with Senna attempting to pass him, Prost for once took a leaf from his team-mate's book and moved across on him. Title number three for Prost.

He took this with him to Ferrari for 1990, a season when Senna got his revenge, winning the title by

deliberately ploughing into Prost at the first corner in Japan. In 1991, the Ferrari team lost the plot and, near the end of the season, took the ludicrous move of sacking Prost. He stayed on the sidelines in 1992, but negotiated a drive with the all-conquering Williams team for 1993.

With a clearly dominant car and a junior team-mate in Damon Hill, Prost's run to a fourth championship was relatively straightforward, his seven wins taking his final tally to 51, ten clear of his nearest rival, Senna. With the latter joining Williams for 1994, Prost took the opportunity of retiring and, in early 1997, took over as owner of the former Ligier team, which was renamed Prost. Now he is looking for a fifth title, but of a different kind.

Ayrton Senna
1988 · 1990 · 1991

Senna was the man who moved the goalposts. He brought to F1 not only an awesome talent, but also an apparent belief that on the track he was justified in any action against anything that prevented him from demonstrating what he knew to be the truth — that he was the best. Such a mix of supreme artistry and on-track thuggery brought him success second only to that of his nemesis, Prost.

By the time Senna graduated to F1 in 1984, it was already apparent that he was something special. He had dominated every category he had raced in, from karts in his native

Left: *A fabulous drive at Suzuka, Japan, in 1988 took Ayrton Senna to the first of his three titles.*

Left: *McLaren's domination of the late 1980s owed as much to Senna as it did to team-mate Alain Prost.*

Brazil to Formula Ford, FF2000 and F3 in Britain. Although the 1984 Toleman was outclassed, Senna came close to winning the Monaco Grand Prix with it, and the graduation to a front-line team – Lotus – followed. Although he took six victories with Lotus in three years, it was clear that the team had fallen behind and did not have the resources to climb back.

He joined McLaren for 1988 and set about taking over Prost's domain. This he did with an unflinching commitment and a greater propensity for risk. Generally he proved even quicker than the Frenchman. He took eight wins to Prost's seven, and clinched the championship with a mesmerising drive in Japan, from 16th place on the first lap to victory.

It had been a close contest, as was 1989. This time, Senna came off second best, even though his victory tally of six was two more than Prost's. With Prost gone from the team for 1990, Senna took another six wins and clinched his second title in Japan by simply aiming his car at Prost's

Right: Monaco yielded Senna a record six victories, but as soon as he perceived McLaren's domination to have faded, he headed for Williams.

Ferrari going into the first corner and keeping his foot down. Both were put out, but Prost could no longer overhaul Senna's points advantage.

In 1991, the challenge came not from Prost, but the resurgent Williams-Renault and Nigel Mansell. Although Senna began the year with four straight victories, it was clear by mid-season that Mansell's Williams was faster. Only some late-season development by Honda rescued Senna's year and allowed him to retain his title.

Senna's remaining two seasons were relatively lean against the backdrop of Williams' superiority, but they saw some of his greatest performances, and his win in the 1993 European Grand Prix at Donington was perhaps his finest. For 1994, he joined Williams, although it was to be a tragically brief relationship, as he succumbed to head injuries inflicted by his Imola crash, when he was leading the field into the Tamburello corner. Just as had occurred when Jim Clark was killed, the sport went into shock.

Nigel Mansell

⚑ 1992

From Formula Ford racer, without a silver spoon to fall back on, to F1 World Champion was a long hard slog for Nigel Mansell. It was a campaign that also saw some of the most exciting, adrenalin-tinged performances of all time.

After winning a Formula Ford title in 1977, Mansell remortgaged his house to pay for a handful of F3 drives in 1978. It was typical of the commitment of the man, as was accepting an F1 test drive with a broken back, courtesy of an F3 shunt. It was Mansell's speed in this test that convinced Lotus boss Colin Chapman to take him on as a regular test driver, a role that led to his F1 début in 1980. Although it gave him his start, Lotus was never able to provide Mansell with a winning car, and many were convinced that despite his speed, he didn't have the psychological make-up of a winner when Williams signed him up for 1985.

He took the Williams-Honda to his first victory at Brands Hatch towards the season's end and immediately followed it with another. In 1986, joined by Nelson Piquet, he won five times, but lost an almost certain championship when his tyre exploded in the final race. In 1987, it was a late-season qualifying crash that stymied him, while in 1988 the Williams, without the works Honda engine, was simply not a winning car. He threw in his lot with Ferrari for 1989 and 1990, winning first time out, but unable to mount a title challenge in either year.

After threatening to retire, he 'unretired' in time for the 1991 season, which saw him back with Williams. The Williams-Renault was an increasingly formidable machine and, by mid-season, Mansell was the pace-setter, winning three times in succession.

Above left: *Despite his well-documented insecurities, Mansell knew how to win, and win with both assurance and flair.*

Left and right: *In 1992 Nigel Mansell finally placed his hands on the steering wheel of a car worthy of his stupendous driving skills. The active-ride Williams FW14B was utterly dominant, and he crushed his World Championship opposition.*

Only Senna's dominant start and late fight back denied him the title. With the active-ride FW14B, however, Mansell had F1's fastest car at his disposal for 1992.

He made devastating use of it, completely obliterating the field in one of the most dominant title campaigns ever seen. Nine Grand Prix wins were the net result, and he'd clinched the championship by Hungary, with five races still to go.

After taking umbrage at Williams for not meeting his pay demands and signing Alain Prost for 1993, Mansell went off and made history by winning the Indycar championship, becoming the only man to have won the titles in successive years (although Andretti, Fittipaldi and Jacques Villeneuve have also won both titles). He made a brief, but

successful, F1 come-back as a Williams stand-in in 1994 – winning the Australian Grand Prix – and a disastrous one in an uncompetitive McLaren in early 1995. A sensational driver, but an emotional and often

Above: *Never at ease with the media, Mansell was nevertheless the darling of the crowds at his home race.*

insecure character, he now runs his own golfing complex in Devon.

Michael Schumacher

1994 · 1995

The German former wünderkind has, by general consensus, assumed Ayrton Senna's role as the 'world's best F1 driver'. His uncanny speed is combined with fabulous racecraft, wondrous wet-weather skills and supreme tactical acuity. In these characteristics – and in his apparent willingness on-track to resort to the professional foul – he is very reminiscent of the great Brazilian. But in addition, he possesses the rare ability to lift a whole team by inspirational leadership.

Schumacher's overwhelmingly successful early days – aided no end by his father's proprietorship of a karting circuit – brought him to the attention of Mercedes-Benz, looking for recruits to its commendable 'junior driver' programme. With the financial help of the car giant,

Schumacher waltzed to success in German Formula Ford and F3, before being included in Mercedes' World Sports Car Team. There, on an international stage for the first time, a racing phenomenon came to be recognized.

After making a sensational F1 début with Jordan, midway through 1991, he was snapped up before the next race by Benetton, thus initiating a lengthy legal battle between the two teams. He took his first victory a year later at Spa, and another in 1993, all the time building up a telepathic relationship with Benetton's technical men, Ross Brawn and Rory Byrne. With Byrne's B194 model, Schumacher was ready to take on Williams in 1994.

His form was immediately sensational, rattling off four straight victories. With Senna's death in the third round at Imola, his mantle as F1's standard-bearer rested easily on

Above: Possessed of devastating speed and car control, Michael Schumacher nevertheless stands as one of the most controversial World Champions of all time.

Right: At France in 1994 he celebrates after crushing the Williams-Renault opposition. A race later his season would fall apart.

Above opposite: Always brilliant on a wet track, Schumacher heads his Benetton-Renault to further success in the 1995 Belgian GP.

Right opposite: The switch to Ferrari yielded further successes, but as yet no World Championship.

Schumacher's shoulders, and a further four wins followed. Despite being banned for two races amid controversy over an alleged illegal 'launch control' device on the Benetton, Schumacher arrived at the final round in Adelaide, vying with Williams' Damon Hill for the world crown.

They immediately outpaced everyone else, Schumacher ahead, and a tense battle took shape. It was Schumacher who cracked first, sliding into the wall and damaging his suspension, although he rejoined the track with his crippled car still in front of Hill. As Hill pounced for the inside at the next corner, Schumacher moved across, and the ensuing contact crippled Hill's car, too. The German maintains it was a misunderstanding, a racing incident, but the net result was that he

became 1994 World Champion.

Armed with a Renault engine in his Benetton, to match that in the Williams, Schumacher enjoyed a much more clear-cut title win in 1995. Race after race, Schumacher and Benetton would make the Hill/Williams combination's race strategy look inept. The title was wrapped up with three races still to go, and another nine Grand Prix victories were added

to his tally, matching Mansell's record for a season.

Thereafter, Schumacher opted for the new challenge of trying to bring World Championship glory back to Ferrari. In 1998 he fought a close race with Hakkinen for the top spot, and 1999 looks like his best year yet. Whatever the result, the quality of his drives has secured his reputation as one of the best.

Damon Hill

 1996

The first son of a World Champion to take the crown himself, Damon Hill's name has joined his late father Graham's in the sport's roll of honour.

A late starter in the sport, after spending some years racing motor bikes at club level, Hill was in his mid-twenties by the time he had made a reputation in the sport's junior ranks, and in his early thirties when, after some impressive performances in F3000, he landed the job of Williams' test driver. His input played a crucial role in developing the active-ride FW14B, which Nigel Mansell used to such dominant effect in 1992. In the meantime, he made his F1 début with Brabham, although it was a sad shadow of the team it had been a few years previously, and Hill did well to qualify occasionally.

His big break came with Mansell's defection to Indycars for 1993. Hill was the natural choice for a seat in the Williams race team, alongside new signing Alain Prost. He took his first win in Hungary that year, and immediately followed it with two more to take third in the championship. With Prost's retirement and Senna's death, he became team leader from early 1994, and only his final-round run-in with Schumacher denied him the title. In 1995, there was more disappointment at the hands of the Benetton/Schumacher combination.

With Schumacher hamstrung initially by his move to Ferrari, Hill's best chance of championship glory was 1996. And, despite competition from his team-mate, Jacques Villeneuve, he grasped the opportunity with both hands. Although a late-season spurt from Villeneuve and a hiccup in Hill's fortunes allowed the contest between them to reach the final round, Hill clinched it with a straightforward and dominant victory as his rival lost a wheel.

Even before he'd taken his title, Hill had been informed that he was not being retained by Williams for 1997. Thus he opted for Tom Walkinshaw's Arrows team, but aside from a heroic near-win in Hungary, it was a desolate year, and for 1998 he accepted an offer to transfer to Jordan, still hungry to prove that he could win without a Williams.

Left: *The first-ever second-generation World Champion, Damon Hill restored faith in sportsmanship during his seasons with Williams and set fresh standards for on- and off-track behaviour.*

Below: *Though beaten by team-mate Jacques Villeneuve in the Portuguese GP in 1996, Hill mustered his defences to triumph in the shoot-out in Japan which clinched him the crown his father Graham had twice worn.*

Jacques Villeneuve

1997

Another second-generation Grand Prix driver to become champion, Jacques Villeneuve has now emerged completely from the shadow of his legendary father, Gilles.

He claims that he was always going to follow in his father's footsteps, although he was just 11 years old when Gilles was killed in 1982. Brought up in Monaco, rather than his native Canada, Villeneuve has been guided from the beginning by Craig Pollock, his former sports master at school. After an initial foray in saloon cars, Villeneuve learned his craft in F3 in Italy and Japan, before moving Stateside and winning the American Formula Atlantic championship.

This campaign was backed by Players cigarettes, which helped his graduation to Indycars in 1994. A promising season was followed by a superb one in 1995, as he took victory in the Indianapolis 500 as well as the Indycar championship. This success, together with the desire by F1 supremo Bernie Ecclestone to see an 'American' driver in F1, eased him straight into the best Grand Prix team in the business for 1996.

After putting his Williams on pole position for his F1 début, Villeneuve scored three wins and took the championship battle with team-mate Damon Hill down to the wire. At Estoril, he also earned the ultimate respect of the F1 world by doing the unthinkable – passing Michael Schumacher around the outside.

Credentials thus established, Villeneuve went into 1997 looking to go one better than his 1996 runner-up position. After beginning the year strongly, he suffered some mid-season 'wobbles' – crashing out of the lead in Canada through pure driving error, and being off the pace in both France and Germany – which was all the

Top left: Like Hill, the son of a famous father, Jacques Villeneuve was quick from the moment he stepped into a Williams F1 car.

Left: Victory in the 1997 British GP proved crucial in the French-Canadian's challenge for the World Championship.

inspired Schumacher needed to take the lead of the series. A strong fight back by Williams and Villeneuve looked like reaping its reward though, until the penultimate round in Japan, where Villeneuve was suspended for a practice yellow flag infringement – his fourth of the season – and Schumacher won.

All of which left Villeneuve virtually neck and neck with the German for a dramatic showdown at Jerez for the European Grand Prix. Although Schumacher made the early running, after both drivers had made their routine stops, Jacques began to hunt the Ferrari down. Once it was in his sights, he decided to surprise Schumacher by diving for the inside from a long way back. It was a beautiful move, and Schumacher was indeed fooled. When he realized his error, he turned into the Williams, but succeeded only in putting

Above: *In all matters Villeneuve is his own man, even when it comes to setting up his car. His preference is particularly for stiff suspension, making his car ride like a kart.*

himself into the gravel trap and out of the race. Villeneuve continued in the lead, and on the last lap allowed the McLarens of Hakkinen and Coulthard to overtake him. Thus his championship was secure, but it had been won the hard way.

CHAPTER **2**

The Challengers
UPCOMERS AND THOSE WHO NEARLY MADE IT

Some, such as Stirling Moss, remain the greatest uncrowned kings of their sport, men upon whom Fate refused to smile. Others, such as Chris Amon, led time after time yet never converted their promise into a single victory. These are some of the great challengers over the years.

Michele Alboreto

The mild-mannered Italian, Michele Alboreto (*above*), led the World Championship for much of 1985, before his Ferrari lost its pace and reliability. He caught the F1 world's attention by winning two Grands Prix for Tyrrell in 1982–3, and subsequently spent five years at Ferrari, winning three Grands Prix. He remained in F1 with lesser teams until 1993.

Jean Alesi

The French-Sicilian former F3000 champion, Jean Alesi (*left*), burst into F1 part way through 1989 with Tyrrell, and ran as high as second on his Grand Prix début. He further impressed by leading the 1990 US Grand Prix in Phoenix in his Tyrrell, ahead of Senna, and momentarily repassing the Brazilian when overtaken. Such form saw offers from both Williams and Ferrari. He chose the latter where, in five seasons of spectacular effort, he won only once, in the 1995 Canadian Grand Prix.

Chris Amon

Unfortunately known as the finest driver never to have won a championship Grand Prix, New Zealander Chris Amon (*above*) was fantastically gifted, but never in the right place at the right time. He made his F1 début at 19 years of age, and four years later, in 1967, was the lead driver for Ferrari. In his three years with the Italian team, he led many times without success, and it was a similar story in his subsequent career with Matra in the early 1970s. He retired from F1 in 1976, after his sheer class had elevated the little Ensign team.

Elio de Angelis

The Roman Elio de Angelis made his way into F1 at an early age, helped by his family's considerable wealth and plenty of talent. After impressing in an outclassed Shadow in 1979, he was signed by Lotus. He stayed with that team for six seasons, winning the 1982 Austrian and 1985 San Marino Grands Prix, and finishing third in the 1984 World Championship. He was killed early in 1986 in a testing accident with Brabham.

Right: Elio de Angelis won two Grands Prix and came third in the 1984 title race before his death in 1986 testing for Brabham.

René Arnoux

The wild-eyed Frenchman, René Arnoux (*right*), will always be remembered for his stirring battle for second place in the 1979 French Grand Prix with Gilles Villeneuve. He gained his initial F1 success with the early Renault turbo cars, winning four Grands Prix, before transferring to Ferrari, where he was in contention for the 1983 World Championship until the final round. Subsequently he raced for Ligier before retiring in 1989.

Giancarlo Baghetti

The only man in history to have won on his début in an F1 championship Grand Prix, Giancarlo Baghetti achieved this feat in 1961, at the wheel of a semi-works Ferrari in the French Grand Prix. Despite such a stunning start, and his subsequent promotion to the factory team, he never again came close to such success and was only rarely seen in F1 after 1962.

▓ Lorenzo Bandini

A popular and effective driver,
Lorenzo Bandini spent most of his
five-year F1 career with Ferrari and
was beginning to show real form
when he crashed fatally in the 1967
Monaco Grand Prix. After fighting
initially with Baghetti for a regular
place on the Ferrari F1 team, Bandini
became properly established there in
1964 and won that year's Austrian
Grand Prix.

▓ Jean Behra

After some wonderful giant-killing
performances in his underpowered
Gordini in the early 1950s,
Frenchman Jean Behra was taken on
by the Maserati team. Once there, he
confirmed his often startling turn of
speed, but too frequently he abused
his machinery and lost. In 1959, he
signed for Ferrari, but was sacked
after punching the team manager. He
was killed later the same year while
racing an F2 car on the dangerous
Avus track.

▓ Stefan Bellof

A very promising future seemed to await the German Stefan Bellof who, in his
début F1 season with Tyrrell in 1984, displayed a stunning turn of speed and
aggression. In the wet Monaco Grand Prix of that year, he was closing in on
leaders Prost and Senna when the race was stopped. He was killed in 1985
during a sports car race at Spa.

▓ Gerhard Berger

After more than 13 seasons and ten
Grand Prix victories for Benetton,
Ferrari and McLaren, Gerhard Berger
(*right*) finally bowed out of F1 at the
end of 1997. He had started with
only a couple of seasons' previous
experience in F3, but was
immediately fast. He earned the
admiration of all in his brave
come-back after a horrific fireball
accident in the 1989 San Marino
Grand Prix.

Above: *Lorenzo Bandini's major F1 success
came when he won the Austrian GP in 1964.*

Above right: *The underrated Tony Brooks was
always at his best on fast circuits, such as Spa
here in 1958, where he won for Vanwall.*

Thierry Boutsen

Acknowledged as a wet-weather specialist, the Belgian Thierry Boutsen won three Grands Prix in his stint with Williams-Renault during 1989–90, two of them in the rain. His F1 career began with Arrows in 1983 and, aside from Williams, took in Benetton, Ligier and Jordan. He has since raced in Touring Cars and sports cars.

Tony Brise

When Graham Hill's light plane crashed in poor visibility in 1975, Tony Brise lost his life along with Hill and other members of the latter's new team. He had just completed his first F1 season with the team and was widely tipped as a future World Champion. Prior to that, he had swept all before him in British F3 and Formula Atlantic, and raised eyebrows when, in a one-off F5000 race at Long Beach, he battled for the lead with Mario Andretti.

Tony Brooks

One of the finest F1 drivers of the 1950s, Tony Brooks became the first British racer to win a Grand Prix in a British car – the 1955 Syracuse race in a Connaught. During the same period, he was studying for his dentistry finals. However it was a non-championship event, but later he went on to record a series of championship-status wins for Vanwall and Ferrari, finishing runner-up in the 1959 championship with the latter. He retired in 1961, aged 29.

Martin Brundle

Although he never managed to win a Grand Prix, Martin Brundle showed great tenacity in a 12-year on-off spell with F1. Senna's match in F3, he arrived in F1 in 1984 and scored a second place in Detroit with the Tyrrell. His best year came as Schumacher's team-mate at Benetton in 1992, when he came close to winning the Belgian Grand Prix and took a series of podium places.

Eugenio Castellotti

Dubbed a wealthy playboy, Eugenio Castellotti was also a seriously quick driver, and although during his short career in the mid-1950s he didn't win a championship Grand Prix, it seemed only a matter of time. As part of the Ferrari team in 1956, his pace was not far adrift of team-mates Fangio and Collins. He died early in 1957 in a testing accident.

Andrea de Cesaris

Although famed more for a spectacularly long list of crashes during his early days, in fact Andrea de Cesaris was a fairly steady hand by the end of his F1 career, which stretched from 1980 to 1993. What was never in doubt was his speed. In 1982, he led for much of the US GP West, and on several occasions in 1983 his Alfa Romeo broke when well placed.

François Cevert

Jackie Stewart's understudy at Tyrrell, François Cevert (below), won the 1971 US Grand Prix, and by 1973 was recognised as one of the best in the business. At the end of that year, he was killed in qualifying when trying to wrest pole position from Ronnie Peterson at the same Watkins Glen track he'd triumphed at in 1971.

✤ Peter Collins

Forever remembered as the man who gave up his own chances of the 1956 World Championship when he handed his Ferrari over to team-mate Fangio, feeling that the Argentinian 'deserved it', Peter Collins was part of the new wave of post-war British talent. He won three Grands Prix for the Italian team before his death in the 1958 German Grand Prix, when chasing Tony Brooks' Vanwall for the lead.

Above: *Peter Collins, remembered as a gentleman and a true sportsman.*

Below: *Patrick Depailler, a beaming daredevil who courted danger.*

✤ David Coulthard

Getting his F1 break as the replacement for Ayrton Senna at Williams placed enormous pressure on the young Scot, David Coulthard, who had graduated through the junior formulae with Jackie Stewart's team. Nevertheless he grasped the opportunity, and within a year had blitzed to four consecutive pole positions and won his first Grand Prix. Since joining McLaren, he's won twice, and in 1998 slid in behind Hakkinen and Schumacher to take 3rd place.

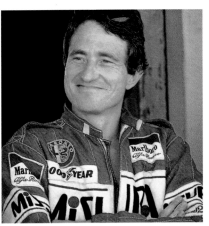

✤ Patrick Depailler

A man renowned for his penchant for danger, Frenchman Patrick Depailler won two Grands Prix before his death in a testing accident at Hockenheim in 1980. He'd arrived in F1 with the Tyrrell team in the mid-1970s, and although he was a regular front-runner it wasn't until 1978 that he made his breakthrough by winning the Monaco Grand Prix. Later he transferred to Ligier and won the 1979 Spanish Grand Prix before breaking his legs in a hang-gliding accident.

✤ Richie Ginther

The Californian Richie Ginther came to F1 through sports car racing with Ferrari, like his friend Phil Hill. In 1961, he was teamed with Hill and finished a strong second to Stirling Moss at Monaco, although his major strength was considered to be his analytical testing ability. After a spell with BRM, he won Honda and Goodyear's first Grand Prix, in Mexico in 1965.

Below: *Richie Ginther celebrates victory for Honda and Goodyear in the 1965 Mexican GP.*

Above: *Scotland's new hope, David Coulthard, a consistent challenger for the World Championship in 1998.*

✤ Frolian Gonzalez

Known as the Pampas Bull, for his huge frame and furious driving style, Frolian Gonzalez was the man who gave Ferrari its first championship Grand Prix, at Silverstone in 1951. As fast as anyone on his day, he lacked the consistency of his great friend and countryman, Fangio. He won the British Grand Prix again in 1954 and finished runner-up in that year's championship, but retired soon after.

✤ Dan Gurney

Arguably America's finest FI driver, Dan Gurney was a formidable competitor during the early to mid-1960s, giving the Porsche and Brabham marques their first GP successes. It was said that he was the only driver Jim Clark considered a threat. Gurney left Brabham to set up his own marque, Eagle, and won the 1967 Belgian Grand Prix in one of its cars. He now runs his All American Racers team in Indycars.

✤ Mika Hakkinen

The furiously fast Finn, Mika Hakkinen (above), won his first Grand Prix in controversial circumstances at Jerez in 1997. Since out-qualifying his team-mate Ayrton Senna in his first race for McLaren in 1993, Hakkinen has been acknowledged as one of the fastest men in FI. He sealed his reputation with the championship in 1998, when he pipped Schumacher.

Above: Jim Clark said Dan Gurney was the only driver he feared, yet the Californian fiddled endlessly and was perennially unlucky.

✤ Johnny Herbert

When Johnny Herbert (*above*) crashed his F3000 car so badly in 1988 that it was feared he would lose his feet, it seemed the end of a hugely promising career. Six months later, he took fourth place in his FI début. It's been a topsy-turvy career since, the highlight to date being two Grand Prix wins for Benetton in 1995. More recently, he's guided Sauber to ever greater heights.

Above: *A magnificent character, Innes Ireland scored Team Lotus' first victory when he won the 1961 US GP at Watkins Glen.*

Right: *Gentleman Jacques Laffite was a universally popular character on the F1 scene.*

Jacky Ickx

When Jacky Ickx qualified his F2 Matra third quickest overall for the 1967 German Grand Prix, he caused a sensation. It led to a Ferrari drive for 1968 and his first Grand Prix win. Another followed with Brabham in 1969. Back with Ferrari in 1970, he was the only man who threatened Jochen Rindt's posthumous title. He took his final win in 1972.

Innes Ireland

A Scot, despite the name, Innes Ireland won Team Lotus' first Grand Prix, in America in 1961. It was the highlight of a career punctuated by several spills, but in which blind courage often overcame second-rate machinery. He drove his last F1 season in 1966 and took to F1 journalism soon after. He succumbed to cancer in 1993.

Jean-Pierre Jabouille

In débuting F1's first turbocharged racer in 1977 with Renault, Jean-Pierre Jabouille made history. He did so again, two years later, by winning the first Grand Prix with such a car, then took another win in the 1980 Austrian Grand Prix. However his career came to an end not long after with a crash that badly broke his legs.

Below: *Jean-Pierre Jabouille, the first man to win with turbo power.*

Jacques Laffite

The brother-in-law and former mechanic of Jean-Pierre Jabouille, Jacques Laffite went into the final round of the 1981 championship with an outside chance of taking the crown, although eventually he finished fourth in the standings. Lafitte graduated to F1 with Frank Williams' team in 1974, but won all six of his Grands Prix with Ligier between 1977 and 1981. His F1 career was brought to a close in 1986 after fracturing a leg very badly.

Right: Another universally loved character was New Zealander Bruce McLaren, whose team lives on.

Below: The king who was never crowned, Stirling Moss was arguably the greatest-ever all-rounder.

Stuart Lewis-Evans

Alongside Stirling Moss and Tony Brooks in the 1957/8 Vanwall team, Stuart Lewis-Evans proved just as quick, although a history of ill-health meant that sometimes his stamina proved to be a problem. He sat on pole position for the 1957 Italian Grand Prix, but his death from burns inflicted in the final round of the 1958 season was a major factor in Vanwall pulling out of the sport.

Onofre Marimon

As an extremely promising young Argentinian driver, Onofre Marimon first appeared in Grand Prix racing in 1953, driving for the Maserati team. He featured in the lead battle for that year's Italian Grand Prix and, under the guidance of his mentor, Fangio, was tipped for great things. He was killed in practice for the 1954 German Grand Prix.

Bruce McLaren

Although his surname is now more familiar because of the race team that he founded, Kiwi Bruce McLaren scored his early F1 successes with Cooper. His victory for the team in America in 1959 made him the youngest ever Grand Prix winner. He remained with Cooper until leaving to found McLaren in 1966, and two years later scored the marque's first win at the Belgian Grand Prix. He died testing a Can-Am McLaren sports car in 1970.

Stirling Moss

It is one of motor racing's ironies that Stirling Moss, one of the greatest drivers of all time, never won a world title. His performances as a privateer, in a Maserati in 1954, earned him a place with Mercedes for 1955, when he won his first Grand Prix. Thereafter, in a variety of cars – Maserati, Vanwall, Cooper and Lotus – he won regularly. After Fangio had retired, and up to the time of the accident that ended his own career in 1962, he stood head and shoulders above his contemporaries. He deserved much more than history records.

Luigi Musso

For a brief time – the 18 months between rival Eugenio Castellotti's death in 1957 and his own in 1958 – Luigi Musso was Italy's top driver. He shared a Grand Prix win with Fangio in 1956, and a year later took third place in the World Championship. Teamed at Ferrari with the faster Mike Hawthorn and Peter Collins in 1958, he was under pressure. He crashed to his death in the French Grand Prix.

Alessandro Nannini

The official winner of the 1989 Japanese Grand Prix after Ayrton Senna was disqualified, Alessandro Nannini was emerging as a genuine world-class driver with Benetton when, in 1990, his arm was severed in a helicopter crash. Although surgeons sewed it back on, his F1 career was over. He has since scored much success in sports and touring cars.

Carlos Pace

The winner of his home Brazilian Grand Prix in 1975 for Brabham, Carlos Pace was killed in a light aircraft crash two years later. He arrived in F1 with Williams in 1972, and impressed at Surtees in the following year by setting fastest lap at the daunting Nürburgring. Taken on by Brabham in 1974, he remained with that team for the rest of his career.

Left: *Pace, heading for victory in Brazil, 1975.*

Riccardo Patrese

The most experienced F1 driver there has ever been, Riccardo Patrese (*above*) amassed 256 Grand Prix starts between 1977 and 1993, winning six of them for Brabham and Williams. Considered wild, but fast, in his early days, he matured into one of the most consistent drivers of all. However the raw speed had disappeared by the time of his final season, in 1993, as team-mate to Schumacher at Benetton.

Ronnie Peterson

Considered the fastest driver in F1 in the mid-1970s, Ronnie Peterson was twice runner-up in the championship. The Swede made his F1 début in 1970 after winning the Monaco F3 race in the previous year, and although he finished second to Stewart in the 1971 title race, it wasn't until 1973 and his spell with Team Lotus that he started winning races. He returned to that team after a two-year break in 1978 and supported Mario Andretti's title campaign, but died from a pulmonary embolism after breaking his legs in the Italian Grand Prix.

Didier Pironi

Prior to the accident in practice for the 1982 German Grand Prix that ended his career, Didier Pironi appeared to be on his way to the world title for Ferrari. His win earlier in the season at Imola had enraged team-mate Gilles Villeneuve and had led, indirectly, to the French-Canadian's death in practice for the Belgian Grand Prix. Pironi had arrived at Ferrari after an early career with Tyrrell in 1978/9 and a season at Ligier in 1980, when he won his first Grand Prix. He died in a power-boat accident in 1987.

Tom Pryce

Dubbed a future world champion, Wales' Tom Pryce had an F1 career that lasted from 1974 until his death in the 1977 South African Grand Prix, caused by a marshal with a fire extinguisher running across the track in front of his car. All but one of his races were with the Shadow team. He won the non-championship Race of Champions in 1975.

Clay Regazzoni

With five Grand Prix wins leading to a third place in the World Championship for Ferrari, Clay Regazzoni's F1 début season in 1970 was nothing short of sensational. Belying an early reputation for wildness, he developed into a steady hand and was a close runner-up in the 1974 championship, again with Ferrari. In 1979, aged 39, he won the Williams team's first Grand Prix. An accident at Long Beach, in 1980, left him confined to a wheelchair.

Right, clockwise from upper left: *Injury cut short Alessandro Nannini's career; Tom Pryce died in a senseless accident in South Africa; poor medical attention killed Ronnie Peterson in 1978; Clay Regazzoni was paralysed in an accident in 1980.*

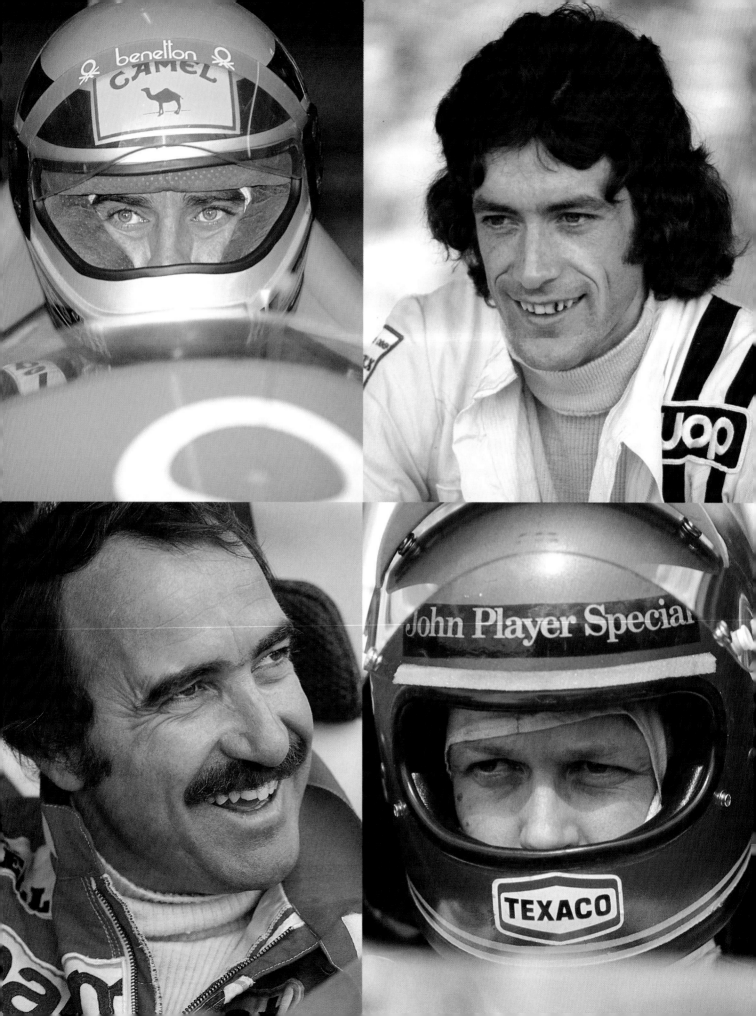

Carlos Reutemann

A few months after coming tantalisingly close to winning the 1981 World Championship for Williams, Carlos Reutemann retired from racing. This brought an end to an F1 career of enormous potential, which was never fully realized. After scoring pole position on his Grand Prix début in 1972, he went on to win 12 Grands Prix for Brabham, Ferrari and Williams. Today he is tipped as a future president of his country.

Peter Revson

An heir to the Revlon cosmetics family fortune, Peter Revson disassociated himself from the business and took to motor racing in the 1960s, making his F1 début in 1964. However it wasn't until his second stint in F1, after establishing himself in America as an Indycar star, that he scored Grand Prix success, winning two races in 1973 for McLaren. He was killed in practice for the 1974 South African Grand Prix.

Pedro Rodriguez

One of the finest wet-weather drivers the sport has ever seen, Mexican Pedro Rodriguez was initially overshadowed by his younger brother, Ricardo. Some time after Ricardo's death, he devoted himself fully to racing and won two Grands Prix: one with Cooper in 1967, the other with BRM in 1970. He was killed in a sports car race in 1971.

Ricardo Rodriguez

Aided by an extremely wealthy family, Ricardo Rodriguez was winning international sports car races when in his mid-teens. Rodriguez made a sensational F1 début, qualifying on the front row for the 1961 Italian Grand Prix. Such promise was never fulfilled, however, for he died after crashing in practice for his home Grand Prix in 1962.

Jo Siffert

A tough former motor-cycle racer, Swiss Jo Siffert enjoyed his first taste of F1 success with Rob Walker's privateer team, winning the 1968 British Grand Prix in a Lotus. He furthered his reputation with some epic battles in sports car racing with Porsche team-mate Pedro Rodriguez, whom he joined at BRM in 1971. He won that year's Austrian Grand Prix, but was killed in a non-championship race at Brands Hatch at the end of the season.

Above left: *Carlos Reutemann.*

Above: *Pedro Rodriguez, brilliant in the wet.*

Left: *Ricardo Rodriguez made a sensational impact for Ferrari at Spa in 1962, as he pressured Phil Hill.*

Wolfgang von Trips

On the verge of the 1961 World Championship, the legendary Wolfgang von Trips crashed to his death in the Italian Grand Prix. The German count's car flipped after a clash of wheels with Jim Clark's Lotus and was launched into the crowd. The accident killed 15 spectators. He had entered F1 in the late 1950s with Ferrari after showing strongly in the team's sports cars.

Left: Like Rindt, von Trips was the victim of cruel misfortune at Monza in 1961 when he was killed.

Below: Never say die: Gilles Villeneuve leads the pack into the hairpin at Long Beach in 1979 – one of his great victories.

Gilles Villeneuve

One of the fastest and most spectacular drivers ever seen in F1, French-Canadian Gilles Villeneuve was a former snowmobile champion who made it to F1 after beating James Hunt in a North American Formula Atlantic race. His F1 début with McLaren in 1977 was sensational and earned him a drive with Ferrari, where he was to stay throughout his career. In 1979, he finished runner-up in the championship to team-mate Jody Scheckter after obeying team orders, but thereafter rarely had a competitive car. He suffered a fatal crash in practice for the 1982 Belgian Grand Prix. His son, Jacques, went on to become 1997 World Champion for the Williams team.

Below: Let the champagne fly – John Watson celebrates a stunning victory at Long Beach in 1983.

Derek Warwick

The immensely popular Derek Warwick never had a race-winning drive in an F1 career that stretched from 1981 to 1993, although he led several times and earned a reputation as one of the toughest competitors on the grid. He now drives more successfuly for his own team in Touring Cars.

John Watson

Five times a Grand Prix winner, and runner-up in the 1982 championship, Northern Ireland's John Watson endured an initial reputation as F1's 'bad luck' man in the mid-1970s. However he went on to achieve success with McLaren in the 1980s, the highlight of which was a win in the 1981 British Grand Prix.

2 | THE CIRCUITS

CHAPTER **3**

Lap Records
THE WORLD'S TEN GREATEST CIRCUITS

Wʜat makes a great Grand Prix circuit? Down the years views have frequently differed, not the least during the troubled 1960s when safety campaigns gradually changed the entire face of the sport forever, and set in train the demise of venues which had come to be regarded as classics.

Brands Hatch

If ever a racing circuit represented a natural amphitheatre it was Brands Hatch, England's 'mini-Nürburgring'. From its humble beginnings as a grass track venue, the circuit was nurtured under the dictatorial (but basically benign) stewardship of John Webb, a far-sighted man who understood the value of publicity and was never short of ideas on how to generate it.

Whereas the Silverstone of the 1960s looked exactly what it was – a fast track based on an old airfield – Brands offered variety: from the plunging Paddock Hill

Right: Elio de Angelis highlights the natural amphitheatre that was Brands Hatch, during the 1985 GP of Europe.

Below right: Ayrton Senna leads the start of that race, which was to give Nigel Mansell his first taste of F1 victory.

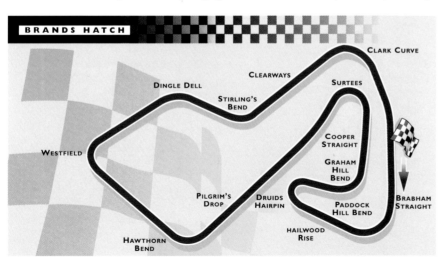

BRANDS HATCH

CLARK CURVE

CLEARWAYS

DINGLE DELL

SURTEES

STIRLING'S BEND

WESTFIELD

COOPER STRAIGHT

GRAHAM HILL BEND

PILGRIM'S DROP

DRUIDS HAIRPIN

PADDOCK HILL BEND

BRABHAM STRAIGHT

HAWTHORN BEND

HAILWOOD RISE

Bend at the start of the lap and the ensuing climb up to the Druids hairpin, to the flat-out blast into the country along the main straight, which ended in a slight dip (Pilgrim's Drop) before the right-hander of Hawthorn Bend. There followed a series of tree-lined curves before expectant spectators on the pit straight caught sight of the cars again as they burst back into the light on the run down to Clearways, the final corner later renamed in Jim Clark's honour.

Perhaps the carnival atmosphere that Webb encouraged was a little too garish for the purists, but enthusiasts knew that Brands Hatch was where you went to be entertained, and to watch good racing. Few would forget the fight between Jo Siffert and Chris Amon in 1968; or the sight of Derek Warwick's tank-like Toleman passing championship leader Didier Pironi in 1982 at Paddock where eight years earlier Jacky Ickx had woven a spell on Niki Lauda. Or the crowd's reaction when it seemed that James Hunt might be banned from the restart in 1976, or the reception that greeted Nigel Mansell's maiden GP win there in 1985.

An argument between Bernie Ecclestone and the new owner of Brands Hatch, John Foulston, led to the circuit's demise as an F1 venue. However, a new agreement is now in place and Brand's Hatch will host a British Grand Prix from 2002. F1's coming home.

Interlagos

Those who raced there still swear that the old Interlagos was one of those circuits that separated the men from the boys. It was bumpy. It possessed corners that generated a force of 15g, which sapped strength. It tested the very mettle of a driver. Frequently, to add to the discomfort, the conditions were humid. The 7.97km (4.95-mile) giant of a circuit was just outside São Paulo, where the enthusiasm of the Brazilians was bettered only by that of the Italians at Monza.

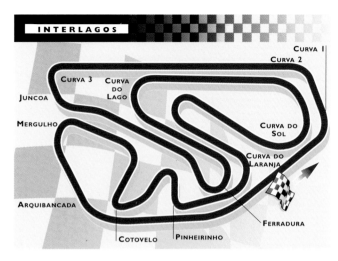

Interlagos dated back to 1940, although it was not until 1973 that the circuit hosted its first Grand Prix. It was entirely fitting that local boy Emerson Fittipaldi should win this in his Lotus since, as the country's first World Champion, he had been so instrumental in winning Brazil the first round of the World Championship. The circuit was packed into a tight space, which meant that the corners were a mixture of very, very fast curves and tight infield bends, few of which gave the drivers any respite on a hot afternoon. And its unusual anti-clockwise orientation could make life hard for neck muscles.

Eventually the ground-effect cars of the late 1970s simply made things too unbearable for the drivers, the rock-hard springs making hard work of the bumps. The Grand Prix moved to Jacarepagua in Rio, home track of Nelson Piquet. But then Interlagos was revised, over a 4.31 km (2.68-mile) design, which broadly retained the characteristics of the old, albeit deleting the fabulously fast opening part to the lap. It was, like Spa, that rare thing: an acceptable modernisation. And it bore the name of its departed son, Carlos 'Moco' Pace, the winner in 1975. A poignant touch. The drivers still complained of the bumps, though. Some things never change.

Left: Interlagos was a spectacular venue in its old form, separating men from boys with its mix of very high-speed sweeps and curves.

Below: Gilles Villeneuve temporarily leads the 1980 race after a blistering start for Ferrari.

Right: Kyalami, too, was a spectacularly fast track. Here Mansell heads for his second victory, in the 1985 South African GP.

Kyalami

In days gone by, Kyalami, South Africa's Grand Prix circuit, conjured up images of unlimited speed on the main straight, and cars slithering through the ensuing Crowthorne and Barbeque bends on the very limit of adhesion before negotiating the Jukskei Sweep and blasting on to the left-hander, Clubhouse Bend, and the Esses. Then the speed continued mounting and mounting on the long upward right curve drag back to the straight again.

Invariably it was hot and sunny there in the days when the race kicked off the season in January or, later, March, and the air was festive as the new cars came out for the first time. The atmosphere was expectant, as it always is at the beginning of a new season when anything seems

possible. Kyalami is 1829m (6000ft) above sea level, which robbed the normally aspirated cars of power and, when they raced together, gave the turbos further advantage, but the racing was usually good.

Kyalami is remembered for surrendering to Jimmy Clark his 25th, and last, GP victory in 1968; for Jack Brabham's swan-song triumph in 1970; for Mike Hailwood's heroic rescue of Clay Regazzoni from his burning BRM in 1973; and for the

needless tragedy that befell Tom Pryce in 1977 when he was hit full in the face by a fire extinguisher carried by a foolhardy, but well-meaning, marshal who ran across the road in front of him just as his Shadow crested the slight rise on the main straight.

It is forgotten, however, for the excuse for a circuit that was created, using the Jukskei/Clubhouse section of the old, for the revival of the 1990s. It deserved so much better.

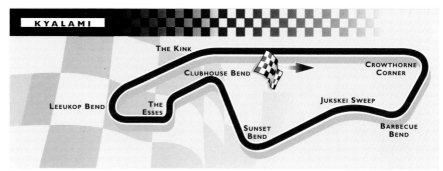

Monaco

In April 1929, William Grover
Williams steered a Bugatti 35B to
victory in a race around the streets
of Monte Carlo, home to the
Grimaldi family for more than 600
years. Motor racing captured hearts
in the principality and, as spectators
discovered that they could almost
touch the very fabric of the sport,
the Monaco Grand Prix became the
jewel in F1's crown. It is the epitome
of motor sport, rivalled only by Le
Mans and the Indianapolis 500.

Monte Carlo is one of the few
tracks where a driver's true brilliance
can make up for deficiencies in his
machinery. It's a narrow grey ribbon
that threads its way between concrete
walls and steel barriers. The smallest
mistake is penalized out of all
proportion. It suits a particular type of
driver, which is why Graham Hill won
it five times. But the record is held by
Ayrton Senna who, in his heyday with
the Marlboro McLaren team, pushed
the mark to six remarkable victories.

*Right: Monaco in the playground of the rich
and famous. It is also a fabulous venue for a
Grand Prix, with the climb up the hill to the
Casino, and the tight sweeps and squirts
through the tunnel by the seafront and the
round the swimming pool by the harbour.*

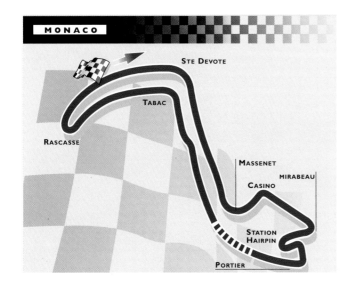

MONACO

STE DEVOTE

TABAC

RASCASSE

MASSENET

MIRABEAU

CASINO

STATION
HAIRPIN

PORTIER

Damon Hill, from whom an emotional victory was
snatched by engine failure in 1996, said, 'Monaco is a classic
race, unique in that the track surface and the demands
from the car are completely different from anywhere else.'

For spectators, Monaco is mecca, a unique place to
watch a Grand Prix driver displaying his artistry at close
quarters, changing direction at breathtaking speeds, shaving
walls, dancing from bump to bump. The extraordinary
juxtaposition of street course, with its mental connotations
of road cars and everyday motoring, and sheer feral speed
creates Monaco's unique charisma as high society meets
high speed.

Monaco redefines the risks that racing drivers accept so
blithely, and reminds you why some do, and why the saner
majority are content simply to watch in awe.

Monza

The spirits of FI still walk at Monza. Built in 1922 as a road course and, with full banking, last used in the tragic 1961 race, the Italian track has seen everything that has happened to FI in the intervening years. Located in park land outside Milan, it is the treasure chest of the sport's romantic side, with the ever-enthusiastic tifosi acting as guardians lest anyone should become too cynical to enjoy an atmosphere that is redolent of a heady blend of yesterday and today.

In its heyday, before the chicane blight cursed it, Monza was the home of slipstreaming epics, when not just two cars might charge side by side for the finish line, but when four, or even five, would vie for victory on the last lap.

Looked at in plan view, it resembles a child's slot racing set, complete with cross-over where the old banked circuit overlaps. From the cockpit, it was the place for unfettered speed. Today it is still a circuit that places the smallest premium on sheer handling, and more on power and good brakes to slow cars for the numerous chicanes. And its glorious atmosphere remains as a lasting tribute to the sheer spirit of the Italians and their love of the sport. As an enthusiast, to be in Monza, as in Imola, is to feel as if one has come home.

In 1961, its darker side saw the clash between Jim Clark and Wolfgang von Trips that killed the latter as he stood on the brink of the World Championship; likewise Jochen Rindt died nine years later as the silver chalice was raised virtually to his lips. Ronnie Peterson, too, perished there. But in 1993, Christian Fittipaldi had a miraculous escape when his Minardi somersaulted over that of his team-mate, Pierluigi Martini, on the finish line. To see the crowd savouring a Ferrari victory there is truly to see Italian motor racing with its heart on its sleeve.

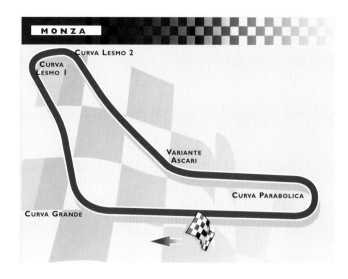

MONZA

CURVA LESMO 2
CURVA LESMO 1
VARIANTE ASCARI
CURVA PARABOLICA
CURVA GRANDE

Below: Monza has been one of the spiritual homes of motorsport since its construction in 1922. In the lower photo can be seen part of the steep banking, last used for FI in the tragic 1961 Italian GP.

The Nürburgring

The 'old' Nürburgring is one of F1's ghosts, a guilty secret from its distant carefree past, a monument to a bygone age of heroes. Of all the race tracks ever devised, it is surely the greatest.

Jackie Stewart used to call the Nürburgring the Green Hell: 'I was always relieved when it was time to leave. The only time you felt good thinking about the 'Ring was when you were a long way away, curled up at home in front of a warm fire on a long winter night. You know, I never ever did one more quick lap there than I absolutely had to.'

The 24.3-km (15.1-mile) track was every racer's dream and nightmare as it wound around the Eifel mountains and the Gothic Nürburg Castle, plunging between the hedgerows and the trees, its 176 corners bearing exotic names such as Quiddelbacher Hohe, Flugplatz, Fuchsrohre (the Foxhole), Wehrseifen, Ex-Muhle, Breidscheid and Bergwerk – where Niki Lauda came to grief. Most famous of them all was the Karussel, a 180-degree banked left-hander. Then there was Brunnchen – where

photographers snapped the cars with all four wheels off the ground – Pflantzgarten and Schwalbenschwanz (or Swallow's Tail), a mini Karussel. Dottinger-Hohe led on to the long hump-backed straight. Blind brows hid the next apex, and being 30cm (1ft) off line could mean the difference between the successful negotiation of a corner and a long walk home. Or much worse.

It was on the brutal sweeps, dives and twists of this monster that great drivers such as Tazio Nuvolari, Bernd

Rosemeyer, Rudolf Caracciola, Dick Seaman, Juan Manuel Fangio, Stirling Moss and Jackie Stewart carved their names with pride.

All of the circuit would be far too dangerous by today's standards, and Lauda's fiery accident in 1976 confirmed that it was simply too long to marshal properly. But in its heyday, this most majestic of all tracks was the most significant challenge a driver would ever face. To have won a Grand Prix there was to have laid claim to true greatness.

Top: No greater circuit was ever devised than the 'old' Nürburgring, where Niki Lauda leads the field in 1975.

Left: An endless string of challenging corners, the 'Ring was the greatest test of any driver's skill.

Osterreichring

Grown men sighed with nostalgia and regret when the F1 circus moved back to Austria, and the new A1-Ring, for the 1997 GP. One, looking at what remained of the old Rindtkurve, expressed his dismay that it had been left to grass over.

The Styrian countryside was as beautiful as it had been ten years earlier, when F1 paid its last visit. But in those days, the race was still held on the majestic Osterreichring, surely one of the most beautiful race tracks in history.

What made the Osterreichring so special was that it was fast. In 1986 and 1987, pole-position lap speeds had reached 256km/h (159mph). And its curves swept up and down hill, pre-senting challenges that only 'real men' overcame. 'That first corner, going up to Hella Licht,' Jackie Stewart mused one day in 1997. 'You know, I'd say that was one of the great underrated corners of motor racing. It was quick and very hard to take really fast. Because you approached it up a gradient, you couldn't see the apex

until you were right on top of it. Oh, that was a real challenge.'

The American driver Mark Donohue crashed there in 1975 and, although conscious afterwards, he died in hospital days later of head injuries. But even the chicane they installed there did not fundamentally alter the character of the track.

Time and again, the Osterreichring created unusual results: Jo Siffert triumphed for BRM in 1971; John Watson for Penske in 1976; Alan

Jones for Shadow 1977; and in 1982, Elio de Angelis beat Keke Rosberg to the line by all of 0.05s. But perhaps the most memorable occurred in 1975, when the rain-soaked race was halted before half distance and the winner, the erratic Italian Vittorio Brambilla, crashed going across the line as he punched the air in triumph.

Now the Osterreichring lies largely forgotten, the A-1 Ring squirming within its confines like an irritating tapeworm.

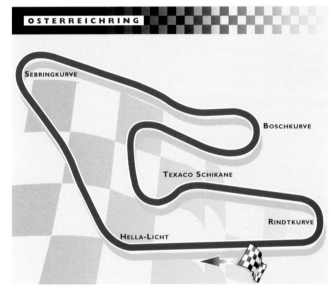

Below: *Like the Nürburgring, the Osterreichring was a daunting challenge. In its present incarnation, the circuit is a shadow of its former self.*

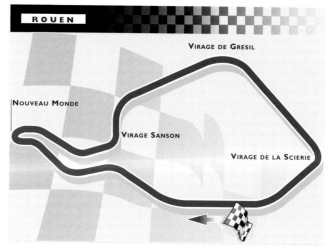

Left: *Denny Hulme leads John Surtees early in the tragic 1968 French GP at Rouen.*

Below: *The chequered flag awaits Jacky Ickx for the first time as a winner in his FI career, as he heads for the finish line at Rouen in 1968.*

[Rouen

In common with Clermont-Ferrand, Rouen was one of the greatest circuits on which the post-war French GP would ever be held. In its 6.44km (4 miles), Rouen-les-Essarts, situated in Normandy, east of Beauvais and north-east of Paris, followed the popular French ploy of utilising sections of the RN138 and the RN840 public roads. The wooded section past the pits ran downhill through a series of curves to the attractively named Nouveau Monde hairpin, and it was here that David Purley said he would use the old paratroopers' technique of screaming into his helmet to pump adrenalin and prevent himself from lifting his foot from the throttle. From there, the track climbed to the village of Sanson and up to Gresil, where it rejoined the Rouen-bound RN138. It was relatively simple in plan form, but another of those circuits where bravery reaped its own reward.

Rouen hosted the French GP on only five occasions: in 1952 when Ascari dominated; 1957 when Fangio's

glorious four-wheel drifts on the downhill curves became part of racing folklore; 1962 and 1964 when the race fell each time to Dan Gurney; and finally 1968 when Jacky Ickx scored his maiden FI success at the wheel of a Ferrari in truly appalling weather conditions. That was the race in which the unfortunate French veteran Jo Schlesser perished when his experimental Honda V8 slid

off the road and crashed into a bank on the approach to Nouveau Monde.

Jochen Rindt took pole position for that final race, at more than 210km/h (125mph), while the abnormally brave Pedro Rodriguez set the fastest lap at a remarkable 178km/h (111mph), despite the rain. The only consolation when Rouen was dropped was that at least Clermont-Ferrand offered a similar steely challenge.

Spa Francorchamps

Jimmy Clark hated Spa Francorchamps, the ultra-fast tree-lined track set in the Belgian Ardennes. The first time he raced there, in 1958, he watched Archie Scott-Brown crash to his death in a sports car race. Two years later, in his first Grand Prix there, Clark narrowly avoided what was left of the unfortunate Chris Bristow, and also lost team-mate Alan Stacey.

Ever the professional, however, Clark won at Spa four times in a row, from 1962 to 1965, yet the nature of the place spooked not only the Scot, but also his fellows. Spa, they all knew, was a life-taker that commanded respect.

In the old days, the circuit measured 14.0km (8.7miles), all of them fast apart from the hairpin bend at La Source at the end of the lap. In 1970, in the last GP held on the old track, Chris Amon's fastest lap was 245km/h (152mph). Later, sports cars would take that to an astonishing 262km/h (163mph), despite the hairpin slowing them to 80km/h (50mph).

Like Clark, Jackie Stewart detested the place after the accident that befell him on the first lap in 1966, when the start was dry, but drivers encountered a sudden wall of spray part way round. That was the problem at Spa: the weather was unpredictable, and it could be dry in places, but wet elsewhere. With the 322km/h (200mph) Masta Straight punctuated by a kink that could just be taken flat out in the 3-litre F1 cars if a driver really screwed up his courage, it was terrifyingly dangerous. After 1970, the race moved elsewhere, but eventually Spa was redesigned.

The Osterreichring and Kyalami died under such circumstances, emerging as pale shadows of their former selves, but Spa remained as glorious as ever. The daunting Eau Rouge was still intact, and only a foolish 'bus stop' chicane marred the circuit's 6.9-km (4.3-mile) symmetry. It was uplifting to see how the old could be blended into the new, if only sufficient thought was given to the problem of adapting something great to the fresh demands of a different era.

Below and right: *Spa offers spectators fabulous scenic views, and the drivers a blistering high-speed challenge that is a throwback to the old days of the sport.*

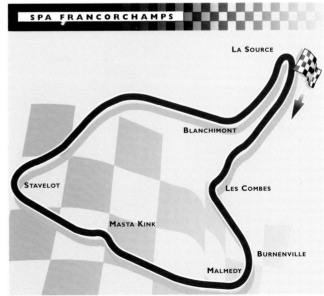

SPA FRANCORCHAMPS

LA SOURCE

BLANCHIMONT

LES COMBES

STAVELOT

MASTA KINK

BURNENVILLE

MALMEDY

Watkins Glen

Nestling by the Finger Lakes in New York State, Watkins Glen was both fast and beautiful in its heyday. As the home of the US GP, it offered the biggest prize fund of the season. Amid autumnal reds, yellows and browns, it went through a period when its beauty was tarnished by the activities of the infamous Bog People, who captured and torched the vehicles of anyone foolish enough to trespass upon their muddy domain. However, as a track that often produced an unusual result, it could be both benign and cruel, giving with one hand, only to take away with the other.

Here, in 1961, Innes Ireland won his only Grand Prix, and the first for Team Lotus. But a few weeks later, Colin Chapman sacked him. Eight years on, Jochen Rindt finally found the magic key to victory, yet within a year he was dead, killed at Monza at the height of his powers. That same season, Chapman's shattered team returned to racing for the first time since the tragedy, and rookie Emerson Fittipaldi, in only his third Grand Prix, secured Rindt's posthumous World Championship by scoring an astonishing victory to throw things beyond Jacky Ickx's reach.

Graham Hill won at Watkins Glen almost as often as at Monaco, yet shattered his legs there in an accident in 1969, which hastened his decline. In 1971, the dashing François Cevert scored his first Grand Prix triumph, only to be killed there two years later in an awful twist of fate, as he stood on the verge of donning Jackie Stewart's mantle within the Tyrrell team. But it was financial problems which killed the Glen as an F1 venue, in its own way just as tragic a loss.

Right: Denny Hulme threads his McLaren through the woods of Watkins Glen during the 1974 US GP at the scenic upstate New York track.

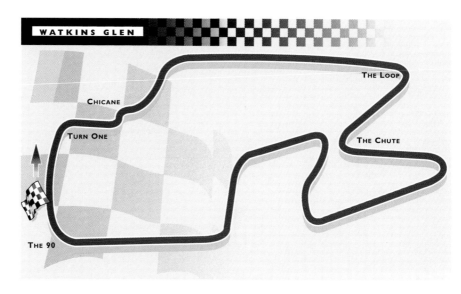

CHAPTER **4**

Keeping Track

THE WORLD CHAMPIONSHIP VENUES, COUNTRY BY COUNTRY

Since its inauguration in 1950, the FIA Formula One World Championship has visited 61 circuits in 22 countries. Few venues have survived intact to the present day – Silverstone, where the championship kicked off in 1950, is a notable exception – for the rigours of change have frequently given individual circuits, and even countries, only a limited role before the exigencies of economics or politics have swung the FI pendulum in the opposite direction.

⋙ Italy, 69 GPs

Imola: '80, '81, '82, '83, '84, '85, '86, '87, '88, '89, '90, '91, '92, '93, '94, '95, '96, '97, '98.

Monza: '50, '51, '52, '53, '54, '55, '56, '57, '58, '59, '60, '61, '62, '63, '64, '65, '66, '67, '68, '69, '70, '71, '72, '73, '74, '75, '76, '77, '78, '79, '81, '82, '83, '84, '85, '86, '87, '88, '89, '90, '91, '92, '93, '94, '95, '96, '97, '98, '99.

Pescara: '57.

In many ways, Italy is the spiritual home of motor racing, even though the French claim to have invented it, and the British to have FI's 'Silicon Valley'.

Monza is one of the oldest tracks, and the greatest, staging the Italian GP almost without exception since 1950. The only year in which it foundered was 1980, at the height of

Left: In Italy, one of the most enduring and amazing features of FI is the fanatical tifosi.

local politicking, then Imola stepped into the breach. This proved a popular venue, too, so much so that from 1981 it has held its own San Marino GP in deference to the tiny principality 30 miles away. It says everything about Imola, and Italian motor racing in general, that although it was the place where Roland Ratzenberger and Ayrton Senna died in the 1994 race, the circuit has none of the stigma associated with Hockenheim or Zolder.

A third Italian circuit also staged a Grand Prix: in 1957, Pescara provided a taste of what was to come at Imola when it hosted the Pescara GP, just before Monza finished off the season. In 1924, Enzo Ferrari won the first GP ever staged there, but Stirling Moss' win in 1957 marked the beginning of the end for the 24.57km (15.273-mile) track on the Adriatic coast.

⟫⟫⟫ United States, 54 GPs

Dallas: '84.

Detroit: '82, '83, '84, '85, '86, '87, '88.

Indianapolis: '50, '51, '52, '53, '54, '55, '56, '57, '58, '59, '60.

Las Vegas: '81, '82.

Long Beach: '76, '77, '78, '79, '80, '81, '82, '83.

Phoenix: '89, '90, '91.

Riverside: '60.

Sebring: '59.

Watkins Glen: '61, '62, '63, '64, '65, '66, '67, '68, '69, '70, '71, '72, '73, '74, '75, '76, '77, '78, '79, '80.

The United States is one of those 'black eyes' that FI has had to endure. Back in the 1960s, the US GP was a regular fixture, firmly established at Watkins Glen after early dalliances at Sebring, in Florida, and the wonderful Riverside in California. At one

glorious point, there were even two US GPs: the East at Watkins Glen, and the West on the semi-street track at Long Beach in California. But then things fell apart.

The picturesque Glen was abandoned after 1980, charged with financial difficulties and with having insufficient hotel space. Then Long Beach promoter Chris Pook called Bernie Ecclestone's financial bluff in 1983. The day the two failed to agree terms, Pook signed a deal with the Indycars and never looked back.

Therein lay the problem, for America had domestic championships such as NASCAR and Indycar, which were far more familiar to the public. FI staged some weak and embarrassing events, such as the Dallas race in 1984, the two events around the Caesar's Palace car park in Vegas in 1982 and 1983, and the Phoenix trio from 1989, where a local ostrich race was said to have drawn a bigger crowd.

The events held on the street course in Detroit were acceptable, but when plans to shift to a better track on nearby Belle Isle foundered for 1989, the Indycars pounced again.

Indianapolis itself was held to be a round of the World Championship for the first 11 years, although there was never any cross-over of driver entries, and it was really a matter of paying lip service to the notion, as the regulations for the two series were completely different. Since CART split with the Indianapolis 500, some have suggested that the latter should be run for FI cars, but although this is never likely to happen, talks continue annually in an effort to secure the return of FI to America, on a proper circuit that would allow the cars to show their pace. The FI world lives in hope.

>>> Britain, 53 GPs

Aintree: '55, '57, '59, '61, '62.
Brands Hatch: '64, '66, '68, '70, '72, '74, '76, '78, '80, '82, '83, '84, '85, '86.
Donington: '93.
Silverstone: '50, '51, '52, '53, '54, '56, '58, '60, '63, '65, '67, '69, '71, '73, '75, '77, '79, '81, '83, '85, '87, '88, '89, '90, '91, '92, '93, '94, '95, '96, '97, '98, '99

The World Championship was inaugurated at Silverstone, the former airfield circuit that styles itself today as the home of British motor sport.

During the 1950s and early 1960s, the Northamptonshire circuit shared the British GP with Aintree, the horse racing venue near Liverpool, which staged the race on five occasions and enjoyed huge crowds.

From 1964, the race alternated on a bi-annual basis between Silverstone and Brands Hatch, until Brands owner John Foulston fell out with Bernie Ecclestone in 1986. Thereafter, the Kentish circuit never again hosted an F1 race, and it was left to Donington Park, in Leicestershire, to augment Silverstone's monopoly. Prior to World War Two, Donington had

staged two full-blown Grands Prix –
in 1937 and 1938 – and in 1993 the
circuit's enthusiastic owner, Tom
Wheatcroft, realized his long-held
ambition to stage a Grand Prix of his
own when he was granted the
European GP.

*Below: Silverstone at Grand Prix time,
the home of British motorsport.*

⟫⟫ Germany, 52 GPs

Avus: '59.

Hockenheim: '70, '77, '78, '79, '80, '81,
'82, '83, '84, '86, '87, '88, '89, '90, '91,
'92, '93, '94, '95, '96, '97, '98, '99.

Nürburgring: '51, '52, '53, '54, '56, '57,
'58, '61, '62, '63, '64, '65, '66, '67, '68,
'69, '71, '72, '73, '74, '75, '76.

New Nürburgring: '84, '85, '95, '96,
'97, '98, '99.

The first German GP was held way
back in 1927, when the fabulous
Nürburgring was first opened. That
giant of a circuit produced all manner
of famous victories, and between
1951 and 1976 the only interruptions
to its use came when the 1959 event
was run at Avus, and when
Hockenheim staged the 1970 race.

Avus, near Berlin, was a flat-out
blast down two straights, which were
linked by high bankings, resulting in
victories for the brave drivers or cars
with strong engines, whereas
Hockenheim will always be

*Above: The new Nürburgring.
Not a patch on the old.*

remembered as the track that killed
Jimmy Clark. It was roundly criticized
back then, yet today it is held as an
example of the so-called high-speed
track, despite the three chicanes
and the infield section, which break
up the otherwise flat-out nature of
its design.

Although it bears the same name,
the 'new' Nürburgring has nothing in
common with the old. A purpose-
built track, it too was criticized as
being bland back in 1984 and 1985
when it staged the European and
German GPs respectively; today, after
providing a venue for the European
race again in 1995 and 1996 in
deference to the effect Michael
Schumacher's domination had on
Germany's interest in F1, it hosts the
Luxembourg GP. Thus Germany, like
Italy, regularly holds two Grands Prix
in a season.

Left: *Magny-Cours lacks the challenge of Rouen or Clermont-Ferrand, and the environment of Paul Ricard.*

Right: *Spa's climb to Les Combes offers fabulous spectating opportunities.*

Below: *Monaco, one of the great places to watch F1 cars in action.*

>>> France, 49 GPs

Clermont-Ferrand: '65, '69, '70, '72.

Dijon-Prenois: '74, '77, '79, '81, '82, '84.

Le Mans: '67.

Magny-Cours: '91, '92, '93, '94, '95, '96, '97, '99.

Paul Ricard Le-Castellet: '71, '73, '75, '76, '78, '80, '82, '83, '85, '86, '87, '88, '89, '90.

Reims: '50, '51, '53, '54, '56, '58, '59, '60, '61, '63, '66.

Rouen: '52, '57, '62, '64, '68.

The oldest race of them all, the French GP, was first held over a 64-mile road course near Le Mans in 1906, when it was won by the Hungarian racer Ferenc Szisz in a Renault. In the intervening years, it has moved around more than an American hobo. When the World Championship started, Reims-Gueux – which had staged pre-war events – was its original home. Then Rouen staged intermittent events as a contrast to the flat-out blast around the French champagne vineyards. Clermont-Ferrand was a spectacular host for four seasons, the 8-km (5-mile) track in the Auvergne providing the undulating nature of a mini-Nürburgring and presenting a similarly demanding challenge. Only once did the race return to Le Mans

when, in 1967, it was run on what was then regarded as little more than a car park: the so-called 'Bugatti' circuit, which took in the main pits of the 24-hour endurance classic and the first part of the lap, before winding back to the pits via a 'Mickey Mouse' infield section. Back then, the drivers were so critical that the race never returned; it was the forerunner of the sort of sanitized venue that is exemplified by Magny-Cours, current home to the race since 1991.

There are still hopes that the French GP may eventually return to the south-coast track at Le Castellet, named after its wealthy founder, Paul Ricard. This fast, challenging circuit staged 14 races between 1971 and 1990, and with its long back straight was very popular with the drivers. So, too, was Dijon, in the heart of the Burgundy wine region, which staged six races, one of them the Swiss GP of 1975! Although the organisers had a reputation for dourness and the brutality of their security men, Dijon will always be remembered for the fabulous fight between Gilles Villeneuve and René Arnoux during the French GP of 1979 when, ironically, their wheel-to-wheel scrap completely overshadowed Renault's first Grand Prix victory since that inaugural 1906 event.

>>> Belgium, 47 GPs

Spa Francorchamps:
'50, '51, '52, '53, '54, '55, '56, '58, '60, '61, '62, '63, '64, '65, '66, '67, '68, '70, '82, '85, '86, '87, '88, '89, '90, '91, '92, '93, '94, '95, '96, '97, '98, '99.

Nivelles: '72, '74.

Zolder: '73, '75, '76, '77, '78, '79, '80, '81, '82, '83, '84.

Belgium has been a staple of the World Championship since its inception, although Spa Francorchamps took a break in the 1970's while it was reworked over a shorter distance.

During this hiatus, the race was either cancelled, or held at less majestic venues. Nivelles, outside Brussels, provided a singularly sterile track for the 1972 and 1974 races, and a portent of things to come, as overtaking proved almost impossible. Had it been, it is debatable whether the spectators could ever have got close enough to what little action there was to have been able to see it without binoculars.

Zolder, which had a run of races between 1975 and 1984, was reasonable enough, but has been overshadowed by Gilles Villeneuve's death there in practice for the 1982 race.

>>> Monaco, 46 GPs

Monte Carlo: '50, '55, '56, '57, '58, '59, '60, '61, '62, '63, '64, '65, '66, '67, '68, '69, '70, '71, '72, '73, '74, '75, '76, '77, '78, '79, '80, '81, '82, '83, '84, '85, '86, '87, '88, '89, '90, '91, '92, '93, '94, '95, '96, '97, '98, '99.

There have been 46 Monaco Grands Prix since the 1950 season, but the event dates back to 1929. And although the Monte Carlo circuit has changed significantly over the years, its fundamental challenge still remains. Monaco is Monaco, and we should all be thankful for that.

⟫⟫⟫ Spain, 31 GPs

Barcelona: '91, '92, '93, '94, '95, '96, '97, '98, '99.

Jarama: '68, '70, '72, '74, '76, '77, '78, '79, '81.

Jerez: '86, '87, '88, '89, '90, '94, '97.

Montjuich Park: '69, '71, '73, '75.

Pedralbes: '51, '54.

The Spanish GP is another that has moved around a good deal. The first two events were held on the 4.4-km (2.7-mile) Pedralbes circuit, just outside Barcelona. The revival in 1968 came at Jarama, an all-new 3.4-km (2.1-mile) track north of Madrid, which was another to be derided as being 'Mickey Mouse' at the time, but which would fit in perfectly with today's different requirements.

Jarama alternated with the fabulous track at Montjuich Park, outside Barcelona, until the 1975 race at the latter ended in tragedy as Rolf Stommelen's Embassy Hill crashed into the crowd after its wing broke.

There had already been acrimonious argument over the standards of safety at the track earlier in the meeting, and thereafter F1 remained at Jarama until 1981.

After a four-year break, F1 went back to Spain, this time to the southern sherry region, Jerez, which hosted the Spanish GP. Then, when it was superseded by a purpose-built track outside Barcelona, Jerez was revived in 1994 and 1997 as host to the European GP.

⟫⟫⟫ Holland, 30 GPs

Zandvoort: '52, '53, '55, '58, '59, '60, '61, '62, '63, '64, '65, '66, '67, '68, '69, '70, '71, '73, '74, '75, '76, '77, '78, '79, '80, '81, '82, '83, '84, '85.

Designed by John Hugenholtz (who also penned Suzuka), Zandvoort was a superb track on which overtaking was genuinely possible throughout its reign as an F1 venue. The long pit straight led into the 180-degree hairpin right-hander called Tarzan, where outbraking moves and round-the-outside efforts regularly enthralled spectators. It says everything about Zandvoort that when the F3 cars went there in the 1980's, even they passed and repassed each other.

Sadly Zandvoort is also associated with appalling standards of marshalling, and few can forget the way that David Purley was abandoned by marshals as he tried single-handedly, and in vain, to rescue Roger Williamson from the fire that took hold in his upturned March during the 1973 race.

Zandvoort continued to stage the race until politics killed it after the 1985 event had narrowly been won by Niki Lauda. Today it has been shortened and still hosts F3 meetings, but the glory days of F1 are long gone.

⟫⟫⟫ Canada, 30 GPs

Montreal: '78, '79, '80, '81, '82, '83, '84, '85, '86, '88, '89, '90, '91, '92, '93, '94, '95, '96, '97, '98, '99.

Mont Tremblant: '68.

Mosport: '67, '69, '71, '72, '73, '74, '76, '77.

Canada was a relative latecomer to F1, its first race being held in the rain, in 1967, at the challenging Mosport Park, near Toronto. A year later, the event was transferred briefly to Mont Tremblant, an equally interesting circuit close to Montreal, before returning to Mosport until 1977. Mosport is best remembered for the completely confused race held there in 1973, when initially the organisers faced a choice of Emerson Fittipaldi,

Above: Montreal is always packed with race fans.

Howden Ganley, Jackie Oliver or Peter Revson as the winner after a fragmented event held in poor weather conditions; eventually they opted for Revson!

Since 1978, the Canadian GP has been held on a track close to the old Olympic rowing basin on an island in the St Lawrence River, just outside Montreal. The track is now named in honour of the late Gilles Villeneuve, who won his first race there in that inaugural year. Another venue to produce unusual results, it was the scene of the unfortunate Riccardo Paletti's death in 1982, and of Jean Alesi's sole victory 13 years later.

>>> Brazil, 27 GPs

Interlagos: '73, '74, '75, '76, '77, '78, '79, '80, '90, '91, '92, '93, '94, '95, '96, '97, '98, '99.

Jacarepagua: '81, '82, '83, '84, '85, '86, '87, '88, '89.

The Brazilians have always been very enthusiastic supporters of F1, and the country has spawned great champions in the form of trailblazer Emerson Fittipaldi, Nelson Piquet and Ayrton Senna. In the wake of Fittipaldi's first title in 1972 came the country's first Grand Prix, at Interlagos, which held sway until Piquet's rise prompted a switch to Jacarepagua, in his home town of Rio. In turn, as Senna came to the fore, the race was revived for 1990, again in São Paulo, but on a revised Interlagos circuit.

Above: Kyalami is different today, and despite the enthusiasm of the locals it is now just another modern F1 venue largely devoid of the overtaking opportunities that characterised its predecessor.

Below: Brazil's Interlagos, F1 glamour among the poverty.

>>> South Africa, 23 GPs

East London: '62, '63, '65.

Kyalami: '67, '68, '69, '70, '71, '72, '73, '74, '75, '76, '77, '78, '79, '80, '82, '83, '84, '85, '92, '93.

Like Argentina, South Africa's F1 history embraces three separate periods, starting with the 1962 event, which decided that year's World Championship in Graham Hill's favour. At that time, like Adelaide, the event ended the season, but after skipping 1964, it returned in 1965 as the season opener. This tradition continued for many years, starting at first on 1 January, then moving by popular request in 1969 to March.

From 1967 onwards, Kyalami took over from East London, and in 1981 the circuit hosted a non-championship breakaway race before the FISA/FOCA war was resolved. The following year, 1982, was the last time that the event opened the season's racing; thereafter the race moved towards the end of the year, before falling from favour in 1985.

There was a brief revival on a revised Kyalami in 1992 and 1993, before the political situation again militated against a race. Talk continues of yet another return, however, on a street circuit in either Johannesburg or Durban.

>>> Austria, 22 GPs

A-1 Ring: '97, '98, '99.
Osterreichring: '70, '71, '72, '73, '74, '75, '76, '77, '78, '79, '80, '81, '82, '83, '84, '85, '86, '87.
Zeltweg: '64.

First part of the World Championship calendar in 1964, Austria's Grand Prix became more famous with the switch to the magnificent Osterreichring circuit, which tended to throw up unusual results in the 1970's.

Today's A-1 Ring incorporates parts of the old track, but has little of its majestic atmosphere, despite the beautiful scenery.

>>> Argentina, 20 GPs

Buenos Aires: '53, '54, '55, '56, '57, '58, '60, '72, '73, '74, '75, '77, '78, '79, '80, '81, '95, '96, '97, '98.

With Juan Manuel Fangio winning his first world title in 1951, it was scarcely surprising that Argentina staged a World Championship Grand Prix as soon as 1953. The event has enjoyed three distinct periods. After Fangio's retirement, it lasted until 1960, was revived in the 1970s as Carlos Reutemann became prominent, then came back from decline for a third time in 1995 as part of F1's global expansion.

>>> Japan, 17 GPs

Aida: '94, '95.
Mount Fuji: '76, '77.
Suzuka: '87, '88, '89, '90, '91, '92, '93, '94, '95, '96, '97, '98, '99.

F1 racing went to Japan in 1976 when the dangerous Fuji track hosted the Orient's first Grand Prix, but after an accident involving Gilles Villeneuve and Ronnie Peterson in 1977, in which spectators in a prohibited area were killed, F1 stayed away. However, given the rise and rise of Honda in the mid-1980s, it was only a matter of time before the Japanese giant brought its own Suzuka circuit into play. It staged the first Japanese GP for ten years with the 1987 event, which was won by Gerhard Berger's Ferrari. Over the years, Suzuka has seen controversy, including the collisions between Ayrton Senna and Alain Prost in 1989 and 1990, but remains one of the best current tracks.

By contrast, Aida, which hosted two races in the mid-1990s, was condemned as a 'Mickey Mouse' track that was anything but worth the two-hour ordeal by bus required to get there.

>>> Portugal, 16 GPs

Estoril: '84, '85, '86, '87, '88, '89, '90, '91, '92, '93, '94, '95, '96.
Monsanto: '59.
Oporto: '58, '60.

F1 went to Portugal towards the end of the 2.5-litre formula, first to Oporto, then to Monsanto, just outside Lisbon, and back to Oporto. Then interest waned until the race was revived at Estoril, in 1984, and until 1996 it proved a popular part of the series. Estoril was used regularly as a test track by teams seeking good

Right: Estoril is politically troubled, but missed as a race track.

off-season weather, but politics and poor finances resulted in the 1997 race being cancelled after years of argument over the standards of its facilities. It remains to be seen whether the 1998 return goes ahead, but the place will always be remembered as the venue for Ayrton Senna's first GP triumph, in the rain in 1985, and for dramatic near misses on the pit straight for Riccardo Patrese in 1992 and Gerhard Berger a year later.

>>> Mexico, 15 GPs

Mexico City: '63, '64, '65, '66, '67, '68, '69, '70, '86, '87, '88, '89, '90, '91, '92.

Mexico staged a non-championship F1 race at the end of 1962, partly at the behest of wealthy Don Pedro Rodriguez, whose sons Ricardo and Pedro were beginning to make a huge mark in international racing. Ricardo was the quicker, and even when he was killed during practice for the race in his Rob Walker Lotus, Rodriguez Snr insisted that plans for a full-blown

Mexican GP should continue. Thus it provided the finale for eight seasons, notably settling the outcome of the World Championship in 1964 and 1968 in out-and-out dramatic style, and in rather more subdued fashion in 1967. It also provided Honda and Goodyear with their first win, courtesy of Richie Ginther in 1965. When the crowds refused even Pedro Rodriguez's request to keep off the edge of the track, the 1970 race marked the last GP for 15 years.

The Mexican GP was revived in

1986 and lasted until 1992, when Nigel Mansell turned the 1991 tables on Williams team-mate Riccardo Patrese.

The Autodromo Hermanos Rodriguez was a great circuit, with the very quick 180-degree banked Peraltada right-hander representing one of the truly unchanged challenges of F1. Sadly politics got the better of an event that brought curious contrasts of exhilaration and pity for the sheer poverty that was evident outside the track.

Opposite top:
The Osterreichring isn't what it was, but remains a scenic venue.

Opposite middle:
High-rise flats overlook Argentina's Autodromo Oscar Galvez in the Parc Almirante Brown.

Opposite bottom:
Suzuka: great track, great people, great atmosphere.

Right: Mexico, one of the truly great places to watch F1 cars in action.

>>> Australia, 15 GPs

Adelaide: '85, '86, '87, '88, '89, '90, '91, '92, '93, '94, '95.

Melbourne: '96, '97, '98, '99.

Although F1 cars raced 'down under' in the 1950s, it was not until the mid-1980s that an official World Championship round was staged in Australia. Then Adelaide formed a highly popular finale to the season for the next decade, until politics and financial matters saw the event relocate to Melbourne for 1996.

Because the traditional Melbourne Cup horse race was held at a similar time to the old Grand Prix, the F1 race was moved to the beginning of the season, the better to spread the city's sporting benefits.

Below: The protestors don't like the GP, but Melbourne's picturesque Albert Park is all the cleaner after its re-development as a race track.

>>> Hungary, 14 GPs

Hungaroring: '86, '87, '88, '89, '90, '91, '92, '93, '94, '95, '96, '97, '98, '99.

New to the calendar in 1986, Hungary has become a popular event because of the sheer enthusiasm of the people, but the Hungaroring is a deadly dull circuit on which over-taking is almost impossible. How else could Thierry Boutsen, worthy driver that he was, have held off Ayrton Senna for the entire 77 laps in 1990? What it needs is an extension with a long straight followed by a hairpin; then it might just provide the focal point for overtaking that it so desperately needs.

⟫⟫ Sweden, 6 GPs

Anderstorp: '73, '74, '75, '76, '77, '78.

The Swedish GP was yet another example of F1 enthusiasm being stirred by a national driver's success at international level. In this case, it was Ronnie Peterson whose exploits proved the catalyst. And Ronnie came incredibly close to winning the inaugural race in 1973, which would have also been his first F1 triumph. However, he was slowed by a puncture and had to wait another race before breaking his duck. Despite the sterility of the Anderstorp circuit (which was built on reclaimed swampland), the Swedish GP remained on the calendar until 1978.

Opposite top: Hungaroring, where the enthusiasm of the spectators is unfortunately not matched by the spectacle of the cars as they chase at high speed around the circuit.

⟫⟫ Switzerland, 5 GPs

Bremgarten: '50, '51, '52, '53, '54.

Switzerland was an enthusiastic follower of F1 in the early 1950s, and the Swiss GP at Bremgarten was an intrinsic part of the early World Championship.

The track was a dangerous, but beautiful, 7.2-km (4.5-mile) road course that taxed drivers to the limit, while changing light conditions and road surfaces added further hazards. It killed the great Achille Varzi in 1948, and ended the equally prominent rainmaster Rudolf Caracciola's career four years later.

In the wake of the Le Mans disaster of 1955, the Swiss immediately renounced Grand Prix racing. Since then, the only Swiss GP was held in 1982 – across the border at Dijon.

Above: Sweden's Anderstorp was built on reclaimed swampland, and the race there frequently threw up some unusual results. Here Andretti momentarily leads the Brabham fancar in 1978.

⟫⟫ Morocco, 1 GP

Casablanca: '58.

Only once did North Africa stage a Grand Prix, when the circus went to Casablanca in 1958 for the race that would decide that year's World Championship. The 7.6-km (4.7-mile) circuit met with general approval, and the race saw Mike Hawthorn do all that he needed in finishing second to Stirling Moss to beat him by one point for the championship crown. However, it is principally remembered for the sad accident that took the life of Moss' Vanwall team-mate, Stuart Lewis-Evans.

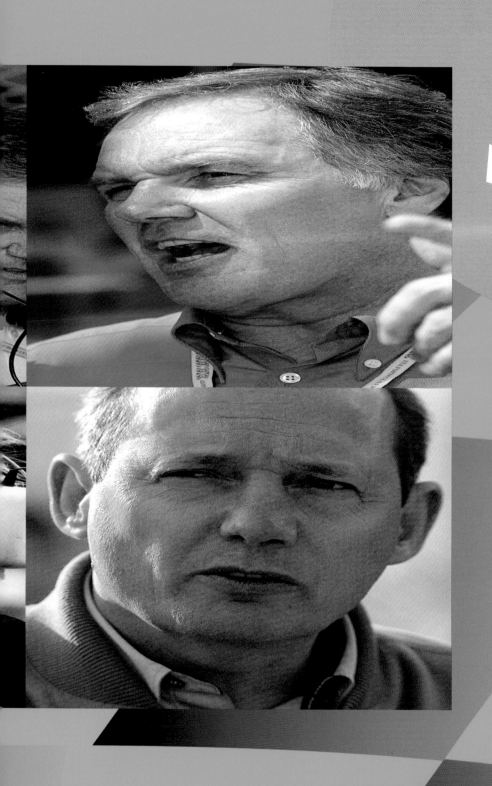

3 PERSONALITIES

CHAPTER **5**

Pioneers

MEN WHO SHAPED THE FACE OF MOTOR SPORT

Some were merely followers or interpreters, men who took the ideas of others and moulded them to their needs. But inevitably a sport as dynamic as motor racing bred its own special characters, whose fertile minds created fresh concepts and led design and development, management, or safety facilities down new avenues.

Left: *Enzo Ferrari, the autocratic and charismatic creator of the world's most famous F1 team.*

⭐ Enzo Ferrari

Ferrari is the only team that has contested the World Championship since its inception. There have been times when the red cars have been missing from races, and these usually coincided with one of Enzo Ferrari's periodic rants against perceived injustice. But always he came back, usually stronger than ever.

Although he died in August 1988, Ingeniere Ferrari's spirit still pervades Maranello, where his cars have always been built, and the prancing horse still exudes the charisma it did in his heyday. A former race driver who enjoyed limited success for Alfa Romeo, Ferrari really made his name running that manufacturer's Grand Prix team before starting his own marque in 1947. Before long, Ferrari had attained legendary status, and the 'Old Man' assiduously did all he could

Above: It was small wonder that Ferrari compared Gilles Villeneuve to pre-war great Tazio Nuvolari. Here he dominates the wet US GP in 1979.

to foster it. Driven by grief for the death of his son, Dino, he could be autocratic, bombastic, frequently petulant, irascible, wheedling and inspired. He ran his team with an iron hand and almost complete disdain for the majority of his drivers who, he believed, should be happy simply to sit in a red car. In 1961, he did nothing to stop all of his World Championship winning managers from walking out after internal strife

initiated by his wife, Laura. Backing down in an argument was not within his character unless, of course, he felt that he could benefit from it.

For all Enzo Ferrari's shortcomings, his cars are part of the very fabric of Grand Prix motor sport, an intrinsic aspect of sporting legend. He came from the pioneering days of motor racing, and was part of the new wave in the period when it graduated from the old city-to-city road races to the

structured World Championship that was inaugurated in 1950. Like Frank Williams, for Ferrari it was never yesterday that mattered, nor even today, but tomorrow. His cars, like his drivers, were usually discarded when they had achieved their purpose.

⭐ Tony Vandervell

Guy Anthony Vandervell was the real-life equivalent of the movie industrialist who decides to create his own Grand Prix car. Wealthy from the business he had built around the replaceable 'thinwall' engine bearing, to which he acquired the British rights in 1930, Vandervell was part of the BRM Trust in its early days until he despaired of the British GP car project ever getting to the track. By the time BRM's V16 was really race ready, it was too late, for the original 1.5-litre formula had collapsed through lack of entries and a new 2.5-litre F1 was already on the stocks for 1954. Vandervell, impatient to see a challenge to the cars from Ferrari and Maserati, decided to do the job himself.

First he purchased a 4.5-litre Ferrari, for experience, although typically this gruff and intimidating fellow rejected the first two cars that were delivered, as they had not been assembled to his satisfaction.

The first Vanwall appeared in 1954, and by 1955 it was beginning to show promise. Vandervell, like Enzo Ferrari, insisted on making both the chassis and the engine. But it was when he enlisted the help of the emerging Colin Chapman to design a new chassis for 1956, and commissioned aerodynamicist Frank Costin to clothe it in sleek bodywork, that the British Racing Green cars really began to challenge 'those bloody red cars'. Stirling Moss was sufficiently impressed to join the team for 1957, together with Tony Brooks, and at Aintree that July the pair of them made history by sharing a car to become the first Britons ever to win the British GP in a British car.

In the following season, Moss narrowly missed the Drivers' World Championship, but Vanwall won the inaugural Constructors' title. However, although Vandervell seemed the archetypal hard-edged industrial tycoon, he was devastated when the upcoming Stuart Lewis-Evans succumbed to injuries sustained in the final race of the season in Morocco. Vandervell had taken British cars and drivers to the top, beating the Italians at the World Championship game, but reluctantly he disbanded his team in the aftermath of the tragedy.

⭐ John Cooper

They rowed frequently, and their characters could scarcely have been more different, but between them, father and son Charles and John Cooper built the little cars that would revolutionize F1 in the 1950s.

Charles had a background that encompassed motor racing at Brooklands, allied to an almost pathological hatred of spending money and a fearsome temper. John was much more easy-going and had a far-sightedness that sat ill with his father, leading to frequent disagreements between them.

Shortly after World War Two, the Coopers began constructing small single-seater cars for the new Formula 500, a training category similar to today's Formula Three. Since they used chain drive, it made sense to mount the engine at the back, ahead of the rear axle. This endowed the cars with excellent roadholding, and over the ensuing years all manner of future stars cut their racing teeth in the little Coopers, among them Stirling Moss, Peter Collins, Stuart Lewis-Evans and Ken Tyrrell. The cars were no-nonsense designs, reliable and effective, and gradually the Coopers evolved F1 versions of the concept. When Moss used one to go non-stop through the Argentinian GP in 1958, and won the race, it ushered in a new era: the age of the rear-engined car.

Thanks to the cheap machines manufactured without fanfare in a small dark garage in Surbiton, England, the hitherto dominant Continental manufacturers, who had ruled Grand Prix racing, were brought to their knees.

Left: Guy Anthony 'Tony' Vandervell (with Innes Ireland) was the wealthy industrialist to whom British motorsport owes a debt of gratitude. His unstinting efforts with Vanwall put Britain on the F1 map in the 1950s.

Above: *What Vandervell started, John Cooper
and his father continued with their rear-engined
racers, albeit in dramatically different style.*

✪ Colin Chapman

If Charles and John Cooper brought about the rear-engined revolution in FI, it was Colin Chapman who took it a stage further with his monocoque-chassis Lotus 25 in 1962. At a stroke, he introduced a stronger, lighter structure, which was simpler to build than the old welded space frame and was so much more rigid that it also handled better.

Possessed of one of the most fertile minds the sport has known, Chapman followed the 25 with the 49 in 1967, echoing Lancia's D50 of 1954 and BRM's 1966 P83 by using the Ford Cosworth DFV engine as a stressed part of the chassis structure. At the same time, he created a car that was lighter and slimmer, yet more powerful, than anything the opposition could present.

The 1970 Lotus 72 introduced side radiators, the wedge shape and torsion-bar suspension. The 1977 Lotus 78 brought the concept of ground effect, and its successor, the 79 of 1978, developed the concept of under-car downforce sufficiently to

dominate that year's World Championship. Where Chapman led, his rivals were forced to follow.

Together with McLaren, Colin Chapman pioneered carbon fibre chassis, then came his final legacy to FI: computer controlled 'active' suspension, which maintained the ideal ride height to optimize a car's handling and aerodynamic behaviour.

Chapman pioneered all these things in a glittering career that embraced Drivers' World Championships for Jim Clark, Graham Hill, Jochen Rindt, Emerson Fittipaldi and Mario Andretti, and seven Constructors' World Championships. But there was another legacy. In 1967, Lotus enjoyed exclusive use of the new Ford Cosworth DFV V8 engine, and only minor mechanical problems prevented Clark from taking another championship. But when Ford's Walter Hayes approached Chapman with the idea that the unit should be sold to his rivals for 1968, the Lotus boss just shrugged and agreed. As a result, the DFV went on general sale, and teams such as McLaren, Matra, March, Williams and Brabham proceeded to challenge Lotus' superiority. It was the act of a selfless and supremely confident man.

Above: Spirited genius Colin Chapman had a fertile mind that forever probed for fresh ways of solving engineering problems.

Below: The Lotus 25 of 1962 took FI on a fresh course of technical development.

Left: *The Williams-Hondas of the mid-1980s were the class of the FI field.*

Below: *The relentless commitment of Frank Williams and Patrick Head has ensured that the Williams team remains at the forefront of FI, more than two decades after it was founded.*

No team has ever hit the century of wins more quickly.

Early in 1986, Williams' penchant for over-driving on the road caught up with him and he was paralysed after crashing his car on the way back from a test at Paul Ricard. When he returned, wheelchair-bound, to the paddock at Brands Hatch, he received a standing ovation. When he says that he never felt sorry for himself for a moment, you can believe that his incredible tenacity sustained him during the dark months of recovery.

Today Frank Williams exhibits greater energy and commitment than a dozen able-bodied men. He is unpopular at times for the way he treats his drivers, but there isn't an individual in the paddock who doesn't regard him with complete and absolute respect.

✪ Frank Williams

For years, Frank Williams' efforts in FI were regarded as little more than a joke by his rivals, as his little team struggled for survival in the 1970s. Yet if you cast your attention back to the 1969 season, when he first entered the category with a private Brabham-Ford for his friend Piers Courage, there were clear signs of the success that was to follow.

That year, Courage finished second in the Monaco and US GPs, each time beating the works Brabhams of Jack Brabham and Jacky Ickx. At Monza, he twice led the Italian GP before falling back with fading fuel pressure.

But a year later, Courage died in Williams' de Tomaso during the Dutch GP at Zandvoort, and the way back was to prove long and tough.

Williams was a dealer, a fitness fanatic who was happiest thinking on his feet. As a race driver, he was erratic; as a team manager and owner, he possessed that indefinable

something that is the key to survival. When his team was taken over by oil man Walter Wolf, Frank eventually quit and started over. And between 1979 and 1997, he and his technical partner, Patrick Head, masterminded more than 100 Grand Prix victories.

⭐ Ron Dennis

His detractors suggest that Ron Dennis never forgave the world for making him start as a mechanic and work his way up. Frequently they point to the chips he appears to carry on both shoulders, and his habit of putting his foot in it with untimely comments at public functions. He is, they say, humourless and snobbish.

Much of this attitude is sour grapes, and those grapes can become very acidic indeed when you have watched a rival such as Dennis win 15 of the season's 16 races, and only lose the remaining one through a cruel twist of fate. That is exactly what occurred in 1988. In that season, Dennis must have been on cloud nine, for he readily admits that the first thing he feels on the Monday morning after a race that his cars have not won, is pain.

Sniping at Dennis is a favourite pastime in the F1 paddock, and very often his apparent arrogance does him no favours, but a look at his achievements is instructive. He worked initially with such greats as Jochen Rindt and Pedro Rodriguez at Cooper, before following Rindt to Brabham in 1968. Later he formed his own junior formula team with fellow mechanic Neil Trundle. They were planning their own F1 entry with a revolutionary carbon fibre-chassised car designed by John Barnard, when Marlboro's John Hogan massaged the marriage with McLaren, which resulted in McLaren International in 1980. Dennis never looked back.

His gift for identifying the required ingredients for success saw him commission a TAG financed turbo engine from Porsche in 1983. A year later, he partnered Alain Prost with Niki Lauda, and they won 12 of the 16 races en route to Lauda's third title. Four years after that, he put Senna and Honda together with his double champion Prost to form the greatest superteam since Fangio and Moss, or Clark and Hill.

Testimony to McLaren's success are 112 Grand Prix wins, nine Drivers' Championships and seven Constructors' Championships. Arrogant Dennis may possibly be, but not without good cause.

Left: *Ron Dennis took McLaren to greatness again after its troubled early 1980s era.*

⭐ Professor Sid Watkins

He is the guardian angel of FI, a man craggy of face and, more often than not, armed with a large cigar and a cheerful, but irreverently unprintable, comment. He is the one man to whom Bernie Ecclestone regularly defers. They call him, simply and affectionately, 'The Prof'. He is Sid Watkins, graduate of Liverpool University Medical School and the Radcliffe Infirmary in Oxford, one of the world's foremost neurosurgeons and the FIA's medical delegate.

Since 1978, The Prof has overseen FI races, following an approach by Bernie Ecclestone, which led to him taking up the position of Grand Prix surgeon. His first race was that year's Swedish GP at Anderstorp where, in his outspoken way, he let it be known

Right: *Amusing, irreverent, outspoken and brilliant at his job, Professor Sid Watkins is FI's guardian angel.*

that he did not think much of the safety standards.

Since then, Watkins has worked tirelessly to raise those standards, never accepting no as an answer, and digging in his heels whenever occasion has demanded. A typical example of this occurred at Imola in 1987, when he refused to let an unwell Nelson Piquet countermand his advice that he should not race following a heavy accident in practice. That set a precedent that is observed

Left: *McLaren's involvements with Marlboro, TAG Porsche and Honda led to FI domination in the late 1980s and early 1990s. West and Mercedes haved helped McLaren to rise again.*

to this day: what The Prof says, goes.

At Imola in 1994, Watkins was first on the scene of Rubens Barrichello's accident, and his prompt action saved the young Brazilian from choking to death after swallowing his tongue. The next day, Roland Ratzenberger was killed, followed a day later by Watkins' close friend, Ayrton Senna. This was, understandably, the lowest point in a career that had seen plenty of unpleasantness. But still The Prof continues his crusade for perfection, striving to give every driver the best chance of surviving an accident. And, as ever, his face remains the one that any injured driver wants to see most. Cigar and all.

CHAPTER **6**

Power Brokers
MOVERS AND SHAKERS

Any competitive endeavour will demand leaders, and motor racing is no different. A dynamic sport with its own life, it has always called for strong masters but men with sufficient blend of vision, management skill and the power to harness its disparate elements have always been few and far between.

◗ Bernie Ecclestone

The name Bernie Ecclestone is one of the best known inside Formula One motor racing circles. But whereas the identities, personalities and backgrounds of the star drivers are familiar to fans the world over, Ecclestone remains an enigma. He is a shadowy figure who usually remains firmly in the background, but as everyone knows, he is the man who pulls the strings. With wry humour, his faxes are headed simply by the name 'Mr E' – mystery. And a mystery he remains to many, although the sudden explosion in his public status brought about by his plans to float F1 in 1997, and then by the controversy surrounding the British Labour Government's handling of his £1,000,000 donation at the end of the year, when a ban on all tobacco advertising seemed imminent, elevated him to the front pages of the national dailies. Now, in public as well as in F1, Ecclestone is perceived to be the modern equivalent of Croesus.

But who is he?

His office is an elegant, glass-fronted building in London's opulent Prince's Gate region, close by Hyde Park, and nothing happens in Formula One without him knowing and, largely, without his specific approval.

He was born in October 1930, and his father was a trawler skipper. He studied chemistry and worked initially as a laboratory technician, but in the days when the old short track at Brands Hatch used to run in an anti-clockwise direction, Bernard Charles Ecclestone, dealer, was a fierce and respected contender. Motor cycles were his first love, and in 1947 he was racing them on grass before graduating to Formula 500 events, at that time the equivalent of what we know today as Formula Three.

Motor cycles also played another vital part in his background. In the late 1940s and early 1950s, he established a large dealership in Bexleyheath, 32km (20 miles) south of London, called Compton & Ecclestone. At the time, leatherclad motor cyclists had an uncouth, lank-hair and oily-fingernail image, but Compton & Ecclestone had the clinically clean air of a modern Formula One team. Everything was just so. Motor cycles were lined up neatly, their front wheels and handlebars in perfect symmetry.

Stories, apocryphal or not, abound about him. He is said to have walked into the Brabham factory one day and discovered that a new wall-phone had been installed. It was not correctly aligned, so he tore it down and, after dashing it to the floor, snarled, 'Get that put up properly, or I'll close the whole place down.' As shocked staff picked up the debris, he reportedly added, 'And don't think that I won't, because you're not dealing with a rational man!'

Right: From the late 1940s onwards Bernie Ecclestone has in some shape or form been involved in Motor sport. In his early days it was motor cycles, latterly it has been with Formula One and its maintenance as one of the foremost sporting series in the world.

Ecclestone does nothing to confirm or deny such stories, having appreciated very early that making other people uncertain about you can be a valuable weapon, especially during negotiations.

Early on, he befriended, then managed, a pugnacious young racer called Stuart Lewis-Evans. Later he managed Austrian hotshoe Jochen Rindt. Both died on the track.

Subsequently he prospered in the property boom, then bought the Brabham team in 1971. Steadily he built up F1 via FOCA, the teams' association. Today his powerbase is Formula One Administration, through which he negotiates television deals and organizes many of the F1 races. Over the years, he has made both himself and many team owners extremely rich. In 1994, a British business magazine ran a list of the 500 wealthiest people in sport. Ecclestone finished well up, albeit some way behind the likes of Nigel Mansell. FIA president Max Mosley smiles and says, 'I think they may mistakenly have thought that Bernie's annual income was his overall wealth.'

Ecclestone — variously known as 'Mr E' or 'The Bolt' (from the 1970s television game show *The Golden Shot*, which featured the character known as Bernie the Bolt) — still fusses over minor things. If curtains aren't drawn neatly, he can become very agitated. He insists that all of the transporter trucks in the paddock are perfectly aligned. Even cars in the car parks must all face the same way, to look better in overhead television shots. His black, grey and silver FOCA bus, with its sinister darkened windows, is always spotlessly clean and has its own prime spot in the paddock, chosen so that it overlooks everything.

Within Formula One, it is sensible not to quarrel too much with him, but at the same time Ecclestone appreciates fighters. One of the reasons why the racer Perry McCarthy was granted a Superlicence in 1992 was because he absolutely refused to give up in Brazil, when the licence he had been given to drive for Andrea Moda was temporarily revoked. Ecclestone admired McCarthy's refusal to give up, and saw to it that he was 'assisted'.

His bark is usually worse than his bite, although he doesn't actually bark at all. His voice is smooth and soft, and even when angry he maintains a chilling ability to keep it quiet and of even tone. After being involved in a traffic altercation with a truck driver, Ecclestone sat with his customary glacial expression as the truckie bawled him out, questioning both his antecedents and his intelligence. When the man's diatribe was finished Ecclestone nodded, and said, very quietly, 'You're absolutely right. I'm not very intelligent at all. That's why you're driving a truck for a living, and I'm sitting here in comfort in this air-conditioned Mercedes-Benz.'

Such quiet restraint makes his anger even more compelling as he transfixes hapless targets of his wrath with an unwavering glare.

Life is a poker game to Bernie Ecclestone: bluff and counter-bluff. Winning is everything. It's a long while since he raced, or even owned a team, but the man who dragged Formula One into the multi-million-dollar era and made it what it is today, with its massive world-wide audience and 17 regular World Championship races every year, remains what he has always been: an out-and-out racer.

Left: *Ecclestone enjoys the attention of Eddie Jordan and David Richards, two men whose influence on motorsport over the years has been immense, but who defer to Ecclestone simply because he is the power behind much of what happens in their sport.*

⊃ Max Mosley

If Max Rufus Mosley was born with a silver spoon in his mouth, as the younger son of Sir Oswald Mosley and Diana Mitford, one of the famous Mitford sisters, the taste of whatever syrup may have been on that spoon was soured by the controversy that surrounded his family. It cannot have been easy having a father in wartime Britain who was the exiled leader and founder of the British League of Fascists. Indeed he was born in 1940, only weeks before his unfortunate mother was interned in Holloway Prison. She had flouted convention, in her own way, seven years earlier by leaving her first husband, the Hon. Brian Guinness of the famous brewing family, for Sir Oswald.

Mosley Jnr went up to Oxford, where he studied physics and became immersed in the Union as its secretary, before going on to specialize in patent and trademark law. Shortly after he qualified as a practising barrister, he discovered motor sport and was soon competing in a Clubman's car before taking the plunge and graduating to Formula Two in 1968. He was competing at Hockenheim on the day that Jim Clark was killed, and recalls 'overtaking Graham Hill on the straight at one point, but only because I didn't see him in the gloom!'

Like Ecclestone, Mosley was honest enough to accept that his future lay elsewhere, and by 1969 he had joined his friends Robin Herd (a brilliant engineer whom he had met at university), Alan Rees (a competitive F2 racer) and businessman Graham Coaker to form the acronymous March team. Initially they planned to build F2 and F3 cars for sale to customers; yet within months, they had been unable to help themselves when it became clear that World Champion entrant Ken Tyrrell and

World Champion driver Jackie Stewart would no longer be able to run Matra chassis. They took the bold decision to jump straight into F1 as well! Stewart, in Tyrrell's private March, and works driver Chris Amon set the fastest times in South Africa for the F1 car's first race, although that was to prove one of few real high points for the company.

A year later, Bernie Ecclestone made his return to F1, as owner of the Brabham team, and Mosley quickly realized that he had discovered a kindred spirit as they witnessed with growing dismay the disorganized manner in which the Grand Prix Constructors' and Entrants' Association (GPCA) conducted its business. Each was determined to do something about it. The GPCA spawned the Formula One Constructors' Association (FOCA), and as Ecclestone took on

more and more of its organisation, his fellow constructors were relieved to give him virtual *carte blanche* as they concentrated solely on their racing. Ecclestone, with Mosley's assistance, now negotiated appearance deals with circuits, giving the constructors, who hitherto had lacked unity, negotiated television deals. They also worked out the complex prize fund allocation, which today remains a matter cloaked in utmost secrecy. Under their management, significant travel concessions accrued to teams placing in the top ten in any preceding year's World Championship. The team owners prospered, and they owed much of that prosperity to Bernie Ecclestone and Max Mosley.

The two faces of Max Mosley – in his days with March (below) and as President of the FIA (right).

In 1978, the mercurial Jean-Marie Balestre was elected president of the FISA, the FIA's sporting subsidiary. It soon became clear that the chauvinistic Frenchman believed strongly that all sporting power should devolve to the FISA, making confrontation with FOCA simply a matter of time.

The inevitable fight with the FISA finally occurred during 1980 and rumbled through a winter of discontent into 1981, with each side deadlocked. With Mosley handling the legal side of things, Ecclestone threatened to form a break-away F1 championship, which Balestre and the FISA prepared to counter with a threat to revoke the licence of any driver who participated. As with all wars, this one ended with a peaceful settlement, the principal instrument of which was the document by which F1 would henceforth be governed: The Concorde Agreement. This was

named after the FISA's opulent premises in the Place de la Concorde in Paris, where matters had been thrashed out. The document owed much to Ecclestone, but also a great deal to Mosley's agile legal mind.

If Ecclestone's negotiating skills and Mosley's legal background created a formidable team during these troubled times, even greater things lay ahead. Whether it was the plan all along is unclear, but in the ultimate poacher-turned-gamekeeper scenario, it was Mosley who, in the autumn 1991, challenged the dictatorial Balestre for the presidency of FISA. Ecclestone had already taken a role as vice president (promotional affairs) within the FIA, back in 1986, and when Mosley achieved a landslide victory over Balestre, it was the dawn of a new era. Once the outlaws, they were suddenly the Establishment.

There are many who believe that Mosley would have pursued a career

in British politics, but for the stigma still associated with his father's controversial political leanings. Now, however, he had the perfect platform for a political career based in Europe which, by the 1990s, had become the seat of power in any case. After bringing the sport back under the wing of the FIA and doing away with the FISA, he exploited fully the consultative status that the governing body enjoyed at both the European Parliament and the United Nations. And he was instrumental in guiding F1 through the trauma of 1994, in the troubled aftermath of the deaths of Ayrton Senna and Roland Ratzenberger at Imola, and Karl Wendlinger's accident at Monaco a fortnight later, which left the

Below and opposite: *With his partner and fellow F1 enthusiast, Ecclestone, Mosley turned the sport around to make it into a huge commercial and sporting success.*

unfortunate Austrian temporarily comatose. Mosley acted decisively, if controversially, to stave off threats by several countries to take steps against the sport, exhibiting sound political skills as he steered it to safety.

Further controversy has followed Mosley's periodic re-election. The Concorde Agreement, which was originally thrashed out in 1981, provided for the FIA to lease the commercial rights to F1 to the teams and FOCA for a four-year period, with the stipulation that they had to acknowledge the governing body's ownership of those rights. The Concorde Agreement was renewed periodically, and Ecclestone continued to deal with commercial matters on his own, taking his own financial risks. The 1992 Concorde Agreement ran its course at the end of 1996, after its usual five-year span, but this time Mosley took the controversial step of assigning the commercial rights directly to Ecclestone's Formula One Administration, thus effectively cutting out the teams. This is the new contract that formed the basis of Ecclestone's planned stock-market flotation. The move tore apart the F1 fraternity and saw Ron Dennis at McLaren, Ken Tyrrell and Frank Williams adamant in their refusal to sign unless they received what they saw as their due share in the new company. Mosley played a hard line, just as he did when he decided unilaterally that treaded tyres and narrow suspension would be mandated for the 1998 regulations, on the grounds of 'safety'. This was a very unpopular decision, which nevertheless he ramrodded through. It remains to be seen whether he can do the same to slap down the dissident teams that he and Ecclestone helped to make wealthy in the first place, and yet have contributed so much to the fabric of the sport.

⟃ Jean-Marie Balestre

As the president of the sport's governing body between 1978 and 1991, Frenchman Jean-Marie Balestre was the man most loved to hate during the 1980s. In all things, this controversial figure seemed to provoke strong feelings.

During World War Two, Balestre acted as an undercover agent for the French Resistance, for whom he posed as a member of the French Waffen SS. But when peace returned, his motives and allegiances were subjected to frequent query, and it was not without difficulty that he was able to convince those in power of the veracity of his claims. Indeed he was continually to fight battles to

clear his name from periodic slander and libel, and it was not until he was retrospectively awarded resistance decorations that such speculation ceased.

Balestre enjoyed a reasonable relationship with his national press, which owed much to his background in the same business. In 1950, he had established a magazine called Autojournal, in partnership with his friend Robert Hersant. They went on to parlay that into a highly successful publishing empire. Balestre had always been keen on motor sport, and in 1959 he founded the French national karting authority. Later he would create the International Karting Commission. Within a decade, he

would also be secretary-general of the French national motor sport authority – the FFSA – and in 1973 he was elected its president. He was angered, however, that the FIA's upper management appeared to have little interest in motor sport, and in 1978 he gave vent to his mounting frustration by proposing to them that they set up a separate sporting offshoot, similar to the now defunct Commission Sportif Internationale

Below: *In the pitlane with Ecclestone in 1980. At this point Balestre, as president of the FISA, was about to confront FOCA.*

Opposite: *Ballestre at a press-conference the year before, as president of FISA.*

(CSI), which had overseen sporting responsibilities in the 1960s. The FIA agreed, relieved perhaps to have found somebody willing to take over such a task, and when the Federation Internationale du Sport Automobile (FISA) was formed for 1978, it was no surprize when he was elected as its founding president.

Possessed of very strong views on how motor sport should be run, and determined to garner as much power as he possibly could for the FISA, Balestre immediately began to confront Bernie Ecclestone and Max Mosley, whom he perceived to be intent on taking overall control. Within months, the two parties had locked horns as he sought to reassert the governing body's influence in all areas.

The ultimate result was the FISA-FOCA war of 1980–1, a frenetic battle that – perhaps inevitably, given the strength of the respective players' hands – ended in the compromize that came to be called the Concorde Agreement. Under its terms, the FIA received a guaranteed cut of the not inconsiderable revenue from the sale of the sport's television rights, while FOCA, under the management of Ecclestone and Mosley, would still handle, and benefit from, such sales. Thus Balestre's dream of controlling everything faded, but despite that his success in garnering such income for the FISA impressed voters at election time for the FIA presidency, to which he graduated in 1987.

History largely remembers Balestre as a bombastic and egotistical character, who was more concerned about his own image than anything else, but this is both unfair and misleading. There is no doubt about his love for the sport, but because his political adroitness frequently left much to be desired, he tended to become labelled. Behind the scenes, he made tremendous steps in the

realm of safety, introducing specific constructional standards and later mandatory crash tests, which were designed to verify and enhance the structural integrity of the cars. Without question, these were instrumental in saving lives and preventing serious injuries, and they helped pave the way for the high safety standards that exist today. Balestre has always received insufficient credit for his work in this area.

Balestre had a tradition for high-handed behaviour (which Mosley would follow) and had no qualms about banning ground effect for 1983, or the turbos for 1989. Moreover, he never gave in to the significant opposition such rulings inevitably provoked.

By the late 1980s, however, he was adjudged by many to have outlived his shelf life, particularly after the controversy surrounding the 1989

Japanese GP, when he had Ayrton Senna excluded. After a fascinating duel, the volatile Brazilian had clashed with team-mate Alain Prost in the chicane, but whereas Prost had retired (with what transpired to be an apparently undamaged car), Senna had regained the track, made a pit stop to have repairs effected, then driven like a man possessed to snatch the lead from Alessandro Nannini's Benetton and roar home to a fabulous victory. Then Balestre decided that the manner in which he had rejoined the track after the incident rendered him liable to disqualification. In the acrimonious aftermath, Senna accused him of chauvinistically favouring Prost, who went on to win that year's title, and was called to Paris to apologize before his licence was granted for 1990.

The matter blew over eventually, but when Max Mosley challenged Balestre in the 1991 FISA presidential election, the latter was defeated. Voting of 43 to 29 in Mosley's favour ushered in a new era for FI.

Despite failing health, 70-year-old Balestre continued as FIA president until 1993, but did not contest Mosley's plan to merge the FIA and the FISA. After lending his support to the idea, which saw Mosley assume overall control, he was elected to the effectively honorary position of president of the FIA Senate.

Opposite above: *A thumbs up at the 1983 British GP.*

Opposite below: *Balestre with Nigel Mansell during the 1994 season.*

Below: *President of the FIA*

4

THE CARS

CHAPTER 7

Top Marques
The Great Racing Stables

While some racing car manufacturers over the years have come and gone, some sinking without trace, others have found the elusive key to superior performance and have left their own indelible mark in the history books. These are 10 of the teams whose exploits have shaped the face of the sport.

Brabham

Established by world champion driver Jack Brabham in 1962, the team that carried his name took three drivers – one of them Jack himself – to four World Championships before its demise 30 years later.

Once Brabham and Cooper had changed the face of F1 design with their success in 1959-60, Cooper's rivals soon leapfrogged ahead. But Brabham had a plan. He left Cooper, recruited designer Ron Tauranac – an old friend from their days in Australian dirt-track racing – and together they drew up plans for a car that was neat, efficient and simple.

Such qualities became hallmarks of the Tauranac Brabhams, and when the new 3-litre formula of 1966 created the vacuum of change, the Brabham cars filled it, thanks to a combination

Left: *Having abandoned Repco in favour of Ford, Brabham's BT26As were back on the pace in 1969, and remained the only non-monocoque cars in F1.*

of these Tauranac core values and Brabham's shrewdness. The doubling of the permitted engine capacity had most teams looking to outright power as the new key to success. Brabham reckoned otherwise, reasoning that, in the formula's early days at least, reliability would be more important. That, and light weight.

The Repco V8 was based on a production Holden motor and was simple – with a single cam per bank – which helped it achieve both of Brabham's aims. The Brabham-Repcos cleaned up in both 1966 and 1967, giving a title apiece to Brabham and Denny Hulme.

With the advent of the Ford Cosworth DFV engine – providing off-the-shelf reliability with real power for anyone who wanted one – a different approach became necessary. This didn't really occur at Brabham until its second phase, when Bernie Ecclestone acquired the company

Above: *Gordon Murray's elegant Brabham BT52 was championship-winning material in 1983.*

after Brabham's retirement and employed young South African designer Gordon Murray.

Free thinking and progressive, Murray designed a series of Brabhams that were superbly effective in both the DFV and following turbo eras. These cars – which won races with Carlos Reutemann, Carlos Pace and Niki Lauda in the 1970s, and Nelson Piquet in the 1980s – also displayed Murray's eye for aesthetic perfection. Piquet was World Champion in 1981 with the DFV powered BT49, and in 1983 with the BMW turbo-engined BT52.

After Piquet left in 1985, Brabham never won another race. When Murray departed and Ecclestone sold the company, its days really were numbered. It lingered on, ever less competitive, until the end of 1992, when it closed its doors for good.

BRM

The original vision former racer Raymond Mays had for British Racing Motors, when he formed it in the immediate post-war years, was for a world-beating, British-built Grand Prix car, funded by British industry. The idea designer Peter Berthon had for the machine in question was of huge power borne of vast mechanical complexity. When BRM finally achieved a world title, over a decade later, it was with neither complexity nor the backing of industry.

The original supercharged V16 BRM produced the awesome power envisaged by Berthon, but rarely for very long and not at any point on the power band that was of much use to the driver. Added to this were interminable delays in the project, and it quickly became a laughing stock. Initial investors were equally swift to disassociate themselves from it. Thus a superb idea was lost to poor execution.

Above: *1971 marked BRM's last real year as a leading contender, with the sleek P160.*

The company was rescued in the mid-1950s by industrialist Sir Alfred Owen, of the Rubery Owen Group, one of the original investors. A more conservative car was designed for the 2.5-litre formula, and Jo Bonnier took it to the marque's first victory, in the 1959 Dutch Grand Prix.

But it was the switch to rear engines and the 1.5-litre formula that brought the team full glory: Graham Hill winning the 1962 world title in the V8 BRM P56. BRM remained a front-rank team for the duration of the formula, also introducing Jackie Stewart to F1 in 1965. But early mistakes were repeated by a complex H16, followed by an underpowered V12 engine in the early days of the new 3-litre formula.

Eventually BRM won races in the period 1970–2, although it was never again a championship threat. The Owen money became insufficient, the team management increasingly out of touch, and the V12 engine ever less competitive. Sadly, by its final days in the mid-1970s, it was regarded as just as much of a joke as the original BRM V16 had been 25 years earlier.

Cooper

Father and son Charles and John Cooper are credited with changing the face of F1 car design with their switch to rear-engined cars in the late 1950s. These machines took Jack Brabham to consecutive world titles in 1959 and 1960, but the team never recaptured such glory.

The Coopers were Surbiton garage owners who established themselves as race car manufacturers in the wake of the post-war 500cc Formula Three boom. It was natural for the motor cycle engines of these cars to be mounted at the rear so that their chain drives could be connected to the rear wheels.

It was only as the Coopers constructed bigger-engined cars to this concept that the inherent

Right: *The first F1 Coopers may have been inelegant, but they were remarkably effective in the face of more powerful opposition.*

advantages of lower weight, smaller frontal area and more responsive handling became apparent. Stirling Moss took an F1 version to a shock win in the 1958 Argentinian Grand Prix, and the revolution was under way.

After Brabham's title successes, every rival team had to accept the inevitable and copy the Cooper formula. At this, Cooper's fortunes went into decline, and without any further innovations that allowed it to return to the forefront, its last F1 season was in 1968.

Ferrari

The most famous and evocative team of all, Ferrari has contested the World Championship right from the very start, winning nine Drivers' and eight Constructors' world titles. It is unique among current F1 teams in producing the entire car – including engine and transmission – the necessary investment being provided by its parent company, Fiat.

Realising his limitations as a race driver in the 1920s with Alfa Romeo, Enzo Ferrari took to managing the team instead. When Alfa withdrew from competition, his own team, Scuderia Ferrari, took over, ostensibly as an independent entrant using Alfa cars, but in reality still with a direct link to the factory. Ferrari and Alfa eventually parted just prior to the outbreak of World War Two, and shortly after

resumption of peace, he had built the first Ferrari Grand Prix car.

The first championship Grand Prix win came in 1951, the first title a year later with Alberto Ascari. Since then, Juan Manuel Fangio ('56), Mike Hawthorn ('58), Phil Hill ('61), John Surtees ('64), Niki Lauda ('75 and '77) and Jody Scheckter ('79) have all taken world titles in the red cars. Fiat acquired control of the Ferrari company in 1969, although the operation of the race team was left in the hands of Enzo until his death.

Long-term sustained success has not been seen since the 1970s, something not helped by a succession of Fiat-dictated management changes. But under the leadership of Luca di Montezemolo Ferrari is making a comeback, and with 2nd place in 1998, and the Constructor's Championship in 1999, the future looks golden.

Above: *No marque has the same mystique and charisma as Ferrari. Here Alesi creates sparks in Portugal in 1994.*

Lotus

The dominant team of the 1960s and 1970s, Lotus – under the guidance of its design genius proprietor, Colin Chapman – was responsible for a host of radical innovations that tended to keep the team one step ahead of the game. The last of six Drivers' and seven Constructors' World Championships came in 1978, and although the team continued after the death of Chapman in 1982, it was a downward spiral, which finally ended in 1994, despite the valiant efforts of Peter Collins and Peter Wright to resurrect past glories.

Chapman formed Lotus Cars to meet the demand for replicas of the Lotus Mk6 sports car he had taken to spectacular success in British club racing in the 1950s. He used the sales of this and subsequent road cars to fund the establishment of Team Lotus, the works race team. The first F1 car appeared in 1958, but it wasn't until Chapman produced his first rear-engined design, the 18, that a Lotus

Above: Man and machine in complete harmony: Jim Clark and Lotus.

won a Grand Prix, courtesy of Stirling Moss at Monaco in 1960.

The car that truly set Lotus on its road to glory arrived in 1962, in the elegant form of the type 25. This was the first Grand Prix car designed to monocoque principles, whereby the aluminium skin of the body actually acted as the chassis, unlike the previously universal arrangement of steel tubes covered by non-structural

Below: Senna had Clark's class, but his Lotuses often let him down.

panels. Its extra stiffness made for superior roadholding, its lighter weight for better performance. With this car, and a development of it, Jim Clark won two world titles, as well as the Indianapolis 500.

Chapman's next advance was to combine this method of construction with the use of the engine as a structural member in the Lotus 49, the first car to use the Ford Cosworth DFV engine. Graham Hill took this to a world title in 1968. A wedge shape, advanced torsion-beam suspension and inboard brakes were the innovations of the type 72, which won world titles for Jochen Rindt and Emerson Fittipaldi. Chapman's final triumph was to introduce the ground-effect principle to F1, making a quantum leap in aerodynamic grip, which helped Mario Andretti to the 1978 world crown.

After Chapman's death, Lotus enjoyed some success with Renault turbo-engined cars, driven by Ayrton Senna, but when the Brazilian left, the winning stopped. After a few more barren seasons, the sponsorship finally dried up. Ownership of the race team had been separated from the road car operation some years previously.

McLaren

Former Cooper driver Bruce McLaren followed in the footsteps of his ex-team-mate, Jack Brabham, in setting up his own F1 team in 1966. Although he won a Grand Prix in one of the cars that bore his name, he didn't live to see the team prosper and grow into one of the most successful of all time.

After McLaren died testing a Can-Am McLaren sports car in 1970, the running of the team was taken over by its manager, Teddy Mayer. He guided McLaren to its first two World Championships: in 1974 with Emerson Fittipaldi and 1976 with James Hunt. It was during this time that it first formed its alliance with Marlboro.

Dwindling success in the late 1970s led Marlboro to initiate a merger in 1980 between McLaren and the F2 team Project 4, also backed by the cigarette company and run by former Brabham mechanic Ron Dennis. Within a year, Dennis was in sole charge, and he brought with him designer John Barnard, who produced the first carbon-fibre F1 car. With this, John Watson won the first Grand Prix for the new-era McLaren in 1981.

With the help of sponsor – and later partner in the team – TAG, McLaren commissioned Porsche to design and build a turbocharged engine. The resultant McLaren-TAG Porsches completely dominated F1 in the mid-1980s, allowing Niki Lauda and Alain Prost to gain three world titles between them.

When the Porsche engines were replaced by Hondas, from 1988, the levels of success reached an even higher plane. Between them, Prost and Ayrton Senna won all but one of the 16 Grands Prix in 1988, an all-time F1 record. It was the first of four consecutive World Championships for the team, another all-time record.

When Honda withdrew from the sport in 1992, and Senna departed a year later, McLaren tumbled. However, the new potent package comprising a powerful Mercedes engine, the brilliant ex-Williams designer Adrian Newey, and the strong partnership of Mika Hakkinen and David Coulthard realized the dream: the 1998 Championship for Hakkinen, with Coulthard in 3rd.

Below: *1997 saw the beginning of McLaren's re-emergence as the dominant marque after several tough years in the post-Senna era.*

Mercedes

Although ostensibly a commercial car-producing giant, throughout its history Mercedes has periodically entered Grand Prix racing, usually to devastating effect.

Although it was the dominant team at the outbreak of World War Two, Mercedes did not re-enter Grand Prix racing until 1954. When it did so, its car – the W196 – was a sophisticated design, engineered with characteristic thoroughness. Fangio took it to victory in its first race and used it to clinch that year's world title. The following season's domination was even more complete, the team winning all but one round.

But that was the year of the Le Mans tragedy, in which over 80 spectators were killed when a Mercedes sports car launched itself into the crowd. There was an immediate outcry against all motor racing, which overnight changed Mercedes involvement from a commercial asset to a liability. It withdrew at the end of the season.

Mercedes did not return to the sport until the late 1980s, when it began to take part in sports car racing. This involvement was stepped up methodically until it re-entered F1, although this time as an engine supplier only. The partnership with McLaren led to major success: the 1998 Championship with new driver Hakkinen and, in third position, Coulthard. The future looks secure.

Left and below: Mercedes' return to F1 in 1954 continued its pre-war success, whether the cars were in 'slipper' body form (left, at Monaco in 1955) or in streamlined guise (below, on their Reims début in 1954).

Above: Tyrrell's six-wheeled P34, run in 1976 and 1977, was one of the sport's closest kept secrets prior to its surprise launch.

Tyrrell

Founded by timber merchant Ken Tyrrell, around the driving talents of Jackie Stewart, the Tyrrell team achieved World Championship glory on three occasions in its first six years. In the 24 years since, it has won only seven more races, and in 1999 it will be swallowed up by the new BAR tobacco 'super team'.

Tyrrell and Stewart first came together in Formula Three in 1964, and their success together launched Stewart into F1 in the following year.

In 1968, the French Matra team, for whom Stewart had driven in F2, was planning to enter F1, using its own V12 engine. Tyrrell proposed that it should allow him to enter a separate team of its cars, powered by Ford Cosworth DFV engines, then the best in the business, and driven by Stewart.

Matra agreed, and after coming close to taking the world crown at its first attempt, the Matra/Tyrrell combination achieved that goal in 1969. Although that was the last year of the partnership, a new Tyrrell car was ready by the end of 1970, and in

Above: Tyrrell's six-wheeled P34, run in 1976 and 1977, was one of the sport's closest kept secrets prior to its surprise launch.

1971 Stewart took the marque's first title. After winning the crown again in 1973, Stewart retired.

Tyrrell soldiered on, despite the blow, and scored further Grand Prix wins with Jody Scheckter, Patrick Depailler and Michele Alboreto. The last of these occurred in 1983, and since then the team's only competitive season has been 1990, with the aerodynamically advanced Tyrrell 019 driven by Jean Alesi.

Vanwall

Tony Vandervell was an industrialist who, in the early post-war period, dreamt of seeing a British F1 car take on and beat the previously dominant Continentals. Initially he shared this vision with Raymond Mays and became involved in the BRM project, but soon left to achieve his ambition by himself. The marque he created, Vanwall, won the first Championship for constructors in 1958.

After leaving BRM, Vandervell, whose company produced the 'thinwall' bearings that were widely used in the automotive and aircraft industries, persuaded Enzo Ferrari to sell him one of his Grand Prix cars. This and subsequent Ferraris were modified at Vandervell's workshops and christened the 'Thinwall Specials'.

These cars formed the basis of the first Vanwall, which appeared in 1954. A Ferrari-like chassis was combined with an engine inspired by the unit in the Norton racing motor cycle. After

a quiet start, the Vanwalls became ever more competitive, and when Colin Chapman was commissioned to design a new chassis, and Frank Costin an aerodynamic body, the 1957 Vanwall became the fastest car in F1.

It converted this status into the 1958 Constructors' title, after Stirling Moss and Tony Brooks between them won six times. The death of the team's third driver, Stuart Lewis-Evans, in the final round at Casablanca, however, extinguished Vandervell's passion for the project. Although a new rear-engined car was subsequently built and raced, Vanwall essentially came to an end on that sad day.

Top: *Stirling Moss heads his Vanwall to a British car's first British GP triumph, at Aintree in 1957.*

Above left: *Tony Vandervell, the original architect of Britain's current domination.*

Left: *Though he was the class of 1958, Moss missed the championship by a mere point.*

Williams

Vying with McLaren as the most successful team in the modern F1 era, Williams has won seven Drivers' and nine Constructors' World Championships in the past 17 seasons.

Frank Williams came into F1 as a privateer entrant in 1969, and although his team continued a hand-to-mouth existence for the next few years, he sold out in 1976 to oil tycoon Walter Wolf. The following year, he started again from scratch, this time with promising young

designer Patrick Head and some sponsorship from Saudia Airlines.

With Head's first F1 design, the Williams FW06, Alan Jones scored some promising results in 1978. A year later, using the designer's superb ground-effect FW07, Clay Regazzoni scored the team's first win, at the British Grand Prix. Jones scored another three before the year was out, and in 1980 he gave Williams its first World Championship. Another followed in 1982, courtesy of Keke Rosberg.

With the advent of the turbo era, Williams formed a partnership with Honda in 1983. The Williams-Hondas

were the fastest cars in the business from the tail end of 1985, and in the following year, Williams took the Constructors' title, but had to wait until 1987 before Nelson Piquet gave the combination another Drivers' crown.

In a shock move, Honda switched to McLaren from 1988, so in 1989 Williams formed an alliance with Renault. Using the French company's V10 engines, Williams won two races in the partnership's first season, and together they progressed steadily, until by late 1991 the Williams-Renaults were the fastest cars on the grid. They retained that status until 1998.

Nigel Mansell gave the partnership its first World Championship in 1992. This achievement was mirrored in 1993 by Alain Prost, in 1996 by Damon Hill, and in 1997 by Jacques Villeneuve.

Above: The *1985 FW10 continued a winning tradition established within eighteen months of the team's launch in 1977.*

Left: *The indefatigable Frank Williams, 1993.*

Below: *Jacques Villeneuve builds upon the successes of Mansell, Prost and Hill, by taking the 1997 drivers' title. In the 1998 season the rise of McLaren stymied his progress.*

CHAPTER **8**

Ten of the Best
THE TOP GRAND PRIX CARS

Creating a car capable of winning a Grand Prix is a dream that has defeated many, let alone producing one that takes on the mantle of true greatness. These are 10 of the greatest designs, which achieved that rare blend of form and function in the pursuit of ultimate success.

⇢〉 Cooper T51

The first mid-engined car to take the World Championship, the Cooper T51, achieved its success with a fraction of the resources available to the teams that had dominated until that point, and with significantly less power. The lessons demonstrated by its layout changed the convention of Grand Prix car design more fundamentally than any before or since.

It was the T51's immediate predecessor that had first shown the advantages of the layout in F1 in 1958. Putting the engine at the back allowed the driver to be seated far lower, without a propshaft to clear, making for a massive reduction in frontal area. The direct mating of the engine and final drive meant that the frames housing these components didn't need to be so bulky, as their torque reversal cancelled each other out. This, and the loss of the propshaft, provided a major weight reduction. Finally, the concentration of the car's masses towards its centre-line made for much more instantaneous changes in direction.

Although the 1958 car won two Grands Prix, such advantages were not recognized universally, partly because the front-engined Ferraris and Vanwalls were still fighting over the destiny of the championship. The Cooper triumphs were regarded as flukes – perhaps because its compact dimensions were particularly suited to the tight confines of tracks like Monaco – and they were thought to have little real worth.

Yet the only reason that the 1958 Cooper wasn't a more consistent threat was that its Coventry Climax engine was merely a bored-out Formula 2 unit of just 2.2 litres. The full 2.5 litres enjoyed by the others gave them a critical advantage.

For 1959, Climax responded with a redesigned crankshaft to lengthen the stroke and give 2.5 litres. The resultant 172kW (230bhp) was still around 45kW (60bhp) down on the Ferrari, but it proved just about enough.

The Cooper T51 began the season with a win for Jack Brabham at Monaco, but it was his highly competitive third on the flat-out expanses of Rheims, despite his power deficit, that really gained the attention of the front-engine traditionalists. He won again at the British Grand Prix, and Cooper T51s, in the hands of Moss and McLaren, won three of the remaining four rounds; Brabham took the title.

Right: Cooper's revolutionary T51 made up in handling and tyre economy for what it initially lacked in power.

⇥❯ Ferrari 312T

When Niki Lauda took the 1975 World Championship, it brought to a close an 11-year title drought for Ferrari. The Austrian was quick to assign praise to the car that carried him to this success, the 312T model. This car was a remarkably well-balanced blend of power, reliability and superb handling, which was enough to give it a small, but significant and consistent, advantage over the opposition during a period of unprecedented competitiveness.

The 312T's flat-12 engine was based on the power unit that had powered all F1 Ferraris since 1970, and would continue to do so until the end of 1980. It was designed by Mauro Forghieri, and the aim of its horizontally opposed cylinder layout was to put the mass of the engine as low down in the car as possible, giving it an advantage over the vee-configurations of the competition. Twelve small cylinders made for higher engine speeds than the eight larger ones of most of its rivals, so theoretically a higher power output was possible. The downside was that it was thirstier and, therefore, needed to carry more fuel at the start of a race, although through good fuel management this penalty was kept to manageable proportions.

This much had applied to all the 1970s Ferraris up to that point. What swung the balance more fully in Ferrari's favour, however, was Forghieri's transverse siting of the gearbox, behind the engine. Again weight distribution was at the root of his thinking, but this time to bring it as far towards the centre of the car as possible. The aim here was to speed up the car's ability to change direction.

When Lauda first tested the car, he reported that the layout made it feel a little twitchy, but that its ultimate handling balance was superbly neutral. The car's predecessor, the 312B3, had always been limited by its power sapping understeer. Lauda won three races in succession with the 312T, and another two before the end of a victorious season, team-mate Regazzoni also taking a win. It went on to a further three consecutive wins at the start of 1976 before being replaced by the 312T2.

Above: *Everything came right for Ferrari in 1975 with Mauro Forghieri's supremely integrated 312T.*

▸❯ Lotus 25

The Lotus 25 was the first monocoque F1 car, and the advantages of this method of construction allowed it to dominate the 1.5-litre era of F1, in the early to mid-1960s. The car gave Lotus its first World Championship, and a development of it even won the Indianapolis 500.

It was Lotus boss Colin Chapman's fanatical search for lower frontal area that caused him to stumble upon the idea of the monocoque hull. Looking for ways to dispense with the steel tubes of the chassis around the cockpit area to further slim the car down, he made the aluminium skin of the car double as the chassis itself. The previous method of forming the load bearing structure from steel tubes, which were then covered with non-structural panels, was rendered instantly obsolete.

But the monocoque design brought advantages far greater than merely providing a slimmer body. It was much stiffer and more resistant to twisting, allowing the suspension to do its job far more effectively. It was also much lighter.

Chapman had kept the car a secret – even entering early-season non-championship races with the Lotus 24, an update of his previous season's 21 with conventional space-frame chassis – but from the 25's début in the 1962 Dutch Grand Prix, it was evident that this was where the future lay.

In Jim Clark's hands, the Lotus 25 went on to prove conclusively that it was the fastest car of the season, although it was thwarted from winning the championship in the final round by unreliability. This was corrected for 1963, when Clark took a record seven wins on his way to the title. A wider-wheeled version, dubbed the 33, also took the crown in 1965, the same year that a beefed-up Indycar derivative won the Indy 500 with Ford V8 power.

Below: *Clark and the brilliant monocoque Lotus 25 were made for each other. Both set standards the rest aspired to match.*

⇉ Lotus 72

After the widespread availability of the superb Cosworth DFV engine – the use of which Lotus had pioneered in 1967 – made the competing cars of the late 1960s extremely evenly-matched, Lotus moved the game on again in 1970 with its innovative 72 model. This went on to take two World Championships during a remarkable six-year career.

Unlike the 25, there was no single aspect of the 72 that was responsible for its clear superiority over its rivals. Instead there were several minor, but significant, contributory factors, all blended together beautifully. The car's wedge shape was more aerodynamically effective than the 'toothpaste tube' styles prevalent until then. The siting of the oil and water radiators at the side, rather than the front of the car, made for a concentration of its masses towards the centre, which provided more responsive handling. Furthermore its inboard suspension and brakes produced smoother airflow and less unsprung weight, while its torsion-bar springing helped endow it with excellent mechanical grip, traction and rising-rate geometry. It all made for a car that Jochen Rindt claimed 'even a monkey could win races in'.

After winning four Grands Prix in succession with the car, Rindt was killed in qualifying for the Italian Grand Prix, but his points score was not surpassed before the end of the season, and thus he became the sport's only posthumous World Champion. His place as Lotus team leader was taken by Emerson Fittipaldi, who went on to win the 1972 World Championship with the car. Even in its fourth year of competition, the 72 was still the fastest car in the field, Ronnie Peterson using it to gain a record nine pole positions. It won three more Grands Prix in 1974 and did not finally retire until the end of 1975.

Below: *Defying convention, Lotus's 72 introduced the wedge shape and side radiator location, torsion bar suspension and inboard brakes. This is Wisell at Montjuich Park in 1971.*

▸▸ Lotus 79

Colin Chapman's final glory, the Lotus 79 took the 1978 World Championship by storm through harnessing the ground-effect principle. It was yet another of Chapman's radical quantum leaps that changed the convention of F1 design.

In 1977, Lotus had introduced its 78 'wing car'. This used an inverted aerofoil within each sidepod to produce downforce. Special skirts beneath the sidepods helped to channel incoming air through a small aperture, which then opened out into a much wider area. By accelerating the air, this venturi arrangement lowered its pressure and created a vacuum, which was contained by

the sealing effect of the skirts so that the car was sucked to the ground. The 78 was the fastest car in F1 that year, although it was let down by poor engine reliability. For 1978, the concept was refined further. Chapman put all the fuel in a central tank behind the driver, which enabled him to narrow the chassis and incorporate uncompromized venturis. He also added skirts that slid up and down over surface irregularities to enhance the ground-effect seal. All these developments to the 78 gave the 79 a vast performance advantage over its rivals, and the team won six Grands Prix that season – Andretti gaining the championship with five, and his team-mate Ronnie Peterson finishing

as runner-up with one. Consequently, that year Lotus won the Constructors' Championship as well.

Virtually every one of Lotus's rivals had a 79 copy on the grid for the start of the following season, but some – notably Williams and Ligier – had realized that even greater advantage could be taken of the concept if the tubs and mounting points of the cars were sufficiently strong and stiff to withstand the massive aerodynamic loadings. Consequently the weaker 79 became an also-ran to the cars that it had inspired.

Below: *Ronnie Peterson presses on in France in 1978, in the glorious Lotus 79 which was the first car to demonstrate fully the potential of harnessing ground-effect aerodynamics.*

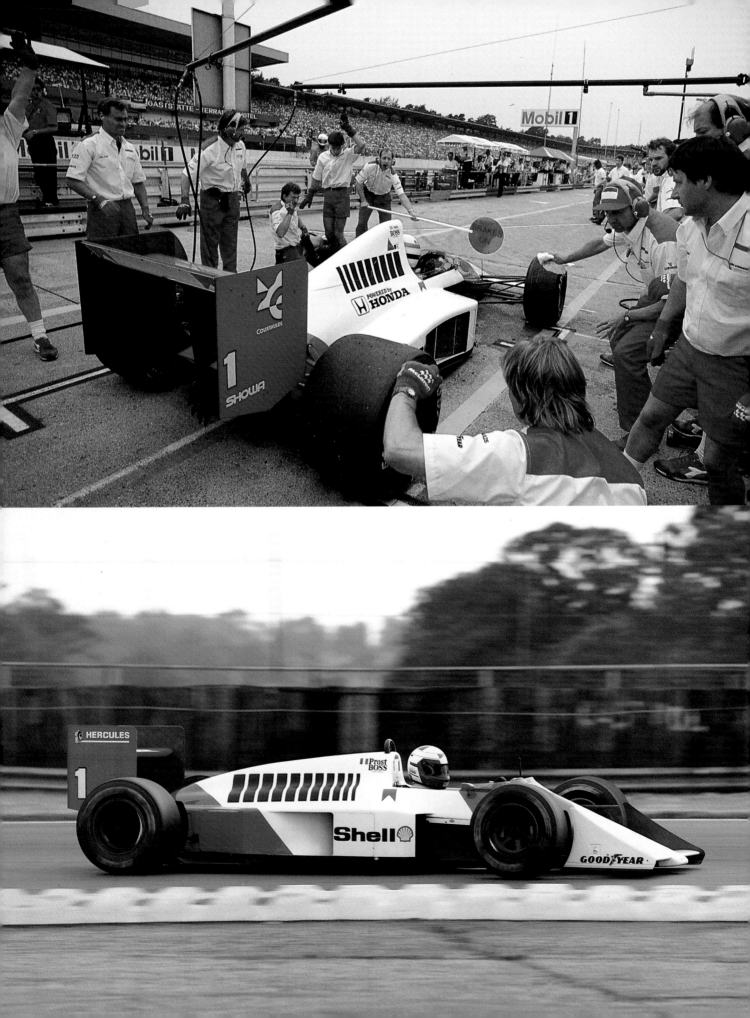

⇥ McLaren MP4/4

The most statistically successful F1 car of all time, McLaren's 1988 MP4/4 won 15 of the 16 Grands Prix comprising that year's championship.

In 1988, Honda had switched from supplying Williams – with which it had won the 1987 World Championship – to McLaren. That was the good news; the bad was that designer John Barnard, responsible for all the McLarens since 1981, had left.

The new car, penned by Steve Nichols and Neil Oatley, essentially retained the aerodynamic essence of Barnard's MP4/3, helped by the fact that, like the Honda, its Porsche engine had also been a V6. The cockpit, however, was noticeably slimmer. Despite this being the final year that turbocharged engines would be allowed, Honda had spared no effort and even produced two engine types – XE2 and XE3 – for use according to the circuit characteristics.

In time-honoured McLaren fashion, the new cars were not completed until the eve of the season, joining pre-season testing at Imola weeks after most of their rivals. Yet instantly the MP4/4s left the opposition breathless. Armed with the most powerful engines and the best drivers – Senna and Prost – and with the best team management, McLaren swept all before it. At the Italian Grand Prix, leader Senna tripped over back-marker Schlesser while lapping him. With Prost already out, it was the only race that the MP4/4 failed to win all season.

Top left: *McLaren's MP4/4 made brilliantly simple use of Honda's 1.5 V6 turbo, and replaced the TAG-powered MP4/3 of 1987 (bottom).*

Right: *The Mercedes W196s of Fangio and Moss enjoyed similarly elevated status throughout 1954 and 1955.*

⇥ Mercedes W196

The devastatingly effective W196 gave a suitably dominant performance for Mercedes-Benz's two-year Grand Prix come-back, winning nine of the 12 races it contested in 1954 and 1955.

At a time of technical stagnancy, the W196, designed by acclaimed Mercedes engineer Rudolph Uhlenhaut, featured many innovations. The most startling of these on the car's introduction was the all-enveloping streamlined body. Then, unlike now, enclosing the wheels with bodywork was not forbidden, and the visual effect made existing cars look obsolete. However it was found to induce high-speed handling problems, so the car usually appeared as a conventional-looking open-wheeler.

But beneath the skin was the further novelty of a straight-eight engine, which was canted over for a lower centre of gravity and which featured desmodromic, springless, valve operation. Fuel injection completed the technical specification, some nine years before its use in F1 was widespread.

Fangio took the W196 to victory on its maiden outing in the 1954 French Grand Prix. It failed to win only twice that year and helped Fangio to his second world title. In the following year, it failed only once, and Fangio took his third crown.

⏩ Renault RS01

Although the Renault RS01 failed to win a single Grand Prix, it ushered in a new era for F1. Not only was it the first of the turbocharged F1 cars, but it also signalled the start of a substantial investment in F1 by major car producers that changed the commercial scale of Grand Prix racing.

When the 3-litre formula was devized in the mid-1960s, an allowance was made for forced-induction engines – supercharged or turbocharged – of half that capacity. It was not seriously expected that anyone would take up such an option, but Renault did. In the mid-1970s, having been involved in an F2 racing programme, the company decided that the commercial possibilities of F1 were too good to

ignore. However, to give itself the image of an innovator, it was keen on looking at the turbocharged option.

Renault's F2 engine was a 2-litre V6. Based on this, a turbo 1.5 V6 was devized, and Renault built a chassis in which to install it, co-designed by Andre de Cortanze and Jean-Pierre Jabouille, the man who had taken the 1976 F2 championship for the company in a self-penned car. Jabouille would also be the driver.

Although the engine gave in excess of 433kW (580bhp) at a time when the best normally aspirated units were producing little more than 373kW (500bhp), it rarely did so for long, and terrible throttle lag made it exceptionally difficult to drive. It made its début at the 1977 British Grand Prix, qualifying well down the field. Progress through the next two seasons was steady, interspersed by

many spectacular blow-ups. Jabouille took his first points with a fourth place in the 1978 US Grand Prix, and in South Africa in early 1979 – aided by Kyalami's high altitude affecting the performance of the normally aspirated engines, but not the turbo Renault's – Jabouille sat the car on pole position.

It would be another few months before he won his first race, in a ground-effect version of the car, the RS10. But the RS01 had started the ball rolling, and within a few seasons the entire grid would be turbo powered, while factories such as BMW, Alfa Romeo and Honda would all be involved in F1 after Renault had demonstrated its commercial worth.

Below: *Renault's RS01 was laughed at initially by nervous rivals, but by 1979 the laughter was beginning to turn to tears.*

Right: *The supremely competitive edge of the Williams FW07 series in the early 1980s had its echo in the similarly gifted FW14s a decade later.*

➤❯ Williams FW07

In only the second year of the team's participation in F1, Williams Grand Prix Engineering produced the FW07. This was the car which established a winning sequence for the team, which 18 years later has still to cease.

Although the Lotus 78 had already shown the way forward with ground effect, when Head designed the conventional FW06 chassis, he did so because he wished to keep things simple in Williams's first year as a constructor. It would also allow him time to properly understand how ground effect worked.

The result of his studies was devastating. The FW07 appeared some way into the 1979 season, but by the second half of the year, it was far and away the fastest car in F1. Although ostensibly it looked similar to the Lotus 79, it featured a much stiffer monocoque that was better able to deal with the huge loadings produced by the ground-effect design.

Clay Regazzoni duly gave the Williams marque its first Grand Prix win at Silverstone, while Alan Jones delivered four more before the season was out. In the following year, Jones gave Williams its first title, after a close battle with Brabham's Nelson Piquet.

Into 1981, the FW07 remained a front-runner, Carlos Reutemann leading the championship for most of the year, but falling at the final hurdle. In its last Grand Prix, at Long Beach 1982, Keke Rosberg used the FW07 to take a strong second place on his way to a world title. It had been a glorious reign.

➤❯ Williams FW14B

The most dominant of all Williams's many winning cars, the FW14B took Nigel Mansell to a crushing 1992 World Championship.

Aside from its superb Renault V10 engine – which was vastly more fuel-efficient than the Honda V12 in the car of chief rival McLaren – the key to the dominance of the 14B was its active-ride suspension. Williams had first tried such a system back in 1987, following the lead of Lotus some years before that. But reliability problems in the 'active' car of 1988 had seen designer Patrick Head subsequently steer away from it.

However wind tunnel data showed that there was a major aerodynamic benefit to be had from keeping the car completely flat and level at all times and, urged on by aerodynamicist Adrian Newey, Head gave the go-ahead for a new active suspension system to be fitted to the team's 1991 chassis, the FW14. Thus was born the FW14B.

It completely trounced the opposition, Mansell winning the first five races of the season, and four more later in the year, as well as sitting on pole position for all but two of the races. He had wrapped up the title with five rounds still to go.

CHAPTER **9**

Oddballs

TEN OF THE MOST UNUSUAL F1 RACERS

Why follow the herd? Motor racing has never been short of designers prepared to hang their tails in the wind and to go out on a technological limb in the quest for a performance advantage. Some have succeeded admirably, others have failed miserably. But the point is that they tried, and in doing so they added much-needed variety.

Bugatti 251

1956

Ettore Bugatti was to motor sport in the 1920's and 1930's what Enzo Ferrari would become in the post-war years. The man who once described the Le Mans Bentleys as 'the world's fastest lorries', Bugatti created engineering masterpieces of outstanding elegance and beauty. Although Italian born, he lived in France and is widely regarded as French by motoring historians: his works cars always raced in French blue.

Bugatti's achievements were largely confined to pre-war racing, although the French ace Jean-Pierre Wimille used a 4.7-litre Bugatti to win the Coupe des Prisonniers for large-engined cars when motor racing began again on the Bois de Boulogne in 1945. Ettore Bugatti died in 1947, and with him died the company's racing activities as his son, Roland, took command. But in 1956, the marque made a remarkable return with a brace of unusual cars for the 2.5-litre F1. These were inspired by Jacques Bolore, who had married Madame Bugatti and begun to exercise control over the business.

The Bugatti 251 was the work of former Ferrari designer Gioacchino Colombo, and it had some remarkably advanced features. At this time, F1 cars were still front-engined, and John Cooper's little rear-engined 'roller skates' had yet to point the way forward. But the 251's 183kW (245bhp) straight-eight power unit was mounted transversely behind the driver. Drive was taken from the centre of the two blocks of four cylinders to a Porsche designed five-speed gearbox. This and the final drive were mounted in unit with the engine, creating weight distribution similar to that enjoyed by today's cars. The chassis was a tubular space frame, while rigid de Dion axles were employed front and rear, at a time when everything else had independent front suspension at the least. Fuel was carried alongside the driver, in the sort of pannier tanks that would become popular in the late 1960's and early 1970's.

In late 1955, the 251 was unveiled on an airfield at Entzheim, near Bugatti's Molsheim plant. Driver Maurice Trintignant tested it there in March of the following year, and it was entered for that year's French GP at Reims. At this time, Bugatti's financial position was precarious, while Trintignant's testing had revealed that the chunky little car had some serious shortcomings. Bolore wanted it to race; Colombo and Trintignant were of the opinion that it needed a lot more development. Further tests at Reims, in the week before the Grand Prix, confirmed the latters' suspicions, but two cars were duly taken to the race.

Out of the Thillois hairpin in particular, the 251's weight distribution endowed it with excellent traction, but its high-speed handling was vague and did not inspire confidence. Trintignant was 18s off Fangio's pole position pace in practice, qualifying 18th out of 20. In the race, he was an also-ran until the team withdrew the car after 18 laps when the throttle began to stick. Before further development could be implemented, the company ran short of funding and the interesting project was sold off.

Left: *Bugatti's unusual T251 promised much but delivered nothing.*

Right: *ATS's own F1 effort in 1963 was awful.*

ATS

1963–4

Enzo Ferrari was the best prepared when the regulations required a change to 1.5-litre F1 cars for 1961, and as his shark-nosed racers swept the board, only Stirling Moss was able to get the better of them in a straight fight. But despite the superiority of his cars, all was not well within the empire over which Ferrari ruled. At the end of the season, he issued a number of his senior engineers with an ultimatum they could not tolerate, and they walked out *en masse*. They were led by Carlo Chiti, a roly-poly character with a volatile temper that disguised genius and a heart of gold.

Chiti was a fundamental part of the Ferrari 156 design team, but he and team manager Romolo Tavoni moved on to set up the adventurous Automobili Turismo Sport (ATS) F1 team with financial backing from industrialists Count Giovanni Volpi di Misurata, Jaime Ortiz Patino and Dr Giorgio Billi. In incredibly short time, Chiti created a factory and a foundry at the new Sasso Marconi

site near Bologna, while simultaneously designing the car and its new V8 engine.

The ATS made its first appearance at the Belgian GP at Spa Francorchamps in 1963, when the team stopped its transporter at Malmedy, far from the paddock, and simply sent its cars around to the astonishment of onlookers in the pits, who wondered what on earth they were and where they had come from. Sadly, after all the effort, the cars were terrible. In their initial state, they even had to have chassis tubes sawn through and rewelded if an engine change was required. They ran in Belgium, with former World Champion Phil Hill at the wheel of one and 1961 French GP winner Giancarlo Baghetti in the other, but were hopeless. After other fleeting outings over the next two seasons, the project died.

Hill still fondly recalls Chiti's love of animals: 'When we were all at ATS, we were in this farmhouse he'd bought, and the animals – pigs, sheep – just used to walk right in! He was one hell of a guy.'

BRM H16

1966–7

The new 3-litre F1 of 1966 promised a return to power and, at BRM, engine designer Tony Rudd opted for the bold expedient of flattening two of the company's successful 1.5-litre V8s and gearing them together, one atop the other, as an H16. He'd been impressed by the Napier Dagger H24 aero engine, and reasoned that such an engine might be coaxed into producing 447kW (600bhp) in the long term.

Sadly the H16 proved horrendously unreliable at first: no sooner had one source of internal vibration been eliminated than another would begin to wreak havoc. The H16 BRM only began racing towards the end of 1966, and even though it was more reliable by 1967, it lacked the expected power.

'It was a dreadful car,' recalls former BRM star Jackie Stewart. 'It was so bad that it would reach a performance plateau, and anybody could do a similar lap time in it. The only time that changed was when you got to really difficult circuits, such as Spa or the Nürburgring. But it was just terrible!'

The problem was not just the engine, for the P83 BRM chassis was a hefty piece of equipment, and even the so-called 'lightweight' P115, which appeared part-way through 1967, was still significantly heavier than the opposition.

The H16 engine did win a Grand Prix, however. Before the Ford DFV was ready for 1967, Lotus chief Colin Chapman did a deal with BRM to use its H16 in 1966 in his type 43. Maurice Philippe and the Lotus design team knew they were in trouble when the first engine arrived and four men were needed to lift it off the truck; subsequent investigation revealed that it weighed as much as the rest of the car. But at Watkins Glen that year, Lotus borrowed the works spare engine after its own had blown up in practice, and in the race Jim Clark nursed his Lotus-BRM to a surprise triumph. It was the only race ever won by a 16-cylinder engine. That victory and Jackie Stewart's second place at Spa, in the following year, would stand as the H16's only decent results.

BRM dumped the H16 in favour of a V12 for 1968, and enjoyed a brief revival of fortune. Years later, Rudd would ponder the situation and say, 'I often wonder what might have happened if we had opted in 1966 for the 3-litre V12 engine derived from the 1.5-litre V8, instead of going to the H16. How different it all might have been, and whether Keith Duckworth would have become such a rich man! I suppose the H16 was the biggest mistake I ever made.'

But it was a glorious failure.

Left: Fiendishly over-complicated and overweight, BRM's H16 boldly misread the requirements of the first 3-litre F1 cars. With Stewart at Spa in 1967 the car still managed a second.

Honda RA302

`1968`

When Honda first entered F1, in 1964, it did so with a complex transversely mounted V12 engine. By the end of the following season, this had been developed sufficiently to win the final race of the 1.5-litre formula, in Mexico. After that, however, Honda's engineers seemed to forget the basic tenet of race car design – that a vehicle should be light and nimble – and saddled its 1966 and 1967 contenders with a hefty V12 engine that weighed 45kg (100lb) more than anyone else's (and there were some heavy old engines about at that time).

By 1968, the team had benefited from John Surtees' technical input, and that season's RA301 design was neater and more powerful, while a lightweight V12 was promised. But behind the scenes, founder Soichiro Honda aspired to sell his air cooled N600 saloon cars world-wide. This desire, together with his motor cycle

experience, told him that Honda needed an air cooled car, and he instructed his engineers to create one. The lightweight V12 project immediately suffered. (Honda would interfere in a similar manner later, when he insisted that the marque emulate Ferrari for the 1991 season by creating a V12 engine – even though a V10 was the optimum package and his own was already the class of the 1989 and 1990 seasons.)

The RA302 at least relied on the basic design principles. It was small and light, its 120-degree V8 engine being slung quite neatly beneath a cantilevered arm at the back of its monocoque chassis. But when the former Lotus racer turned journalist Innes Ireland encountered the car on its first test at Silverstone, in June, he was appalled by its handling behaviour. Surtees himself was miffed when the car simply arrived, unannounced, from Tokyo, along with instructions that it be raced in the French GP at Rouen. Clearly it was substantially underdeveloped, and he

Above: Schlesser at Rouen in 1968 driving the underdeveloped Honda RA302. On lap two the engine cut out and he was killed.

refused, whereupon Honda arranged for it to be entered by Honda France. Jo Schlesser, a solid F2 driver with Grand Prix aspirations, understandably jumped at the chance to drive it.

Schlesser started from the penultimate slot on the grid, while Surtees, in the old car, challenged for the lead in dire conditions. On the second lap, Schlesser's V8 cut out on the run down to the Nouveau Monde hairpin. The Honda slewed off into a bank at high speed and burst into flames, which spread across the width of the track. The Frenchman died in the inferno.

Surtees tried a second RA302 V8 at Monza later in the year, before it was mothballed, but at the end of the season Honda withdrew to concentrate on selling cars. Its return in the 1980's would be far more auspicious.

Cosworth 4WD

1969

In 1969, there was a general belief that the increasing power outputs of F1 engines would eventually mean that everyone had to incorporate four-wheel drive on their cars to provide sufficient traction.

That season, Lotus, Matra and McLaren all developed four-wheel-drive cars. So, for reasons that remain unclear, did Cosworth, the company responsible for building the Ford DFV engine, which was well on its way to becoming the most successful Grand Prix engine in history.

Cosworth's founder, Keith Duckworth, had little faith that others were going the right way about four-wheel drive, and after luring designer Robin Herd away from McLaren, he urged him to create the new machine. When it appeared mid-season, it had

an aluminium monocoque chassis with side pontoons, which carried the fuel, and an extraordinarily crude-looking full-width aluminium nose of triangular section. This looked like something that had been knocked up temporarily pending the proper job. The transmission system was Cosworth's own design, while the engine was turned through 180 degrees and mated to a six-speed gearbox.

Duckworth's partner, Mike Costin, tried it first, at Mallory Park. Later Trevor Taylor, Jim Clark's former team-mate at Lotus, tested the car at Silverstone. A man who was fearless enough to race wheel to wheel with men such as the wild Belgian driver Willy Mairesse, Taylor would simply roll his eyes whenever asked to comment on the car. Then motor sport diarist Eoin Young was press-ganged into trying it. Prior to the

Above: *Even Cosworth staff admitted later that they didn't really know what possessed them to create the horrible 4WD prototype of 1969.*

event, he was offered a glass of wine – 'the red infuriator' – by the colourful Jumbo Goddard, in anticipation of an unpleasant experience. Young had no pretensions towards being a racing driver, nor any doubts about his opinion of the angular, unpainted beast: 'It was awful!' he said.

Heavy steering and wild wheelspin – the very problem the car sought to alleviate – were the major limiting factors and, as soon as it had arrived, the Cosworth was axed by Duckworth and Costin. In later years, one Cosworth employee was moved to remark, 'It was an aberration. I really can't think what was in our minds when we undertook the project.'

Amon AF101

1974

As a racing driver, Chris Amon was in the class of Jimmy Clark and Jackie Stewart, but besides being devastatingly unlucky, he was also completely disorganized.

After leading, but losing, countless Grands Prix for Ferrari between 1967 and '69, usually because of trivial mechanical problems beyond his control, he joined March, then Matra, where the trend continued. When the French team pulled out, at the end of 1972, Amon prepared to rejoin March, only to hear on the radio, back home in New Zealand, that he had been 'fired' by director Max Mosley for reasons that were never made clear, but which Amon believed centred around money that would be contributed to the team by a French sponsor if it chose Jean-Pierre Jarier instead.

Thus Amon made the disastrous switch to Tecno for 1973, and when that degraded to the standard of a joke, had brief outings for Tyrrell. For 1974, he attempted to take control of his own destiny by joining with backer John Dalton to produce his own car. The Amon F101 was designed by Gordon Fowell, the man behind one of the drastically underpowered Tecnos. Many features of the car, particularly the central fuel tank right behind the driver and the forward driving position, would appear in the highly successful Lotus 79 of 1978, but the Amon was an utter disaster.

The car's first race was the Spanish GP in 1974, when its shortcomings were manifest. It was seen at a couple more races before Larry Perkins, substituting for an indisposed Amon, crunched it at the Nürburgring.

The tragedy of the car was not so much that it failed, as that Amon stayed with the project as long as he did. Between 1973 and 1974, he received offers to join McLaren, Brabham and Ferrari, all of which had winning cars, but he stayed loyal to Dalton throughout, right until they threw in the towel. If the project called the New Zealander's judgement into question, it also demonstrated his absolute integrity.

'I said no to Bernie Ecclestone's invitation to replace Rikki von Opel at Brabham,' Chris said, 'because if I'd gone off to drive for Brabham, it would have knocked the morale of our team. It wouldn't have been fair to John or the guys, who were working all hours. If I'd got into a Brabham BT44, I'd never have gone back to my own thing.'

But he would have scored the Grand Prix victory that he so definitely deserved.

Below: *The car that killed a career: Chris Amon's terrible AF101.*

Tyrrell P34

1976–77

When Ken Tyrrell took the wraps off his latest Grand Prix challenger, late in 1975, onlookers simply gasped in amazement. From the cockpit backwards, it looked pretty much like anything else. But from the cockpit forwards, it produced the surprise of the decade: there were four front wheels! Moreover they were not the normal 33cm (13in) size. Instead two axles carried 25cm (10in) front wheels and tyres.

The idea had come from Tyrrell's designer, Derek Gardner, and it was not simply an attempt to reduce the car's frontal area. True that was part of the equation, but he was well aware that the rear wheels also had to be factored into any such calculations. What the dramatically unorthodox layout did confer on the Tyrrell P34 (for Project 34) was

leech-like grip. In 1976, when the cars were at the peak of their performance, what drivers Jody Scheckter and Patrick Depailler most frequently praised was the turn-in ability as they approached corners.

Initially Tyrrell had no firm plans to race the car, but when the prototype showed such promise in back-to-back tests against the standard 007 car, race versions were hurriedly prepared. They proved highly competitive.

On the way to third place in the Constructors' World Championship, only 12 points down on Ferrari and three adrift of McLaren, Scheckter and Depailler finished third and fourth respectively in the drivers' title chase. The South African took pole position and won the race in Sweden, with the Frenchman second, and each had gained a fastest lap: Scheckter in Germany, Depailler in Canada.

There were numerous second places, too.

Such promise prompted Tyrrell to continue with the cars' evolution into 1977, when Ronnie Peterson replaced Scheckter. But although the Tyrrells had more aerodynamic bodywork, they could rarely keep pace with the competition, partly because Goodyear was no longer able to develop the bespoke front tyres as it coped with a fresh challenge from Michelin.

Both March and Williams also produced six-wheeled cars, both of them using twin rear axles so that they did enjoy a reduction in frontal area. However, both experienced transmission problems and never raced at F1 level, and in any case such concepts were banned by 1982. But later Jonathan Palmer used the six-wheeled Williams FW08 to win the Goodwood Festival of Speed hillclimb and came away raving about the car's 'phenomenal traction'.

Lotus 56B

1971

It almost goes without saying that
Colin Chapman introduced the gas
turbine engine to FI. What other
designer possessed that incredible
fertility of imagination and freedom
of thought to embrace all manner of
technical experiment?

The pregnant-looking Lotus 56B
that appeared in 1971 was a
hangover from Chapman's days at
Indianapolis, for the 56 had actually
appeared in 1968 as a state-of-the-
art wedge-shaped contender for the
500 mile race. It was intended to
build upon the near-miss run of the
STP-Paxton turbocar in the 1967

*Above: Colin Chapman's bulbous Lotus 56B
was a leftover from the 1968 Indianapolis
500 campaign, and the first FI car to use
turbine power.*

*Left: Uncle Ken's greatest secret was the
six-wheeled Tyrrell which first raced in 1976.
This is Patrick Depailler at Monaco.*

race, when Parnelli Jones had
broken down almost in sight of the
finish line.

Backed by wealthy Andy
Granatelli of STP fame, Chapman
had Maurice Philippe pen the 56.
Jim Clark loved it but was killed
before the race, as was Mike Spence
who stood in for both Clark and
his intended replacement, Jackie
Stewart, who had sustained a wrist
injury. In that 1968 500, Joe Leonard
suffered a similar fate to Jones,
dropping out when victory
seemed imminent. Later that year a
shocked USAC moved quickly to ban
turbines, before another revolution
took place.

When the 56 was conceived,
engine supplier Pratt and Whitney
had planned a turbine suitable to FI.
By 1970 it was ready, but after Jochen
Rindt's death at Monza that year it
was to be 1971 before Chapman's
new super-baby was ready. The four-
wheel drive car with its 500bhp
turbine appeared in Emerson
Fittipaldi's hands in the Brands Hatch

Race of Champions, but bottomed so
much it broke its suspension. After a
crash at Oulton Park it was repaired
for the International Trophy at
Silverstone, where Fittipaldi put it on
the front row. The suspension broke
again in the first heat, but he inherited
third place in the second.

Following further work the car
made a sensational Grand Prix début
in Holland. On a wet track driver
Dave Walker overcame inherent
throttle lag and moved swiftly from
the back of the grid to 10th place by
the fifth lap, only to slide off the road
at the Tarzan hairpin. The great
moment was over.

Fittipaldi drove the car again at
Monza, in the colours of World Wide
Racing to bypass potential lingering
problems over the Rindt accident, but
could only finish eighth. When the
Brazilian finished a weak second in a
non-championship race at
Hockenheim, Chapman quietly
abandoned his turbine experiments
and looked elsewhere for his
next inspiration.

Arrows A2

1978

Rather like Ferrari in 1961, Don Nichols' Shadow team suffered a walk-out at the end of 1977, as sometime driver Jackie Oliver, team manager Alan Rees and designer Tony Southgate left to form Arrows, a loose acronym of their initials.

Due to the tight schedule, Southgate had but two months in which to pen a new car, the Arrows FA1. Miraculously it was ready in time for the Brazilian GP, the second race of the championship. It actually appeared before the Shadow team had completed its own DN9, which Southgate had drawn before leaving. When the two were lined up together, cynics observed that only the paint jobs differentiated them. Of course, this was somewhat inevitable, since the same man had designed both and could not be expected to develop his design philosophy to any dramatic extent in such a short time.

The FA1 proved successful, leading the South African GP, finishing sixth in the US GP West and at Monaco, and second in Sweden. But then came a bombshell when Nichols' won a High Court action in London to have the Arrows declared a breach of Shadow's design. Lord Justice Templeman declared that, in his opinion, 40 per cent of the FA1's components were copies of the DN9's. The FA1 was banned. Southgate had expected this, and

Arrows rushed his new A1 through in time for that year's British GP. But what he really wanted to build was a radical aerodynamic evolution of Colin Chapman's 'something for nothing' ground-effect concept, and he did so with his next design for 1979, the Arrows A2. This was an extremely low bullet-shaped car with faired-in bodywork. Its engine and gearbox were canted upwards at the back to facilitate the use of a full-width under-tray to maximize the amount of downforce generated by the air-flow.

Unfortunately the engine installation raised the centre of gravity and, in this era of experimental engineering, the team never satisfactorily discovered the cure to persistent 'porpoising' at speed. This was an aerodynamic phenomenon in which the central point through which the air forces acted upon the car – the centre of pressure – moved about constantly as it raced. Both factors had an extremely adverse effect on the handling, which drivers Riccardo Patrese and Jochen Mass roundly condemned. The A2 was abandoned for 1980, when the conventional A3 followed Williams' established design thinking.

Below: *After its first FA1 was deemed to be a Shadow DN9 disguise, Arrows hurriedly produced this A1 in 1978.*

Right: *A year later, its unusual A2 sought to break dramatic new ground aerodynamically.*

Brabham fan car

1978

Colin Chapman had harnessed under-car air pressure in his 1977 Lotus 78 to create what became known as 'ground effect', but the slow speed of the car on straights prompted rivals to suspect that the concept had shortcomings. However, when Chapman revised the architecture of his next design, the 79, to produce a slim and elegant car that was far less compromized, it ran away and hid for many of the races of 1978.

Over at Brabham, South African designer Gordon Murray was saddled in his design thinking by Bernie Ecclestone's deal to use the bulky and wide Alfa Romeo flat-12 engine, which ruined any attempts to create a car of similarly narrow girth. Thus it appeared that Brabham was in no position to exploit ground effect to anything approaching the extent of Chapman's cars. However Murray's

fertile mind came up with an ingenious means of challenging the Lotus in the downforce-generation stakes. Working with his assistant, David North, he moved the water radiator of his triangular-shaped BT46 to a horizontal position above the engine, then incorporated a vertically mounted fan at the very back of the car. This was driven by the engine, ostensibly with the primary aim of drawing air over the power unit to cool it. But there was a valuable by-product: Murray incorporated special skirts on the underside of the car's wide under-tray so that the fan also sucked the air from beneath the car. This reduced the under-car air pressure and thereby generated massive downforce by literally sucking the car closer to the ground.

The Brabham BT46 'fan car', as it became known, was tested at Silverstone and Brands Hatch prior to the Swedish GP at Anderstorp on 17

June 1978. John Watson and Niki Lauda qualified second and third behind Mario Andretti in Chapman's hitherto dominant Lotus 79, but in the race Lauda stomped all over the black and gold car, which broke down during a fruitless chase. Lauda swept on as if he was in a different race, winning easily and beating Riccardo Patrese's Arrows by 34s.

The result was uproar as rival team owners called for an immediate ban on the car, which appeared to have rendered their own machines obsolete overnight. Rather like the Indianapolis owners who had claimed that the STP Paxton turbine car of 1967 presented a danger to following drivers because of its heat haze, some argued that the Brabham spat debris at their drivers after sucking it up with the fan. The loophole that Murray and North had exploited stated that any extraction could not have a primary function which was aerodynamic. By the letter of the law, the car was legal, and although fan cars were immediately banned by the FIA, Lauda's result stood. On its one and only outing, the brilliant Brabham

Opposite and above: *The dustbin lid hides the secret of Brabham's fan car, a secret which was revealed to a roar of disapproval at Anderstorp in Sweden, 1978.*

fan car had decimated its opposition.

Lauda and Murray had the last laugh in a way, by winning the British and Italian GPs later that year in a standard BT46.

5

CHAPTER **10**

Hot Wheels
THE TEN BEST RACES

Competition is the lifeblood of motorsport, and in any era great races stand out, be it because of the closeness of the contest, the arrival of a new marque or driver, or for an heroic drive that overcomes opposition or unfavourable conditions.

1953 Italian Grand Prix

This was the final World Championship round to be held under the 2-litre Formula Two regulations, a measure introduced in 1952 because of the shortage of suitable F1 machinery. It was an era that had been completely dominated by Ferrari and its lead driver, Alberto Ascari. But as the 1953 season progressed, the Maserati team posed an increasingly strong threat, particularly from the car driven by Juan Fangio.

Although Ascari was already confirmed as World Champion when the cars assembled at Monza in mid-September, if Ferrari could win this final round, it would make its domination of the two-year 'F2'

Left: *With the Maserati of Fangio separating the Ferraris, Marimon pursues with the intention of helping his team-mate after a long pit-stop to repair his car's holed oil radiator.*

championship total, as it had yet to be beaten.

Ascari duly planted his car on pole position, although Fangio – competing at Monza for the first time since breaking his neck there the previous year – was only 0.5s slower. Farina's Ferrari was third quickest, just ahead of the second Maserati driven by Fangio's young protégé, Onofre Marimon.

Ascari led away, but with the cars so evenly matched on the fast slipstreaming circuit, no one was able to make a break for it at the front. The two Ferraris and two Maseratis constantly swopped the lead between them for lap after lap – the official lap charts showed the lead changing 22 times! The straw bales lining the edge of the track became frayed as the drivers sought to find a vital extra edge, and back-markers were passed on each side by the high-speed four-car convoy.

Above: *Fangio leads the Ferrari of Ascari.*

After 46 of the 80 laps, Marimon pitted with a holed oil radiator, but after repairs had been made, he rejoined the battle for the lead, even though he was three laps adrift, to give support to Fangio. But as the race entered its late stages, it seemed that the Ferraris of Ascari and Farina were slowly, but surely, emerging on top. Going into the final lap, Fangio was only third.

Approaching the double 'porfido' curves, Farina, desperate to beat his team-mate for once, attempted to pass Ascari, but went wide on the exit of the first bend, edging on to the grass and allowing Fangio to nip past into second. Then Ascari turned in early for the second bend, determined that no one was going to get inside him, but began to spin on the way out and was collected by Marimon as Fangio took the lead and the win.

1957 German Grand Prix

This was the race in which Fangio, at 46 years of age, clinched his fifth World Championship. Rarely, if ever, has a title been gained in such majestic fashion.

It was Fangio's Maserati 250F that took pole position in 9m 25.6s, just under three seconds quicker than the Ferrari of Mike Hawthorn. Peter Collins, in the other Ferrari, was on the second row.

With race day dawning blazing hot, tyre wear became a critical part of the equation. Ferrari decided that it would run non-stop, although the drivers would need to be quite careful in the early laps. Maserati and Fangio opted to make a stop and,

thus, to start with the fuel tanks only half-filled.

Although the Ferraris led away, Fangio in the lighter Maserati had passed them both by the third lap and was pulling steadily clear. After 12 of the 22 laps, he came in for his planned stop with a lead of 28s. But the team's pitwork was hopelessly slow, even by the standards of the day, and was not helped by the seat having broken. Fangio rejoined some 80s behind the two Ferraris.

The Ferrari crew relaxed, particularly when it timed Fangio's out lap and found him to be lapping no quicker than Hawthorn and Collins. But that was merely Fangio bedding in his new tyres. His next nine laps were among the finest

anyone has ever driven, being breathtaking in their audacity. Later the maestro admitted that he did things in the car that day that he never wanted to repeat. Furthermore he was already 28 miles into this charge by the time the Ferrari team could alert its drivers via pit signals.

Each successive tour brought Fangio a new lap record, and on the 20th, with Collins in his sights, he lowered it to 9m 17.4s, a staggering 8s faster than his pole time. He passed both Ferraris on the next lap, on the way to the last – and most glorious – of his 24 wins.

Above: Even Fangio admitted that he never wanted to drive as hard again after his brilliant victory for Maserati in the 1957 German GP.

1965 Italian Grand Prix

During the 1965 season dominated by Jim Clark and Lotus, the Italian race stood out as being more evenly matched than the Scot had made the others. It also saw the first win of very many for one of Clark's fellow countryman.

Although Clark took his customary pole position, John Surtees was very much the hero of the crowd, with a time in his Ferrari just 0.2s slower. Also right on the pace were the two BRMs of Jackie Stewart – enjoying his first season in F1 – and Graham Hill.

The crowd let out a collective sigh of disappointment at the start when Surtees was left virtually stationary on the line with clutch slip. As the cars completed their first manic slipstreaming lap, Clark led the pack, while Surtees was down in 14th place. The good news for the Italians was that his clutch was now perfectly okay, and he began to scythe his way through the field.

The usual multi-car slipstreaming battle for the lead developed. Clark, Hill, Stewart, Gurney, Bandini, Spence and Siffert were all in early contention. By the tenth lap, Surtees had joined them, and a lap later he was leading! Alas it was not for long, as the clutch began slipping again and eventually he retired.

Clark, Hill and Stewart – taking turns to lead – began to edge away from the others. Then, on the 64th lap, 12 from the end, Clark's fuel injection pump failed, and he was out. This left the two BRMs, driven by the wily old veteran and the eager new boy.

A lap from the end, Hill, who was leading, got off line through the Parabolica, suffered a huge sideways moment, and Stewart was through. A lap later, he recorded the first of 27 Grand Prix victories.

Below: *It was a case of master v pupil at Monza in 1965, when Jackie Stewart pipped BRM team-mate Graham Hill to win his first GP.*

1968 British Grand Prix

A close contest that lasted virtually the entire distance, and a popular winner, characterized the 1968 British Grand Prix at Brands Hatch.

Brands clearly suited the Lotus 49, for behind Graham Hill's example in pole position were lined up his team-mate, Jackie Oliver, and, in fourth place, the Rob Walker entered 49 driven by Jo Siffert. In third place sat Chris Amon in the Ferrari, looking to take his first win after a succession of near misses over the past season-and-a-half.

Oliver blasted into the lead – for the first time in his F1 career – and for three laps headed Hill, Siffert and Amon. Then Hill took over at the front, while Oliver's car began to trail smoke from an overfilled tank. Hill appeared to be on his way to a home win, something that he'd never managed before, but on lap 26 he was out with a driveshaft failure.

Consequently Oliver reassumed the lead, narrowly ahead of Siffert, but the latter's goggles were badly splashed with oil from Oliver's smoking car and, while attempting to clear them, he was passed by Amon. Siffert retaliated and, just after half distance, regained his second place. This immediately became first place, as Oliver pulled off with a broken crankshaft.

For the remainder of the race, Amon, desperate to record that first win, hounded Siffert for all he was worth. Siffert – equally eager to score what would be his first win – was impeccable in his defence. Through the infield section, the better handling of the Ferrari allowed it to crawl all over Siffert's car, but in the fast section around the back, the Lotus' DFV could stretch its legs.

Thus Siffert took his début win, while Amon, his tyres ruined, was left to wait for another day – a day which would never come.

Below: *Jo Siffert takes the flag in Rob Walker's Lotus, Brands Hatch 1968.*

Opposite right: *Pedro Rodriguez swapped the lead with Ickx at Zandvoort in 1971, despite a fuel metering problem.*

Opposite below: *As track dried, Ickx gained the advantage and pulled fractionally away from Rodriguez to win.*

1971 Dutch Grand Prix

Although 1971 belonged almost exclusively to Jackie Stewart and Tyrrell, torrential rain at the Dutch Grand Prix in June saw the Scot relegated to playing a bit-part, his brand of tyres being unsuitable for such conditions. As a result, a fabulous race-long duel was fought out between the two prominent wet-weather aces of the era, Jacky Ickx and Pedro Rodriguez.

The Zandvoort circuit, with its very long straight, was particularly suited to the 12-cylinder engines of the time. Ickx planted his flat-12 Ferrari on pole, alongside Rodriguez's V12 BRM. Stewart, in the best of the V8 cars, was only third fastest.

Torrential rain on race day ensured that the users of Firestone tyres would be at an advantage. Both Ickx and Rodriguez were on this rubber; Stewart wasn't. Ickx immediately stormed into the lead, with Rodriguez glued to the Ferrari's gearbox. Stewart ran a distant third initially, but spun way down the field on the third lap and eventually finished 11th!

The two leaders were lapping at a completely different pace to the rest of the field and not making a single mistake between them. Their uncanny

skill in such conditions made the others look inept. Fourteen drivers left the road at Tarzan bend alone, so treacherous was the surface. Furthermore the Ferrari and BRM were rarely separated by more than a car's length, building up the tension. On the ninth lap, Rodriguez took the lead. Now it was Ickx's turn to watch the leader's gearbox.

Eventually it stopped raining and, although the track remained treacherously slippery, a dry line began to form in parts, notably at the Hunzerug hairpin. Here the cards began to fall in Ickx's favour. Rodriguez's fuel metering unit had begun to malfunction, making the

BRM's power delivery more peaky than the Ferrari's and obliging the Mexican to take this bend in first gear as it dried. Ickx found he could take it in second, and his consequent speed on to the following straight was higher, enabling him to retake the lead on lap 30.

Although an awkwardly placed back-marker slowed the Ferrari on the next lap, allowing Rodriguez to get back in front, Ickx reasserted himself once more a lap after that. For the remaining 38 laps, Rodriguez shadowed the Ferrari, but never again found a way past. Third-place man Clay Regazzoni was a lap behind these two aces at the finish.

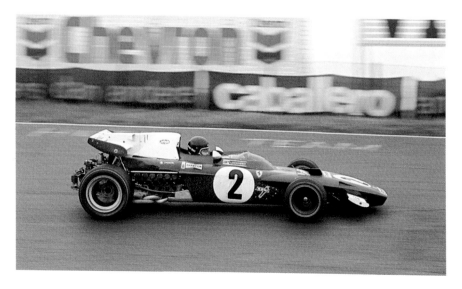

1975 Dutch Grand Prix

The 1975 Dutch race was the
occasion of James Hunt's first Grand
Prix win – and the Hesketh team's
only victory – and it stands as a
tribute to his combination of flair
and intelligence.

It was the year of Niki Lauda and
Ferrari. As the F1 circus gathered in
Zandvoort in June, that combination
had just rattled off a sequence of
three consecutive wins. Thus it was
no great surprise when the Austrian
planted his red car on pole position,
ahead of team-mate Regazzoni.
Hunt's Hesketh, however, was the

Opposite above and below: *James Hunt truly came of age as a Grand Prix driver with his superb victory over Niki Lauda at Zandvoort in 1975, Hesketh's sole championship victory.*

Right: *The 1976 Dutch GP was the drive of James Hunt's life: here he fends of the challenge of Watson's more powerful Penske. Having seen Watson off, Hunt then had to withstand extreme pressure from Clay Reggazzoni.*

fastest of the DFV-powered cars, in third place.

As so often at Zandvoort, the track was wet on race day. It had stopped raining shortly before the start, but everyone still opted for wet-weather tyres. Hunt, however, was certain that the greater part of the race would be dry and had his Hesketh put on dry suspension settings.

Lauda surged into an immediate lead. Hunt, in third place, concentrated intensely on monitoring the state of the track. As soon as he felt a dry line to be going down, on lap seven, he made a bolt to the pits for slicks, laps ahead of anyone else.

He'd timed the move to perfection. On his first flying lap, Hunt's was the fastest car on the track. He knew he had to push mightily during this critical stage of the race, as this was where his eventual advantage over Lauda would be built up. As the others peeled off into the pits, Hunt found himself in the lead. Lauda, who had stopped six laps later than Hunt, rejoined in second, but lost a place to Jarier's Shadow as his tyres warmed, giving Hunt some breathing space.

Once back up to second, Lauda repeatedly caught right up to Hunt on the long straight, but the Hesketh's dry settings enabled Hunt to increase his slight advantage during the rest of each lap. For 62 laps, he withstood the pressure of the Ferrari driver, never once making a mistake. It was a superb performance.

1976 Dutch Grand Prix

The original Zandvoort track, with its long straight followed by a wide hairpin – Tarzan bend – in which a variety of lines could be used, rarely failed to produce a classic race. That of 1976 was no exception.

Niki Lauda was recovering strongly following his near-fatal crash at the German Grand Prix and was due to return in Italy, having missed only two races. James Hunt and the McLaren team were looking to close the points chasm between the Ferrari driver and Hunt before the Austrian returned. Only wins would do, and Hunt had already lost one chance,

finishing a mere fourth in the previous race in Austria. For Holland, Ferrari sent along one car for Lauda's team-mate Clay Regazzoni.

Hunt qualified second fastest to Ronnie Peterson's March, while Regazzoni was fifth quickest. As the lights turned green, Peterson took an immediate lead, and John Watson – who had won in Austria – also surged through the first corner in his Penske to pass Hunt. For the next seven laps, Hunt watched as Watson put intense pressure on Peterson. Hunt was in no position to join the fight, as his car was understeering badly, a condition made worse when one of his brake ducts worked loose and disturbed the airflow.

At the beginning of the eighth lap, Watson committed himself to a move around the outside of the March through Tarzan corner, but Peterson held his ground on the exit, forcing Watson to back right off to avoid a collision. In a flash, Hunt nipped past into second place.

Four laps later, Peterson slid very wide on oil dropped by another car, and Hunt sailed undramatically past. Peterson's handling then began to go off as the March's tyres overheated, and soon Watson was back up to second, looking to find a way past Hunt.

Time after time, Hunt would come down the main straight virtually hugging the pit wall to prevent Watson from moving inside for

Tarzan. On several occasions, Watson would place the Penske alongside the McLaren, to the outside. Whenever he attempted to make a pass around the outside of Tarzan, however, Hunt would stay out wide on the exit, forcing Watson to take to the grass.

On lap 47, with 28 still to go, Watson ground to a halt with transmission failure. Yet still Hunt wasn't home and dry. Unable to run truly fast laps because of his handling problem, slowly but surely he was being caught by Regazzoni. Hunt pressed on as hard as he dared, and although his 10s cushion had dwindled to less than 1s by the end, the win was his. Later it would prove crucial to his success in the championship.

1987 British Grand Prix

By 1987, something of a grudge match had developed between Williams drivers Nigel Mansell and Nelson Piquet. Ostensibly the latter had joined the team as number-one driver the year before, but frequently Mansell had out-performed him, and Williams had declined to issue team orders. Mansell had already won twice by the time they came to his home Grand Prix at Silverstone, but Piquet had yet to open his account.

Qualifying had seen a tense battle for pole position, fought entirely between the two Williams drivers, with Piquet edging out Mansell by 0.07s.

Prost's McLaren dived briefly into the lead, but Piquet and Mansell led the field at the end of the first lap. Mansell was running with less wing than Piquet, hoping to be faster in the later stages when the fuel load lightened. In the meantime, he planned simply to keep pace with the leader.

Mansell got his first inkling that the plan was going awry on the 12th lap as a vibration came up through the steering, the result of a wheel weight flying off. As the vibration worsened, he realised that he would have to pit for new tyres. He did so on lap 36, by which time he was sufficiently clear not to lose his second place when he rejoined. He was, though, 28s adrift of Piquet with just 29 laps left.

He began a quite sensational charge, rattling off a sequence of qualifying-style laps on his fresh tyres. Piquet tried to respond, but his tyres were long past their best, and Mansell steadily tracked the other Williams down. The air of expectation from the home crowd grew as it watched something very special begin to unfold.

Left: *Hunt celebrates, well-satisfied with a hard-fought result in the Dutch GP in 1976*

On the 63rd lap, with just two to go, the two cars came down the 306km/h (190mph) Hangar Straight as one, Mansell tucked in tight behind Piquet. Approaching Stowe, Mansell moved to the left, causing Piquet to do likewise to block him, but immediately Mansell swooped to the right and passed down the inside.

The crowd erupted.

For the rest of the distance, Mansell did just enough to keep Piquet behind. His engine was near meltdown, and he ran out of fuel on the slow-down lap, but he had won and he was mobbed.

Top: Nelson Piquet heads Nigel Mansell early in their fabulous battle during the 1987 British GP.

Above and right: After selling Piquet a dummy at Stowe, Mansell snatched the lead and kept it to the finish to the delight of his fans. Few British GP triumphs were more popular.

1995 European Grand Prix

Amid the late-season battle for the championship between Benetton's Michael Schumacher and Williams' Damon Hill, a superb race was fought at the Nürburgring for the 1995 European Grand Prix.

It had rained heavily on the morning of race day, and even though it had stopped by the time the cars lined up, most of the field opted for wet-weather tyres. Most, but not Jean Alesi and Ferrari. In an audacious bid

for glory, after qualifying only sixth, the Frenchman opted for slicks and dry-weather settings.

David Coulthard's Williams led Schumacher and Hill from the start, with Alesi in sixth place, but soon picking off Herbert and Irvine to run a remarkable fourth. After a dozen laps, with a dry line going down, the leading three made their stops for slick tyres and a refuel. Thus Alesi assumed a substantial lead from Coulthard, Schumacher and Hill, although the German was soon past

the Williams and up to second after some wheel-to-wheel dicing.

Both Alesi and Schumacher made their routine fuel stops on the 34th lap, the Ferrari driver rejoining without losing the lead, although Hill – yet to make his stop – was right with him and attempted to pass. Alesi resisted, and Hill damaged the nose of his Williams, leaving him fourth after pitting, with Schumacher now back up to second, but a long way behind. Later Hill clouted a barrier and retired.

Below: *The battle between Michael Schumacher and Damon Hill at Nürburgring in 1995 was a fabulous celebration of driving on a greasy track.*

Right: *Hill, however, spun and cracked a leg, and his failure to score points gave yet further advantage to Schumacher's championship chase.*

Schumacher got his head down and began to charge as hard as he knew how, setting one fastest lap after another. Initially Alesi looked safe, but then inexplicably eased off the pace. By the time he sped up again, there were only three laps left, and Schumacher was right with him.

Approaching the chicane, the Benetton driver made an outrageous move from a long way back, effectively challenging Alesi to surrender the lead or take them both off. Alesi capitulated, and Schumacher went through to win.

Above: *Jean Alesi was also in on the action at Nürburgring, and came within an ace of victory.*

Right: *Schumacher's smile says it all after a great triumph.*

1997 Japanese Grand Prix

It was the penultimate race in a tense two-man title contest, and it held a couple of unexpected twists. The 1997 Japanese race also saw the most remarkable example of two drivers clearly operating as a single team seen in modern Grand Prix racing.

The drama began in qualifying, when Williams' Jacques Villeneuve committed his fourth offence of the season of failing to slow down for a yellow flag and was banned from the meeting. Although he would be allowed to race under appeal, it was almost certain that the appeal would not stand and that any position he gained in the race would not count.

Therefore it was unclear how Villeneuve would approach this race, starting from pole position with his title rival, Michael Schumacher, sitting alongside in his Ferrari. Schumacher's concern was that, in a marginal situation, the Williams driver may have attempted to take them both

off, knowing he would be losing nothing. However Schumacher, together with his team-mate Eddie Irvine, had a plan.

Villeneuve took off into the lead, aggressively edging out Schumacher as they went into the first turn. But then he ran the early laps at a very gentle pace, hoping to give others a chance to challenge Schumacher. They didn't. Instead the field bunched up behind him, and Schumacher was reluctant to attempt a pass that might take him out of the race. It was at this point that Irvine came into play, passing Hakkinen and Schumacher – with the latter's co-operation – in one brilliant fluid move around the outside of the first corner and rushing up to the back of Villeneuve. On the third lap, he passed the Williams and quickly pulled out an enormous lead.

Villeneuve continued to lap slowly for a while, Schumacher still cautiously sitting behind him. The former was still vainly hoping that one of the drivers behind would try

to pass Schumacher. By the seventh lap, it was clear that this wasn't going to happen and, with Irvine now 13s in the lead, Villeneuve finally got a move on.

After the first round of routine fuel stops, Irvine was 11s ahead, but, crucially, Schumacher just managed to get ahead of Villeneuve as the Williams driver left the pits. Then the next stage of the pre-race plan was ready to be put into action, and Irvine slowed dramatically, allowing Schumacher to pass him, but taking care to prevent Villeneuve from doing the same.

After Villeneuve's second fuel stop went wrong, he played no further significant part in the race, while Schumacher went on to a solid victory. It left the two drivers separated by a point as they went into the final round in Jerez, where the final twist awaited.

Below: *In the penultimate Grand Prix of the 1997 season, Ferrari team-mates Schumacher and Irvine pulled off a brilliant victory.*

CHAPTER 11

Down to the Wire
THE TEN CLOSEST FINISHES

Close competition is what every spectator wants to see, though frequently they are disappointed. But every so often along comes a race so gripping that the result remains in doubt right to the chequered flag. These are 10 of the closest contests, where the stopwatch struggled to differentiate between drivers.

1954 French GP, Reims

▸ 0.1s

In the immediate post-war years, Germany was banned from participation in international motor racing, but the moment the ban was lifted the Stuttgart manufacturer, Mercedes-Benz, was ready with a team of extraordinary cars.

In 1914, Mercedes had entered Grand Prix racing and cleaned up. This happened again in 1934. Now, after another 20-year interval, it occurred for a third time. The silver cars were ready for the French Grand Prix around the champagne country near Reims in France, and they created an immediate sensation. With their unusual full-width bodywork, which enclosed the wheels, they looked astonishingly advanced in comparison to rival marques, whose products did not seem to have changed in appearance in 20 years.

The Argentinian star, Juan Manuel Fangio, headed the team. World Champion in 1951, he already led the 1954 championship (which he would go on to win) after victories for Maserati in Argentina and Belgium. Now he took pole position

Opposite: No luck for Froilan Gonzalez, after his engine quits in the 1954 French GP.

Above and below: Juan Manuel Fangio slowed in the closing stages so that team-mate Karl Kling could close up for a photo finish to Mercedes' successful return to motor racing.

comfortably from team-mate Karl Kling, with double champion Alberto Ascari's Maserati for company on the front row of the grid. On the second row, Fangio's fellow countryman, Froilan Gonzalez, was almost as fast as Kling in his Ferrari.

It was Kling who got away first to lead Fangio and Gonzalez as Ascari botched the start. But Fangio soon slipped ahead, and there he stayed for the remainder of an afternoon that struck an immediate chill into the hearts of Ferrari and Maserati. Try as he might – and he tried very hard indeed – Gonzalez could not maintain the German cars' pace and began to come under threat from Hans Hermann in the third Mercedes. These two fought one another hard until Gonzalez spun at the Thillois hairpin on the 13th lap, an under-bonnet fire adding to his excitement. The symmetry of a Mercedes 1-2-3 was spoiled when Hermann's engine broke on lap 17, but as the two leading Mercedes lapped the field, Fangio slowed until Kling was within a tenth of a second, and in a crushing display of technological superiority that was how they crossed the line after the 61 laps. Mercedes-Benz was back, simply picking up where it had left off prior to the war.

1955 British GP, Aintree
▐▐▶ 0.2s

Did the legendary Juan Manuel Fangio let Stirling Moss win his 'home' Grand Prix at Aintree in 1955? Even to the day that he died, in July 1995 (40 years later to the very race), the great Argentinian champion never let his Mercedes-Benz team-mate know the truth about whether he had been beaten fairly and squarely that day, or had pulled his punch in the interest of sport.

After the German manufacturer's return in 1954, the 1955 season was almost exclusively the preserve of the slipper-bodied Silver Arrows with their straight-eight engines. There were four of them at Aintree, and they took four of the top five positions. As Moss set the fastest qualifying time, only Jean Behra in third place for Maserati spoiled the silver symmetry.

At the start of the race, Fangio took his customary lead immediately, as behind him Moss was followed by team-mates Karl Kling and Piero Taruffi. Already it seemed over bar the shouting, but fortunately Behra livened things up. After suffering too much wheelspin at the start, he made quick work of Taruffi and then Kling to move into third place, but after only nine laps the Maserati cried enough.

The spectators' interest did not subside, however, for Moss had moved smoothly ahead of Fangio to lead on his home turf. Further down the field, the Franco-American Harry Schell was fighting back after a poor start in the British Vanwall that he had qualified seventh. This display lasted until the Vanwall's throttle pedal broke.

Up front, Fangio soon passed Moss again and appeared to discourage his attempts to fight back, but Stirling was ahead once more on the 26th lap, and thereafter Fangio simply sat right on his tail as they sped around. Moss then eased back under pit orders, but speeded up with three of the 90 laps left to match his qualifying time. Fangio responded and out of the final corner drew alongside Moss. They crossed the line side by side, with the Englishman fractionally head. A gripping finale or a stage-managed demonstration?

'I think that race with the Mercedes was my best British Grand Prix,' Moss says today, 'but I still don't know even now whether Fangio let me win or whether he didn't. Whenever I asked him, he always said, "No, it was your day and you were driving really well," and so on. So I don't honestly know. People have said that he said that he'd backed off. He may have done; I don't know. I just don't know. But that was a very important one, obviously, to me, because of what it meant.'

It was the first time a British driver had ever won the British GP.

Opposite: *Stirling Moss never discovered whether Fangio let him win the 1955 British GP at Aintree – all he would say was, 'No, it was your day and you were driving really well.'*

Above right: *Italian novice Giancarlo Baghetti made history when he beat the Porsches of Gurney and Bonnier to win a Grand Prix, first time out.*

1961 French GP, Reims

▶ 0.2s

Enzo Ferrari's famous shark-nosed red cars dominated the 1961 season, with Count Wolfgang von Trips and the Californian Phil Hill fighting for the World Championship while the British contenders counted the cost of prevaricating when it had been announced that the formula regulations would change in 1961 to cater for 1.5-litre cars.

After a brilliant drive in Monaco, Stirling Moss had beaten the Ferraris in Rob Walker's private Lotus, but then Trips won in Holland and Hill in Belgium.

Hill took pole position for the French GP on the fast Reims circuit, comfortably ahead of Trips and their team-mate, Hill's fellow Californian Richie Ginther. Moss had sneaked a slipstream tow from one of the Ferraris, but was still only fourth, ahead of the emergent Jim Clark's works Lotus. Further back, the third Californian, Dan Gurney, was ninth, while 12th fastest was a young Italian called Giancarlo Baghetti. It was his first Grand Epreuve, but already he had the unique distinction of winning his first two non-championship F1 races in a Ferrari entered by FISA, an association of Italian motor clubs.

Ginther led, ahead of Trips, Hill and Moss, but Hill was soon in front, then Ginther spun. Trips moved to the lead on lap 13, but abandoned the race five laps later with a broken engine. Then Hill spun on lap 38 while trying to pass Moss, who had been delayed. He stalled his engine and lost a lot of time restarting. Ferrari's last chance seemed to be Ginther, but he stopped for oil two laps later.

Now, incredibly, it was all up to Baghetti, who led on laps 41 to 43, with the Porsches of Gurney and Jo Bonnier right on his tail. Then Bonnier moved ahead on lap 44 before Baghetti reasserted himself. Gurney and Bonnier dead-heated lap 46, and two laps later Gurney crossed the line side by side with Baghetti in a blistering slipstream race around the champagne vineyards. It came down to the American's experience versus the Italian's clear horsepower advantage.

Gurney led Baghetti into the last lap, but the latter used all of his Ferrari's muscle to slipstream him to the finish line, popping alongside the frustrated American at the very last moment to grab a historic victory by a tenth of a second. It was Baghetti's first GP and his only win – an achievement no one has ever matched.

1967 Italian GP, Monza

▸ 0.2s

Before spoiled by chicanes, the Monza circuit was one of the fastest in the world, and usually its high-speed curves created epic slipstreaming races, the outcome of which was in doubt until the finish line. If a driver sat immediately behind another car travelling at high speed, he could literally be pulled along by the suction of the vortex created in the wake of the leading car. Thus, even if a car lacked horsepower, a canny driver could minimize the disadvantage and be sucked along at similar speed. The art lay in getting a tow at the right time, then pouncing ahead of the leading car at the very last moment.

That season, the new Lotus-Fords of Jim Clark and Graham Hill had rewritten the design rule book, and only Dan Gurney's Eagle-Weslake was a real threat in the power

Left: Early in the race Jack Brabham mixed it wheel-to-wheel with Graham Hill and Jim Clark in the Lotus-Fords, and is seen here indicating to Clark that the Lotus has sustained a punctured tyre.

Below: Meanwhile, John Surtees lay back in the pack, heading Jochen Rindt, Chris Amon and Bruce McLaren before pulling away to challenge the Australian in the closing stages.

stakes. But because this was Monza, other combinations became competitive, too.

Clark took his expected pole position, but alongside him was a championship threat in the form of Jack Brabham in the Brabham-Repco, and Bruce McLaren in his new McLaren-BRM. Gurney led after a ragged start had reshuffled the grid, but after five laps Clark was in the lead and the Eagle's engine had broken. Then, on lap 13, Clark suddenly pulled into the pits; the handling was awry, and Brabham had pulled alongside at one stage to indicate to him that a rear tyre had sustained a puncture.

Now Hill was left to fight with Brabham and his team-mate Denny Hulme, while not too far back came John Surtees in a new and hurriedly built Honda, which was really a Lola Indianapolis chassis fitted with

Honda's heavy, but powerful, V12 engine. Surtees led a group comprising Chris Amon's Ferrari, the McLaren (which Bruce had over-revved at the start, taking the edge off the engine) and Jochen Rindt's Cooper-Maserati.

Hill managed to shake off his pursuers and open up a comfortable lead as Brabham began to suffer a sticking throttle and Hulme dropped out with overheating. Meanwhile, Clark, who had rejoined in 15th place – a lap down – was into a stunning recovery drive.

With only nine of the 68 laps left, Hill's engine wilted under the strain, so Brabham was left with a narrow lead over Surtees, who had broken clear of his pursuers. But the incredible Clark was pulverising the lap record and rapidly gaining ground. After making up a complete lap – something almost unheard of in FI

Above: *As the flag falls at Monza, Surtees pips Brabham by just 0.2s.*

1969 Italian GP, Monza
▶ 0.08s

Two years earlier, John Surtees and Jack Brabham had lunged for the finish tape in the Italian GP. This time, no fewer than four drivers would fight for the spoils in the last-corner drag race to the chequered flag.

A victory for Jackie Stewart would secure him his first world championship title with three races still to go. He and entrant Ken Tyrrell had enjoyed a fabulous year, gaining victories in five of the seven races with their Matra-Ford, and although the Belgian ace Jacky Ickx had just beaten him at the Nürburgring, Stewart's confidence was soaring.

The Austrian challenger, Jochen Rindt, took pole position in his Lotus-Ford from 1967 champion Denny Hulme's McLaren-Ford, while Piers Courage's Brabham-Ford was fourth,

racing – the Scot swept back into the lead on lap 61 and immediately pulled clear of Brabham and Surtees. But as Colin Chapman prepared to welcome his driver over the line, the Brabham and Honda roared into sight. Clark was nowhere to be seen. Approaching the Parabolica Curve, Surtees had cannily obliged Brabham to brake on cement dust, which covered Gurney's oil on the inside line and, as the Australian ran wide, the Englishman sprinted to the inside on the exit to the corner, beating him to the line in a genuine photo-finish. Officially, two-tenths of a second separated them.

And Clark? To minimize the weight of the car, Chapman had gambled on a minimal fuel load for the Lotus, but Clark's brilliant drive had used almost every drop, and the pumps wouldn't pick up what little was left. The Lotus stuttered and slowed, creeping over the line in third place. Jimmy was not amused, as one of the greatest drives went without its just reward.

alongside Stewart and ahead of Bruce McLaren and Stewart's team-mate, Jean-Pierre Beltoise.

The race quickly developed into the expected slipstreaming thriller, and Tyrrell and Stewart had cunningly chosen a fourth-gear ratio that enabled the Scot to punch to the front on the laps when bonus money was paid to the leader! Initially, there was a seven-car fight for the lead between Stewart, Rindt, Jo Siffert in Rob Walker's private Lotus-Ford, McLaren, Hulme, Courage and Beltoise. Then Graham Hill made it eight as he caught up in his Lotus-Ford. Hulme, Siffert and Hill all suffered mechanical trouble, however, in a race that was notoriously hard on equipment. This left Stewart, Rindt, Beltoise, Courage and McLaren to take turns in the lead as the race built up to its nail-biting climax. Then Courage lost ground as the fuel pressure on Frank Williams' car

Above: *In the traditional slipstream epic of pre-chicane Monza, Stewart heads McLaren and Rindt into the Parabolica corner.*

Left: *On the final lap Stewart is still ahead of Rindt, team-mate Beltoise, and McLaren, and would just remain so on the line.*

faltered, leaving the quartet to fight it out.

Beltoise dived down the inside going into the Parabolica Curve on the final lap, grabbing a temporary lead, but he had moved too soon, and it was Rindt and Stewart in the fight to the line. With that fourth gear, Stewart timed his charge perfectly, inching ahead of both Beltoise and Rindt. He beat Jochen by 0.08s, at that time the closest-ever margin of victory. Beltoise was another 0.09s further back, and McLaren only 0.02s behind him. But it was Stewart's day as he snatched his first crown with a brilliantly judged performance.

1971 Italian GP, Monza

⟶ 0.01s

If Monza in 1969 had gone two better than 1967, in 1971 it went one better still, as five cars crossed the finish line separated by only 0.61s.

Pundits had predicted a Ferrari year after Jacky Ickx's performances late in 1970, but Jackie Stewart and Tyrrell had turned the tables and the Scot had wrapped up his second title, even though he had failed to finish the previous race, in Austria.

There BRM had gained some consolation for the death of Pedro Rodriguez in July, as Jo Siffert stormed to victory, so the British team went to Monza with very high hopes. At first, however, the officials had Ickx on pole for Ferrari, but long after the day's crowd had gone home and the journalists' stories of Ferrari

Above: Yet again Monza in 1971 provided a slipstreaming drama. Here Gethin's BRM leads Peterson's March, Hailwood's Surtees, Cevert's Tyrrell and Ganley's BRM.

Right: As a lapped Bonnier (28) stays out of the way, Gethin just pips Peterson to the line with Cevert and Hailwood in their wheeltracks.

supremacy had reached newspaper editors, they 'discovered' a faster time for Chris Amon in the Matra V12. Siffert was third, with team-mates Howden Ganley and Peter Gethin fourth and 11th, while François Cevert's Tyrrell-Ford and Ronnie Peterson's March-Ford were on the third row.

This time, Stewart played a major role for only 16 laps, after which his engine broke, and it was Peterson and Cevert who set the slipstreaming pace, challenged by bike racing star Mike Hailwood, who had returned to F1 in a Surtees-Ford. Siffert had led initially until his BRM became stuck in fourth gear, then Amon pushed the

Matra to the front and finally seemed set for his long overdue maiden GP triumph until disaster intervened.

The New Zealander was well ahead, with nine laps to go, when he tried to pull a tear-off visor from his helmet, only to have the complete visor come away. With his eyes unprotected from the 322km/h (200mph) wind blast, he could only drop away to a distant sixth by the finish.

Thus the final stages were a scrap between Peterson, Cevert, Hailwood and Ganley, with Gethin recovering rapidly after being baulked earlier and losing the tow. That actually helped to cool his overheating engine

and, as the five of them prepared for the last lap, the jockey's son was back in the thick of the fight. Peterson slid wide in the Parabolica, forcing Cevert to take the slower, tighter inside line, but before he could establish himself there, Gethin outbraked him dramatically and gained sufficient momentum to pass the startled Peterson on the line. They were separated by 0.01s, with Cevert 0.08s further back, Hailwood another 0.09s and Ganley 0.43s behind the Surtees driver. It was only Gethin's second race for BRM and, at 242.72km/h (150.76mph), it remains the fastest Grand Prix ever run.

As an amusing aside, he recalled
the puncture sustained by the
limousine that carried him and the
Stanleys – Louis and Jean – from the
circuit. Since they were the owners of
the team, it was unthinkable that the
Stanleys should become involved in
sordid mechanical work, so the man
who had just won the fastest GP in
history found himself on his hands
and knees only hours after the
greatest triumph of his life, changing
the wheel.

1981 Spanish GP, Jarama
➡ 0.21s

Some races are over within laps of
the start, but the 1981 Spanish Grand
Prix went down in history as a nail-
biter from start to finish, as the
French-Canadian Gilles Villeneuve
scored arguably his greatest triumph
in a car that nobody had rated before
the start flag fell.

While Ferrari's new turbocharged
1.5-litre V6 engine was a dramatic
and powerful improvement over the
superannuated 3-litre flat-12 from
1980, the chassis of the 126CK was
still many seasons behind its British
rivals. Its behaviour *in extremis* was
appalling, and only a driver of
Villeneuve's undisputed class had a
hope of taming it.

He had just won the Monaco GP
with it, after a fabulous battle of mind
over matter, but when the cars began
practice at the Jarama circuit in Spain,
three weeks later, the Frenchman
Jacques Laffite took pole with his Ligier-
Matra V12, ahead of the two Williams-
Ford V8s of Alan Jones and Carlos
Reutemann, and John Watson's new
and impressive McLaren-Ford. Alain
Prost's Renault turbo was fifth fastest
from Bruno Giacomelli's Alfa Romeo,
while Villeneuve was only seventh.

On race day, the temperature was
above 37°C (100°F) as Laffite muffed

Above: *Winner of the fastest race ever, Peter Gethin looks suitably satisfied after a great performance.*

his start, and Jones and Reutemann flew into the lead, while Villeneuve immediately minimized his disadvantage with a stunning getaway from the fourth row of the grid, which pushed him straight up into third place.

He made that second at the end of the lap, when his Ferrari horsepower carried him by Reutemann at the end of the pit straight, but already Jones was away, quickly building what seemed a comfortable lead. But then the Australian made one of his very rare mistakes on the 14th lap, spinning off at the first corner. Now Villeneuve was in the lead, and the level of

excitement went up another notch as it became clear that he could not draw away from his pursuers. It seemed only a matter of time before Reutemann, Watson, Laffite or Elio de Angelis (in the Lotus-Ford) would exploit the superior handling of their cars to push him back down the order. Gearbox trouble prevented Reutemann from fending off an attack by Laffite, and Watson also pushed ahead, but still the first five remained in a crocodile, the gaps between the cars increasing and diminishing only marginally.

Villeneuve would out-accelerate his rivals down the main straight, only to have them scrabbling all over the

back of the Ferrari as soon as they came to Jarama's many corners. But he stuck cleanly and fairly to his line, and nobody could do anything about it. They stayed that way for the 67 laps that remained before the flag fell, all five of them being covered by a mere 1.24s.

Villeneuve was hailed by Enzo Ferrari as the spiritual successor to the great Tazio Nuvolari. After his fabulous performance, few disagreed.

Below: *This is the way it was for most of the Spanish GP in 1981, with Villeneuve tantalisingly poised just ahead of Laffite, Watson, Reutemann and de Angelis, who scrabbled in vain for the lead.*

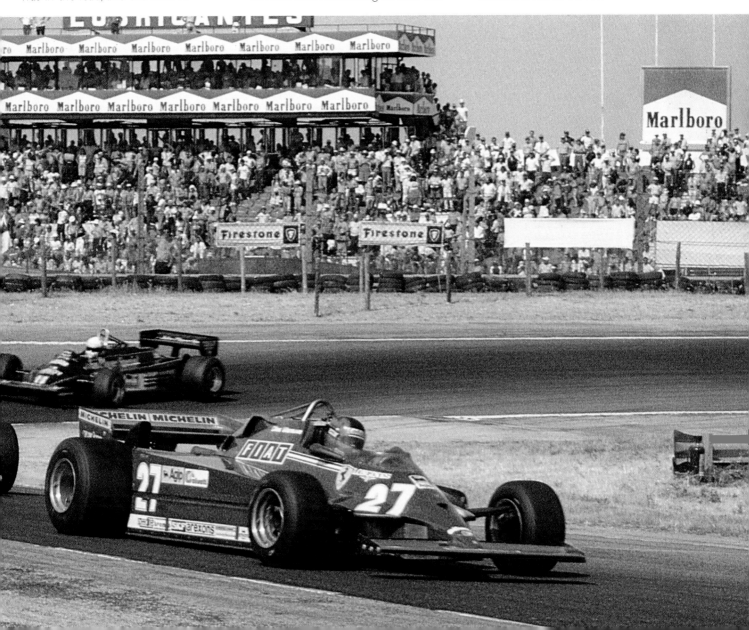

1982 Austrian GP, Osterreichring

⫸ 0.05s

By the time of the 1982 Austrian Grand Prix, at the glorious Osterreichring circuit, F1 had reached a crossroads. In that tragic season, the great Gilles Villeneuve had been killed during practice for the Belgian GP at Zolder, then the Italian novice Ricardo Paletti had died at the start of the Canadian GP after running into the back of Didier Pironi's stalled Ferrari. Pironi himself had suffered horrible leg injuries in a crash during practice for the German GP at Hockenheim, when he ran into the back of Alain Prost's Renault, which had been hidden in a ball of spray. At the same time, the pendulum had begun to swing in favour of the turbocharged 1.5-litre cars and away from the normally aspirated 3-litres, which had ruled since the dawn of the formula in 1966. Thus the sport was in a state of flux as thousand upon thousand of Ferrari fans trekked over the border to see how Patrick Tambay would fare in the lone red car.

However, qualifying belonged to the turbo Brabham-BMWs driven by Nelson Piquet and Riccardo Patrese, with Tambay splitting the two Renault turbos of Alain Prost and René Arnoux. Keke Rosberg (in a Williams-Ford) was the fastest non-turbo, in sixth place, nearly three seconds slower than Piquet and just ahead of Elio de Angelis' normally aspirated Lotus-Ford.

Piquet led the first lap before Patrese sprinted ahead for a 26-lap stint that would end in engine failure. Tambay, however, faded instantly when his Ferrari sustained a puncture from the wreckage of a first-lap accident. He would

recover to fourth by the end, but at this stage the two Brabhams and the two Renaults held sway. De Angelis was into a strong rhythm, in fifth, waiting for the fragile turbo cars to break. He didn't have to wait long, as Arnoux became a casualty with engine failure on lap 15, then Piquet needed fresh tyres on lap 17. The Brazilian was fading by the time Patrese's engine broke, and as Prost led from de Angelis on lap 32, the championship-hungry Rosberg was beginning to line up a challenge to the Lotus driver.

When Prost's Renault engine blew up on lap 49, the normally aspirated battle became one for the lead. Neither de Angelis nor Rosberg had ever won a Grand Prix and both were desperate to do so. Over the last laps, it became clear that Keke was the faster, and bit by bit he chewed into Elio's advantage. By the final lap, they were 1.6s apart, but Rosberg had eliminated that as they came to the last corner, the long, fast sweeping right-hander known as the Rindtkurve. There he challenged, but as de Angelis' engine momentarily misfired, the Italian kept tight to the inside line, forcing Rosberg to follow him. Thus the Finn could not maintain momentum through the corner, and the finish line came just too soon for him to surge past. The Lotus won by 0.05s, the closest margin at that time. For Lotus, it was an apposite triumph. Fifteen years earlier, Jim Clark had won the Dutch GP on the Ford Cosworth DFV engine's maiden outing; de Angelis' victory scored that legendary power unit's 150th win.

Right: *It's mine! De Angelis knows he has just done enough to beat Rosberg to the line in Austria, 1982, and shows his elation by thumping the air.*

1982 Dutch GP, Zandvoort
⟫ 0.232s

Once the fastest man in Grand Prix racing (during his years with Ferrari), Niki Lauda knew that in qualifying he was no match for the younger Alain Prost, as they were teamed together at McLaren in 1984 and 1985. In the previous year, 'The Rat' had used all his cunning to beat Prost to the World Championship by half a point, the

smallest margin in history, but in 1985 the tide was flowing all Prost's way. Lauda knew it was to be his last year in the cockpit and, having announced his intention to retire at his home race, he had lost a possible victory when a turbo broke. Now he had decided that he was going to take any chances that presented themselves.

Prost had won in Brazil, Monaco, Britain and Austria, and as they lined up on the grid at Zandvoort in

Above: There were no orders at McLaren in 1985, when Niki Lauda rose one last time to the occasion to win his 25th GP, narrowly fending off team-mate Alain Prost.

Holland, Lauda appeared to have no chance. He was tenth, with Piquet's Brabham-BMW on pole from Rosberg's Williams-Honda, Prost, and Senna in the Lotus-Renault. But significantly, Niki had headed the morning times. Things went his way in

the race, too, when he turned in a typically controlled and analytical performance.

First, Piquet stalled on the line, leaving fast-starting Teo Fabi in the Toleman-Hart to chase Rosberg and Senna. Prost was fourth, Lauda already up to fifth. Fabi soon fell back, while Prost surged forward. On the 21st lap, Rosberg dropped out and, just as Prost took the lead, the canny Lauda made an early stop for fresh tyres. Prost stopped for tyres 13 laps later, resuming third place behind Senna and, in the lead now, Lauda. By the 51st lap, Niki was 7.1s clear of his team-mate, but ruthlessly Prost slashed the gap lap after lap. With ten laps to go, it was down to 2.6s. In a spellbinding finale, the two red and white cars circulated nose to tail, Lauda refusing to concede any

ground and controlling Prost as they raced through traffic. In the final three laps, it was a gloves-off contest, but Lauda, the old master, proved equal to the task. He crossed the line just 0.232s clear.

Prost would go on to win in Italy, and to cement his first World Championship, but Lauda had proved a point. He finished only tenth in the drivers' championship, 59 points adrift of Prost, but the win was his 25th, and last, Grand Prix victory, drawing him level with Jim Clark. Now he could retire with dignity.

Below: *If Alain Prost was disappointed it didn't show. As Lauda celebrates, the Frenchman smiles happily as Senna uncorks his bubbly. Less happy days lay ahead as a new rivalry would develop between the Frenchman and the Brazilian.*

1986 Spanish GP, Jerez

▶ **0.014s**

Both Nigel Mansell and Ayrton Senna believed they had won the Spanish Grand Prix at Jerez in 1986, and anyone who saw the race could appreciate why. The finish to the 1971 Italian GP had been a smidgeon tighter, but that afternoon in Spain both the Englishman and the Brazilian had crossed the line as if they were in the same car. The official gap was given as 0.014s, after 303km (188 miles) of racing.

Senna, in the Lotus-Renault, had taken pole position from fellow countryman Nelson Piquet in a Williams-Honda, and it was Senna in the less powerful car who surged into the lead. His Lotus was well suited to the tight and twisty little track, and he stayed ahead for the first 39 laps before Mansell finally used all of the extra horsepower from his Williams-Honda to blast by.

The Englishman soon opened a four-second lead, but as Senna came under threat from Alain Prost's McLaren TAG-Porsche, he gradually began to reduce that deficit. With ten laps left, Mansell's tyres were past their best, punished by that extra power, and Senna began to challenge once again. At first, Mansell managed to hold him back, but Senna's

persistence paid off, and as Mansell was compromised, having to lift off, Prost grabbed second place.

With little to lose, Mansell gambled on a stop for fresh tyres, emerging from the pits 20s behind Senna with nine laps to go. In a mighty performance, he began to hack into the Brazilian's lead at a rate of four seconds a lap. And even when he came upon Prost, a potential obstacle, he was not to be denied. Going into the last lap, he was 1.5s behind Senna, but half-way around they were together, and now it was the Lotus driver's tyres that were past their best. By the final corner, they were running nose to tail, and it would all be down to a drag race out of the last hairpin left-hander. The Williams-Honda was quicker, thanks to its superior power, and Mansell surged alongside Senna as they crossed the line, throwing his hand up in victory. Both thought they had won, but the finish line had been moved a mite closer to the final corner since qualifying, and Mansell had actually passed Senna after they had crossed it. Had it been left in its original position, he would have won.

Below and **right:** *Squirting out of the last hairpin and up to the start/finish line, Mansell is poised to vault past Senna at Jerez, but the move came fractions of a second too late.*

CHAPTER **12**

Points of Argument
TEN CONTROVERSIAL RACES

More often than not the victory is clear cut. But sometimes events or conditions conspire to cloak a race in controversy. Perhaps the winner's identity remains uncertain; team tactics backfire or go ignored; or a driver's on-track behaviour shames his reputation and sullies his performance. Here are 10 such races, which remain talking points.

1960 Italian Grand Prix

Although the Italian Grand Prix of 1960 went down in history as the last victory for a front-engined Grand Prix car, it was not a glorious win.

The rear-engined revolution, started by Cooper two years before, had passed Ferrari by. The Old Man's comment that the horse should always pull the cart was illustrative of his reluctance to change. By Monza, the penultimate round, his cars had still to open their 1960 account.

Ferrari's prospects and the size of the crowd that gathers for the Italian Grand Prix are always linked inextricably, so the Monza organisers were downcast. Then they hit upon an idea. Instead of the road course, they would use the full circuit, including the bumpy banked section, giving the powerful Ferraris a chance to stretch their legs and making their mid-engined rivals' handling advantage less significant.

The British teams were not only affronted by this blatant nationalism at their expense; but they also considered the full track to be dangerous. They banded together and threatened a boycott if the organisers did not reverse their decision. The Italians stood their ground, and the entry was reduced to four Ferraris – one of them an F2 car – two F2 Porsches and nine privateers in various hybrids. Phil Hill duly took his first Grand Prix win, ahead of his Ferrari team-mates Richie Ginther and Willy Mairesse.

Opposite left: Willy Mairesse powers his front-engined Ferrari around the Monza banking, on the way to third place.

Above: Mairesse heads Count Wolfgang von Trips in the rear-engined Ferrari Dino 246.

1973 Canadian Grand Prix

The first time that a safety car was used in a Grand Prix was at the 1973 Canadian race, and boy did it show! To this day, no one is really sure who won.

It was wet when Ronnie Peterson led the field away in his JPS Lotus, but in such conditions it was the Firestone tyre users who tended to show well, and Peterson was on Goodyears. On the third lap, Niki Lauda's Firestone-shod BRM – which had qualified eighth – calmly passed Peterson for the lead.

Peterson later spun into a guardrail because of a deflating tyre, and when the track began to dry and Lauda headed for the pits for intermediate tyres, it was Emerson Fittipaldi's Lotus that led from Jackie Oliver's Shadow. Then they pitted, and Jean-Pierre Beltoise's BRM led for a few laps before he, too, pitted.

At this critical stage in the race – when some of the front-runners had pitted and some hadn't – Jody Scheckter and François Cevert, battling for fourth place, collided. With their damaged cars partially

blocking the track, the safety car was scrambled – three laps after the accident.

The Porsche 914 driver duly waved cars past until it picked up Howden Ganley's Iso-Williams. This car definitely wasn't leading, but no one in the pits could agree who was. The Lotus boys were adamant that it was Fittipaldi, the McLaren crew that it was their man, Peter Revson. Some even maintained that it was Oliver's Shadow.

Without the benefit of electronic timing, the official version is that it was Revson, that he'd chanced into the pits at just the right time and was able to make up almost a lap when the pace car came out and picked up the wrong car. Fittipaldi, the story goes, was in second, but almost a lap down on Revson when racing resumed. He was credited with second place and Oliver third. But who knows, since the trophy was initially destined to be given to Ganley?

Left: Mosport Park was not a happy place even before the race began in 1973.

Below: Carlos Reutemann slithers into the lead from Peter Revson (8) and Jody Scheckter, but the start would be much clearer than the finish.

1975 Spanish Grand Prix

Although a fabulous circuit, Montjuich Park never hosted another Grand Prix after the shameful 1975 event.

Set within beautiful park land near Barcelona, Montjuich had alternated as a venue for the Spanish Grand Prix with Jarama since 1969. At that first race, both Graham Hill and Jochen Rindt suffered spectacular crashes in their Lotuses when each experienced rear wing failure over the same crest.

Concerns were expressed over safety in 1975, and the Grand Prix Drivers' Association safety committee inspected the track on the eve of qualifying. It did not like what it found. Much of the Armco barrier was only loosely bolted together, and several of the mounting posts were not properly embedded in the ground.

The drivers said they would not take to the track until this had been rectified. The organizers, rather than attending to the problem, threatened the constructors, pointing out that if no race took place, they would be in breach of contract and that the cars would be impounded. With only one exit from the paddock, it would have been a simple matter for the police to do this, and the ensuing court case would have taken months, which would have jeopardized the championship.

Thus blackmailed into racing, the teams acquiesced, although Emerson Fittipaldi recorded just three extremely slow laps as a protest and then withdrew from the meeting. He was followed in this action by his brother Wilson and by Arturo Merzario in the first lap of the race. At the front, the two Ferraris of Lauda and Regazzoni collided into the first corner, and it was actually the unfancied Hill of Rolf Stommelen that led for much of the distance.

Then the accident everyone had feared occurred. Ironically, over the same crest where Graham Hill's wing had broken in 1969, the same happened to the car he now owned, driven by Stommelen. One of the earliest carbon-fibre wing struts had snapped, and the car flew over the guardrail. In the subsequent impact, a fireman, a photographer and two members of the crowd were killed, while Stommelen broke a leg.

Shamefully the race continued for another four laps before being halted. McLaren's Jochen Mass was awarded the victory, although understandably he came close to assaulting the organising committee that waited to hand him his prize.

Above: *The Ferraris lead off at the start, only to collide seconds later.*

Below: *Ken Tyrrell was so worried about the Armco barriers he went out with his spanner.*

1976 Spanish Grand Prix

The 1976 race at Jarama gave the first indication that the season was going to be something out of the ordinary.

Grand Prix cars were subjected to new regulations that year. They needed to feature more overhang ahead of the driver's feet for his protection; the rear wing overhang had to be reduced from 100cm (39in) to 80cm (31in); the tall airboxes that had featured on the cars in the last couple of seasons were outlawed; and the width of the rear of the car could not exceed 215cm (85in). This last figure had been chosen because it matched that of the widest car that had raced in 1975, the McLaren M23. To give constructors the chance to ready their cars, the new regulations would

not take effect until the fourth round of the season, in Spain.

The first three rounds had been as much a continuation of 1975 in form as in regulation, for Ferrari had won every time: twice with Niki Lauda, once with Clay Regazzoni. James Hunt, however, had a promising start with his new team, McLaren, recording two pole positions.

The new-shape cars duly took to the track in Jarama, and Hunt gained his third pole position, being fractionally faster than Lauda in the new Ferrari. In the race, Lauda took off into the lead, but he had injured his ribs in a tractor accident at home, just days before, and the pain prevented him from defending hard when Hunt came at him and passed.

Hunt duly came home for his first McLaren win, over 30s ahead of Lauda. He was elated . . . briefly. The

scrutineers carefully measured every car, to check that it conformed to the new regulations. All of them passed, but one – the McLaren. It was 1.8cm (0.7in) too wide at the back. The difference between its 1975 width and its current dimension was accounted for by the change in profile of the Goodyear tyres. Nevertheless Hunt was thrown out, and Lauda was awarded the win.

McLaren lodged an immediate appeal, which was heard two months later, and Hunt was reinstated. This was on the eve of that year's British Grand Prix, from which he would also be disqualified.

Above: *First you win, then you lose. Then you win again.*

Right: *Pironi has dived back ahead of Villeneuve as the 1982 San Marino GP draws to its end.*

1982 San Marino Grand Prix

The San Marino race of 1982 became notorious for two reasons. Firstly it witnessed a pull-out by over half of the teams due to an ongoing political argument. Then the ensuing race brought a twist in the tail that ultimately laid down the ingredients for tragedy in the next round.

Grand Prix racing was in the grip of a power battle during the early 1980s. In one corner was FISA, the governing body, in the other FOCA, an organisation comprising the British specialist teams, which made up most of the grid.

The latest in many rows between them had broken out early in the season over the use of 'water cooled' brakes by most of the FOCA teams. This was a ruse whereby the normally aspirated Cosworth runners attempted to keep pace with the turbos by running their cars under weight in the race, then filling up with fluids – which was permitted – afterwards. But the fluids included lots of water for fictitious brake cooling.

After Williams and Brabham were excluded from the first two places in the Brazilian Grand Prix for this practice, FISA ruled that it was officially banned forthwith. In a fit of pique, the FOCA teams responded by claiming that they could not ready their cars in time for the next race, the San Marino Grand Prix at Imola.

Therefore the 12 cars that took to the grid were those closely aligned to FISA: the so-called 'grandees' – Ferrari, Renault, Alfa-Romeo; some small non-British teams; and Tyrrell, which was obliged to attend since it had just secured an Italian sponsor. Yet in its early stages, the race developed into a cracker, with the two Renaults of Alain Prost and René Arnoux fighting it out with the two Ferraris of Gilles Villeneuve and Didier Pironi. Once the Renaults dropped out, the Ferraris were left in first and second, with Villeneuve ahead. At this stage, under no threat from anyone else, the Ferrari drivers were instructed to hold station to the end.

All looked in order as Villeneuve duly cruised around, with Pironi a couple of lengths behind. Then, two laps from the end, Pironi overtook. Villeneuve assumed that his team-mate was merely putting on a show for the crowd, but none the less was surprised at how hard he had to push to regain the lead. Back in front on the final lap, he assumed that all was settled. But instead, Pironi used the final passing place on the lap to overtake once more and go on to a sly victory.

Villeneuve was incensed at what he saw as a betrayal of trust. From this point on, he decided, he would cut off all communication with Pironi and ensure that he always beat him on the track. In practice for the next round at Zolder, Pironi went faster than Villeneuve. It was during the latter's response to that lap that he crashed to his death.

1984 Monaco Grand Prix

Alain Prost won the 1984 Monaco Grand Prix after it was stopped before half-distance because of the weather conditions. There was some debate about whether it should have been stopped, and if it hadn't been, Ayrton Senna – or even Stefan Bellof – may have won his first Grand Prix.

It was a year of McLaren domination, and all looked to be routine in this wet race as Prost eased ever further clear at the head of the field, once Nigel Mansell's five-lap charge in the lead ended when he slid into the wall. Then the heavens opened. Prost had never been entirely happy in such treacherous conditions ever since Hockenheim in 1982. There he had been indirectly involved in the qualifying accident that ended Didier Pironi's career when, in near-zero visibility, the Ferrari driver did not see the back of Prost's car until too late.

Back at Monaco, Prost's turbo McLaren was losing traction even on the straights, so he backed off, sure that the race couldn't continue. But it

did, and catching him hand over fist was a driver in only his sixth Grand Prix, in a second-rate car – Ayrton Senna. Fuelled by the courage of ambition, he was sliding and coaxing his turbocharged Toleman-Hart into contention, recognising what could have been his sole chance of displaying his true capabilities. A second per lap, a second-and-a-half sometimes, Senna was eating into Prost's big lead.

Yet, unbelievably, Senna himself was being caught by another. Stefan Bellof was also in his sixth Grand Prix, and his car was an even less likely contender for victory: a normally aspirated Tyrrell. He had just scraped in on to the back row, but if Martin Brundle had completed the qualifying lap in which brake failure caused him to crash, Bellof would have been bumped off the grid by his own team-mate.

But these dreadful race-day conditions were heaven-sent for the fearless German with fabulous car control, not to mention the razor-sharp throttle response of a good old-fashioned normally aspirated engine.

Each time Prost passed the start/finish line, he pointed to the sky, imploring the clerk of the course to halt proceedings. Finally, just short of half-distance, the decision was taken. The race was declared, with Prost the winner from Senna and Bellof, and half-points were awarded.

There were two ironies in this result. The first was that the clerk of the course was Jacky Ickx, a former F1 driver who, in his day, was acknowledged as 'the rainmaster'. The other was that had the race gone the full distance and Prost only finished second, the six points he would have gained, rather than the 4.5 for his half-race victory, would have won him that year's World Championship.

Above: Prost in his
McLaren fends off the
on-form Nigel Mansell.

Opposite: Mansell
storms past the pit wall
on his ill-fated five-
lap charge.

Left: Rosberg's Renault
and Bellof's Toleman
slip and slide around
the Rascasse in
conditions which would
eventually mean the
race was called off.

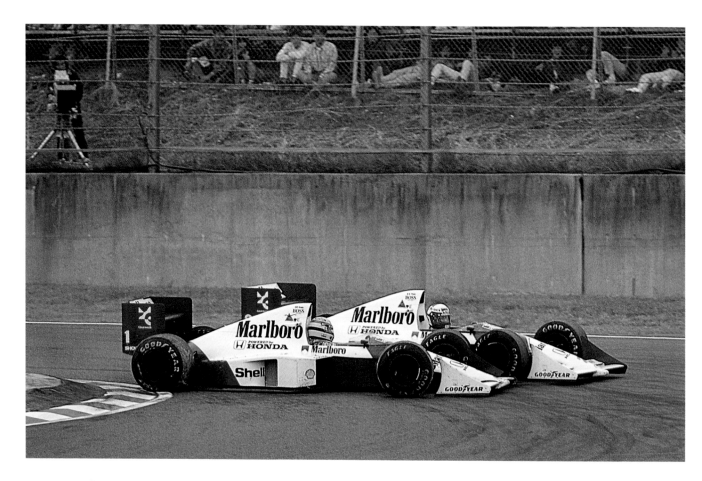

1989 and 1990 Japanese Grands Prix

In 1989, Alain Prost clinched his third World Championship, at the Japanese Grand Prix, in controversial circumstances concerning team-mate Ayrton Senna. This escalated the simmering feud between them into a full-scale war.

Having the world's best pair of drivers in the same team was always going to be difficult, particularly when one of them had the sort of uncompromising commitment to winning displayed by Senna. Right from the start, it had been a relationship with its tensions, but a marker went down in the 1988 Portuguese Grand Prix when Prost began to pull alongside Senna in an effort to pass, and had the Brazilian calmly ease him towards the pit wall at 306km/h (190mph). The message from Senna was clear:

'Back off, or we both have an enormous accident.'

Senna won the title that year, partly through that move. In 1989, the situation was just as delicately balanced between them, but Prost was ahead on points as they headed into the penultimate round in Japan, needing only to finish in front of Senna in this race to clinch the title. Although, so far, he had refused to resort to Senna's brand of latent violence on the track, he warned that in this race he was not going to give way to that sort of behaviour. Quite simply, he had had enough.

Prost took an immediate lead and drove a magnificent early stint, Senna being unable even to get close enough for a look at the lead. For every fastest lap Senna recorded, Prost would pull out a better one. After the pit stops, Prost still led, but Senna began a desperate charge, sliding over kerbs and attacking with

all his might. The gap between them began to close at last.

With ten laps to go, Senna was with the leader, knowing that he had to pass if he was to keep his crown. There seemed nowhere obvious to overtake Prost, so closely matched were they, but on lap 47, six from the end, Senna saw a chink of daylight up the inside at the chicane. He held off the brakes as late as possible and dived for the gap.

It wasn't enough for a clean pass, but it was the sort of move Senna had made work many times before, simply by presenting the other driver with a stark choice. This time, as promised, Prost turned in. Clumsily. He knew Senna was there; he knew he was going to take them both off; he knew that in doing so, he would become World Champion. It was the sort of move that Senna wouldn't have hesitated in making. They collided.

But as Prost climbed from his stalled car, Senna got going again. He took a short cut back on to the track via an escape road, for which he was disqualified from a stunning recovery win. McLaren – which was losing Prost to Ferrari for the following year, but keeping Senna – appealed, but this was quashed. Prost took the world title with him to Ferrari. Senna, meanwhile, felt that he had a score to settle.

One year later, Senna took pole position again at Suzuka, but the FIA obliged him to line up on the right-hand side of the grid, rather than giving him the choice of lane. This put him on the dirty side, favouring arch-rival Prost, who was in very strong contention for the championship in a Ferrari that was superior to the McLaren. Still smarting from the previous year's events, Senna swore before the race: 'If he gets to the first corner ahead of me, he ain't gonna make it round.'

And that's precisely what happened. Prost got a better start from the cleaner side of the track and led Senna into the first corner. But as the Frenchman lifted slightly to get round, Senna kept his foot hard down and simply smashed into the back of the Ferrari, taking both of them into instant retirement. Observers said that the engine note of the McLaren never wavered, and although he denied that he had done it deliberately to ruin Prost's chances of garnering sufficient points to win the title, Senna admitted his guilt in an extraordinary outburst in Japan in the following year.

Opposite : *Full stop one. Senna and Prost come to their ungainly halt at the Suzuka chicane in 1989.*

Right: *Full stop two. This time it's 1990, and Prost is considering striking Senna after their first corner incident in Japan.*

following corner. Schumacher moved across, and the resultant impact damaged the Williams' suspension, too. Schumacher retired on the spot, but with Hill also out, the German became World Champion.

Later he would maintain that the clash had been a racing accident, a misunderstanding.

Above and left: Almost over, certainly out. As Hill dives for the inside, Schumacher blocks him in Adelaide, 1994.

Below: Agonizing moments passed for Schumacher, until he realized that Hill's car was too badly damaged to continue.

1994 Australian Grand Prix

'The Schumacher Incident'. Opinions still differ on the manner in which Michael Schumacher won his first World Championship, at the 1994 Australian Grand Prix.

On the track, Schumacher and his Benetton were usually more than a match for Damon Hill and his Williams. But the issue had been clouded by allegations of Benetton's supposed 'launch control' start-line device, and subsequently by Schumacher's late-season, two-race ban, which stemmed from an earlier driving infringement.

He won magnificently upon his return, and even though subsequently he finished second to Hill in Japan, he

arrived in Australia one point ahead. In essence, whoever finished in front would be champion. If neither finished, Schumacher took the crown.

Although 'guest driver' Nigel Mansell secured pole position for Williams, when the flag dropped, it Schumacher and Hill immediately leapt out front. With a narrow, but comfortable, lead, it all seemed to be going Schumacher's way – until he cracked, sliding momentarily into a concrete wall. He regained the track before Hill, who had been delayed when lapping Heinz-Harald Frentzen, appeared. But his suspension was badly damaged. Hill, presented with the sight of the crawling Benetton, and with no knowledge of its incident, dived for the inside of the

1997 European Grand Prix

'The Schumacher Incident 2'. Again battling for the championship in 1997's final round at the European Grand Prix, this time Schumacher's actions were even more blatant.

In so many ways, it was a repeat of 1994, but this time in Jerez, Spain. Once more, Schumacher had hauled a supposedly inferior car – his Ferrari – into championship

Ferrari's inside. It was a gap that Schumacher hadn't even bothered to defend, so far back was the Williams. But now Villeneuve was alongside him. Schumacher appeared to turn away, but then, just as in 1994, he turned into his rival. Only on this occasion, the Williams was relatively unscathed, and Schumacher was in the gravel.

Same story, different ending. This time, the biter had been bitten.

contention against Williams' lead driver, now Jacques Villeneuve. Again he was one point ahead going into the last round and, if neither contender finished, he would be champion.

Again he got off to a fantastic start, leading without apparent threat. Villeneuve, meanwhile, had become caught up behind his team-mate, Frentzen, and it was some time before he emerged in second place. Even then, he made no real inroads on the Ferrari's useful lead.

After the pit stops, Schumacher still led, but Villeneuve was closer, sufficiently so to be thinking about mounting an immediate passing move to surprise the German. From a long way back, he dived cleanly down the

Above left: Villeneuve and Schumacher have their moment of truth on lap 48 in Jerez.

Above: After you, Mika. Coulthard obeys team orders to let team-mate Hakkinen go on for the victory.

Left: Blond wigs all round, as Villeneuve's crew fetes its champion.

6

TECHNOLOGY

CHAPTER 13

Designer Genes
THE GREAT DESIGNERS

Imagination; the ability to think laterally and to break free of established dogma; a ruthless streak of individuality. These are all prerequisites of the world's leading designers. Gifted free-thinkers they have led the sport to each of its technological eras, established new parameters in the endless quest for greater performance.

✎ John Barnard

The man responsible for introducing the now-universal carbon-fibre construction to F1, John Barnard has designed winning cars for McLaren, Ferrari and Benetton. He learned his trade at Lola Cars in the 1970s, becoming involved in Indycar racing when the company re-entered that arena towards the end of the decade. There he helped the Chaparral team take a Lola to victory in all three of the 805-km (500-mile) Indycar races in 1978 with Al Unser.

When Chaparral decided to build its own car, Barnard was the man chosen to design it. The Chaparral 2K introduced the ground-effect principle – which had been pioneered in F1 by Lotus – into Indycar racing in 1979. It was very successful.

Feeling that Chaparral boss Jim Hall was taking the credit for his design, Barnard responded to Ron Dennis's offer to design a new F1 car for his Project Four team. Eventually this would become the first new-era McLaren, the MP4/1, after Dennis had taken effective control of that company in 1980. Barnard's design was the first Grand Prix car built in carbon fibre, a medium that rapidly replaced the previously universal honeycomb aluminium. John Watson took the car to its first Grand Prix win in 1981.

When McLaren moved into the turbocharged era, Barnard worked with engine manufacturer Porsche in determining the layout and dimensions of its V6 motor so that it dovetailed precisely with his aerodynamic requirements. The McLaren MP4/2-Porsches duly swept all before them in 1984 and 1985.

After a disagreement with Dennis, Barnard left McLaren and, in 1987, joined Ferrari. There he persuaded the company to agree to the unthinkable: that the Ferrari F1 cars would be designed in the UK. Setting up a satellite operation in Surrey, called GTO, he conceived the cars with

Above: *Opinionated, occasionally prickly, but brilliant, John Barnard is the designer's designer in F1.*

which Nigel Mansell and Alain Prost scored much success in 1989 and 1990. They also brought another innovation to F1: semi-automatic gearboxes.

He left Ferrari in 1990 and joined forces with Benetton, designing the B191 model used by Nelson Piquet to win the 1991 Canadian Grand Prix, but it was a short partnership. He'd left by mid-1991 and later rejoined Ferrari.

Although Barnard's GTO operation had been closed down when he left, he set up another British-based Ferrari design centre, FDD. His new designs didn't come on-stream until 1994, but they helped bring Ferrari back to competitive respectability, to the point where his 1997 car – the F310B – almost gave Michael Schumacher the World Championship. By then, his

contract with the Italian team had come to an end and, in mid-season, he joined Arrows.

Above: Man and machine. Barnard with Prost and the carbon-fibre McLaren that the Englishman pioneered

Below: But for a moment's inattention and then rashness in Jerez, Schumacher might have taken Barnard's Ferrari F310B to the title in 1997.

✎ Rory Byrne

In partnership with Ross Brawn, Rory Byrne was the design brain behind the Benetton cars that took Michael Schumacher to consecutive world titles in 1994 and 1995.

South African Byrne was an engineer with the Toleman team as it rose through the ranks of British club racing and into the European F2 Championship in the late 1970s. After using a succession of other manufacturers' cars, Toleman had Byrne pen its own F2 chassis for 1980. This took the European title at its first attempt, with Brian Henton doing the driving.

Then the team made the move into F1, and Byrne designed a car around a turbocharged version of the Hart engine, which had been used in F2. Although this TG181 model was a

disaster initially, the team and engine supplier learned quickly, and by 1982 it occasionally performed quite respectably in the hands of Derek Warwick.

Progress continued into 1983 with Byrne's TG183, the double rear wing arrangement of which was widely copied. His more conventional TG184 and 185 models gained widespread admiration and a reputation as the best-handling chassis in the business.

When Toleman was bought out by Benetton, Byrne's TG185 became the basis of the Benetton B186, a BMW turbo replacing the underpowered Hart. With this car, Gerhard Berger scored his and the team's first Grand Prix victory in Mexico in 1986. Byrne penned a series of Ford-powered Benettons before leaving, in 1990, to design Reynard's new F1 car.

This proved to be a stillborn project, and in mid-1991 Byrne returned to Benetton. The basis of his Reynard design was used for the B192, with its characteristic high nose helping to generate under-car airflow. This eventually developed into the B194, which took Schumacher to his first World Championship. A Renault-engined version, the B195, repeated that success in the following year.

Although Byrne stayed at Benetton when Schumacher left, it wasn't long before the German had recruited both him and his Benetton partner, Ross Brawn, to join him at Ferrari. Byrne joined the Italian team for the 1997 season, in time to pen the 1998 contender.

Below: Rory Byrne's contribution to Benetton's success is often overlooked, but his B194 and B195 designs were winners in Schumacher's hands.

Left and below: *Did anyone bring such fertile flair and innovation to FI as Colin Chapman? Graham Hill drives the elegant 49 at Nürburgring 1967 (left); the Old Man confers with de Angelis (below).*

Colin Chapman

The late founder of Lotus, Colin Chapman, has been widely acclaimed as the foremost racing car design genius of all time. Although many of the concepts commonly attributed to him were not strictly his, he had a flair for incorporating them in an original and highly effective way.

Dealing in cars as a way of supplementing his income while studying for his engineering degree in the early 1950s, Chapman used one of his trade-ins, an Austin Seven, as the basis for a trials car. This was designated the Lotus Mk1. A later special, the Lotus Mk6, proved a formidable machine in British 750 motor club racing with Chapman himself at the wheel. So much so that he set up Lotus Cars to meet the demand for replicas from other competitors. Team Lotus, the works racing team, swiftly followed.

Lotus entered FI in 1958, although it wasn't until Chapman followed Cooper's example and designed a rear-engined car that success came. His designs betrayed an obsessive preoccupation with saving weight and reducing frontal area. It was while searching for further reductions in the latter that he came up with the first monocoque FI car, the Lotus 25.

Introduced in 1962, the 25's method of construction employed the outer skin as a stressed structural part of the car, dispensing with the need for an inner framework of steel tubing, which was prevalent at the time. This revolutionized race car design. Its lightness and aerodynamic efficiency helped Jim Clark give Lotus its first two world titles.

Taking the concept further, Chapman revived the use of the engine as a stressed member in his 1967 Lotus 49, and three years later came up with the 72, featuring torsion-bar suspension with rising-rate springing and inboard brakes. Both cars were championship winners as well as trend setters.

But perhaps his biggest advance came with the Lotus 78 and 79 models of 1977/8. Using information established by his aerodynamicist, Peter Wright, Chapman conceived the ground-effect car, which utilized under-body aerodynamics to suck the car to the ground. It made for massively increased cornering speeds and again revolutionized race car design.

Like Barnard, Chapman was in the forefront with carbon-fibre chassis technology, but his final innovation, before his death from a heart attack in December 1982, was the twin-chassis Lotus 88. This had a softly sprung inner chassis to give the driver a smooth ride, and a virtually solidly sprung outer chassis to cope with the massive aerodynamic downforce then being generated by FI cars. But it was banned by the governing body, a bitter disappointment from which Chapman never fully recovered.

✏ Gioacchino Colombo

Responsible for the Alfa Romeo Alfetta models that dominated the first two years of the World Championship, as well as the original Ferrari Grand Prix car, Gioacchino Colombo's place in history is well and truly assured.

Colombo joined Alfa Romeo in 1924 and was made assistant to the great pre-war designer Vittorio Jano, whom he helped create both the P2 and P3 Alfas, two of the most successful Grand Prix cars of all time. He was finally given full responsibility for a car when Alfa instructed him to produce a machine to comply with the supercharged 1.5-litre voiturette

category. This car, dubbed the Alfetta, featured a rear-mounted gearbox in the interests of weight distribution and enjoyed immediate glory when introduced in 1937. At that time, the Alfa race team was operated by Enzo Ferrari's Scuderia Ferrari, and after the war, when Ferrari was setting himself up as a race car constructor in his own right, he commissioned Colombo to come up with a car.

It was Colombo who conceived the V12 engine configuration with which Ferrari would forever be associated. The 125GP car, introduced in 1947 and progressively developed until 1950, was another 1.5-litre supercharged design, the former voiturette capacity limit now forming

the basis of the post-war Grand Prix formula. Although it won Grands Prix, it was outclassed when Alfa Romeo returned to racing with developed versions of Colombo's old Alfettas.

Thus Ferrari concentrated on a 4.5-litre unsupercharged car, as recommended by Colombo's design rival, Aurelio Lampredi. Colombo, meanwhile, returned to Alfa Romeo, where he squeezed more power from his Alfetta design to stave off the increasing threat from the Lampredi Ferrari in 1951.

After designing the unsuccessful, but highly original, 1956 mid-engined Bugatti 251, Colombo worked for Abarth and MV Agusta motor cycles. He died in 1987.

✏ Mauro Forghieri

Engine man-turned-chassis designer, Mauro Forghieri was responsible for a long line of F1 Ferraris from the 1960s to the early 1980s. The pinnacle of his work was the superb 1975 championship-winning 312T model.

Forghieri's father worked in Ferrari's machine shop and obtained young Mauro a work-experience placement towards the end of his engineering studies. A short time later, he was taken on as assistant to chief designer Carlo Chiti and, when the latter left at the end of 1961, Forghieri found himself as a principal designer.

Initially he specialized in engines and was responsible for a flat-12 unit that produced excellent power, but which was made obsolete by the termination of the 1.5-litre formula. Subsequently he became heavily involved in chassis design, too, and was responsible for the superb-handling 1968 Ferrari 312, which was arguably the fastest car of the season. It was let down by the relatively

Left: *Mauro Forghieri's Ferrari 312T4 recaptured the spell of his mid-1970s creations, and took Jody Scheckter to the World Championship crown in 1979.*

feeble power output of its Lampredi-designed V12 engine.

As a remedy, Forghieri returned to his theme of an engine with 12 horizontally opposed cylinders at the end of 1969, with the aim of keeping the mass as low down in the car as possible. The resultant Ferrari 312B model was F1's pace-setter by the end of 1970.

It was this engine that formed the basis of his sublime 312T. With the flat-12 keeping the engine low – and producing excellent power and

reliability – he sought also to keep the weight as close to the centre of the car as possible by using a transversely mounted gearbox. The result was a superbly neutral-handling and responsive chassis with which Niki Lauda walked the 1975 World Championship.

Forghieri's next engine was Ferrari's turbocharged V6, which triumphed twice in its first year, 1981. He left the team in 1984 and later designed an F1 V12 for Lamborghini before setting up as a freelancer.

Patrick Head

The man behind the cars that have won all of Williams' seven Drivers' and nine Constructors' World Championships, Patrick Head is also a partner in Williams Grand Prix Engineering.

When Frank Williams set up his second F1 team in 1977, he chose Head as the key to his new operation. A former Lola Cars designer – he had worked there alongside John Barnard – Head's first F1 design was the Williams FW06 of 1978. Simple and very compact, it was highly effective and gained Williams real respectability.

Incorporating the latest ground-effect principles, the FW07 of 1979 turned Williams into a winner. It showed Head's strength of taking established principles to the limits by thorough research and engineering. The FW07 instantly outpaced the car that had inspired it, the Lotus 79.

Head's reluctance to dive straight into the latest technology before fully researching and understanding it was apparent when Williams was the last of the front-line teams to adopt carbon-fibre construction for its cars for 1985. Yet his first such chassis, the FW10, was F1's pace-setter by the end of its first season, and a development of it went on to take more World Championships for the team.

Active ride was introduced to F1 by Lotus, but it was Head who, in 1992, took the concept to its logical conclusion with the FW14B, a car that displayed a staggering superiority over its rivals. Aided by the excellent Renault V10 engines, Patrick Head's designs led the way in F1 until 1998 with the resurgence of McLaren.

Above: *'Come and work for me, Patrick!' Head listens to Stewart in full flow.*

Left: *Fast and effective, Williams's 1986 FW11 epitomized Head's pragmatism.*

For commercial reasons, Ecclestone then saddled Brabham with heavy sports-car-derived Alfa Romeo flat-12 engines, and the resultant BT45 and BT46 designs were forced to lose the compact dimensions of the earlier models. However, with the latter car, Murray tried to lessen the weight penalty by designing a system of 'surface cooling', using heat exchangers instead of radiators. Unfortunately it didn't work. His next attempt at finding an advantage was far more effective – the notorious 'fan car'.

Stymied in designing an effective ground-effect car by the configuration of the Alfa's engine, Murray sectioned off the rear under-body with skirts and installed a huge fan at the back, which sucked the car to the ground. It won its only race, the 1978 Swedish Grand Prix, but was banned immediately after.

When Brabham returned to the Cosworth DFV, Murray was able to design a car that reflected his preference for compact and elegant dimensions, the BT49. Nelson Piquet took it to a world title in 1981, and two years later did the same with Murray's turbo car, the BT52.

After leaving Brabham for McLaren, Murray contributed towards the 1989 title-winning McLaren MP4/5. Thereafter he went on to design the McLaren F1 road car, which subsequently achieved great success in international GT racing.

Gordon Murray

One of the most original and free thinking designers F1 has ever seen, Gordon Murray designed a series of effective and beautiful Brabhams in the 1970s and 1980s.

South African Murray had already designed and built his own club racer when he arrived in Britain hoping to widen his design experience with a Grand Prix team. He was picked up by Brabham in the early 1970s and promoted to chief designer by Bernie Ecclestone soon after. The latter's refusal to allow corporate sponsors to place any demands on his team made for the sort of atmosphere in which the laid-back Murray could flourish.

The BT42 and BT44 designed by Murray displayed all the elegance that was to become his hallmark, while their triangular-section monocoques helped to ensure consistent handling over a wide range of fuel loads. They were among the fastest, if not the fastest, of the Cosworth DFV-powered cars in the mid-1970s.

Far left: *Never a man to follow
the herd, Gordon Murray revitalized
Brabham fortunes with a series of
individual designs in the late 1970s and
early 1980s.*

Below: *Murray's BT49 took Nelson
Piquet to his first title in 1981.*

✎ Ron Tauranac

Brabham cars designed by Ron
Tauranac won consecutive World
Championships in 1966 and 1967,
and established the Brabham marque
as a major force in F1.

A friend of Jack Brabham's when
both were involved in dirt-track
racing in their native Australia,
Tauranac was the designer Brabham
sought when he set up as a race car
constructor in 1962. His approach –
no-nonsense and practical – reflected
Brabham's own.

Tauranac's original design, the BT3
(BT for Brabham-Tauranac), was
standard fare for the time, but neat,
simple and light. These, rather than
progressive innovations, became
hallmarks of the Tauranac Brabhams.
Even as rival constructors copied the
Lotus 25 formula of a monocoque
chassis, the Brabhams continued to
be of tubular construction for many
more years.

Among them was the 1966 BT19
model, which used the similarly
unambitious Repco engine, but took
Jack Brabham to the 1966 world title.

Above: *Brabham's design force in the 1960s was
down-to-earth Aussie Ron Tauranac, seen here
discussing his BT34 with Graham Hill in 1971.*

A development of this car, the BT24,
did the same for Denny Hulme in
1967. The light weight of these cars
let them run softer-compound tyres
than their rivals, while their simplicity
made for superb reliability.

The space-frame Brabhams
remained competitive right through
until 1969, the company's first
monocoque only appearing as the
1970 BT33, when regulation changes
effectively ruled out space frames. It
says much that Jack won first time
out with the new car, in Kyalami in
South Africa.

Following Brabham's retirement at
the end of 1970, Tauranac bought the
company. However he stayed for only
a year before selling out to Bernie
Ecclestone, and in the mid-1970s
founded Ralt (his and brother Austin
Lewis's initials), which went on to
become one of the most successful
customer race car constructors until
being merged with the rival March
company in the early 1990s.

A Changing Face
DEVELOPMENT OF THE GRAND PRIX CAR

Look at the Grand Prix car of 1950, then at its 1998 counterpart, and only the existence of four wheels seems to bind them together. But even they are different. What changes led to this complete evolution? What developments took designers to each step along the way?

The development of Grand Prix car design has always been a fascinating battle between technology and the desire of teams to make their machines ever faster on the one hand, and the governing body's need to strike a balance between spectacle and safety on the other. Consequently, as the cars have become faster, various formulae imposing technical limitations have been applied. But the rules can only react to technology, not anticipate it, and history has shown that an inventive mind in a competitive environment will always find a way of circumnavigating the regulations to gain an advantage on the track.

When such men are given substantial budgets to feed their inquisitive and competitive minds, as has been the case in the last 15 years or so, the pace of change can be breathtaking. Thus hardly a year has gone by in the modern era when there has not been some new

artificial limitation imposed on the cars. To do otherwise would mean changing the circuits to suit the machinery, as the sport's golden rule must be to ensure that spectators are not put at risk, while a secondary, but important, requirement should be that racing is not unnecessarily perilous for the drivers.

ALFA ROMEO ALFETTA
Neither of these situations held true in the early days of the World Championship. Such concerns would come much later. At that time, the primary aim had simply been to get motor racing up and running after World War Two, and consequently a formula was devized – Formula One – that encompassed existing machinery. This is why the car that dominated in 1950 and 1951 dated back to 1937.

That car was the Alfa Romeo Alfetta, its 1.5-litre engine eventually being supercharged to such an extent

that it produced around 283kW (380bhp). Ferrari was the first to demonstrate that the 4.5 litres allowed for an unsupercharged engine could be made more effective, since it gave almost as much power, but used

far less fuel. Thus forced induction – supercharging and turbocharging – fell out of favour for several decades.

In fact, engines remained the main focus of the teams during most of the 1950s, through both the 2-litre and 2.5-litre formulae. Ever since racing began, chassis and suspensions had always played second fiddle to pure horsepower in the concerns of race car designers. The simplistic notion that, because there were more straights than corners, the engine was more important was summed up by

Above: Fangio's 1953 Maserati was essentially a minor development of the front-engined Grand Prix car theme that evolved in the 1930s.

Enzo Ferrari, who claimed that he built 'engines with wheels attached'.

COOPER CLIMAX

This all changed through the efforts of one team, Cooper. Its cars had evolved from motor cycle-engined F3 cars, which had chain drives that made it logical to fit the engines at the back. Almost by chance, Cooper discovered that such a layout offered genuine advantages, and its F1 car of 1958 made this apparent to the racing world at large. Although powered only by a bored-out F2 engine of 2.2-litres, it won both the Argentinian and Monaco Grands Prix.

How could a car giving away as much as 67kW (90bhp) to the front-engined Ferraris possibly be competitive? Because its layout meant that it was lighter and aerodynamically more efficient, while its handling was more responsive. That it led to a wholesale adoption of rear-engined – or more accurately mid-engined – cars was significant in that it demonstrated a widespread acceptance that the engine was not the be-all and end-all of race car design.

Nevertheless, the engine specification remained the governing body's main weapon in containing speeds. An appalling safety record in the mid-1950s had caused it to announce in 1958 that, from 1961, the capacity of F1 cars would be reduced to 1.5 litres (unsupercharged). By the time that this formula came to be implemented, there was also a minimum weight stipulation, as it was felt that the ingenious efforts of constructors such as Cooper, in making their underpowered cars competitive through light weight,

Left and right: *Via the Coopers' innovative little cars of the late 1950s, the Grand Prix car of 1961 evolved into the timeless sharknose Ferrari (left) and the boxy but effective little Lotus 18, both seen here at Monaco.*

were compromising their structural safety. The limit was pinned at 450kg (992lb) – the 1958 Cooper weighed just 380kg (838lb), the Lotus 16 360kg (794lb).

Additional safety requirements of the new formula included ignition cut-out switches, electric self-starters, dual-circuit braking and roll-over bars. In addition, enclosed bodywork (as seen on the initial 1954 Mercedes) was banned, although the main reason for this was to keep the machinery recognisable as formula cars rather than any concern about straight-line speeds. Had this not been introduced, there is little doubt that the F1 car of today would look very different.

Lotus 25

The severely restricted power output of these original 1.5-litre engines – around 149kW (200bhp) – intensified the search for advantage through chassis engineering. Colin Chapman's frantic efforts to reduce frontal area caused him to develop the monocoque-chassis Lotus 25 in 1962. Its construction conveyed benefits way beyond those he was originally seeking, including better torsional stiffness, vastly reduced weight and better driver safety. It quickly became the accepted format for a race car.

The technical gains made during the five years of the 1.5-litre formula were evidenced by the lap record at the Nürburgring, which rose from 153km/h (95mph) in 1961 to 163km/h (101mph) in 1965. Incidentally both speeds were faster than the 2.5-litre F1 record set by a front-engined car.

Such gains were applied to the new 3-litre generation of cars from 1966 onwards. The doubling of the permitted engine size came about because it was felt that the 1.5-litre cars failed to provide a spectacle, particularly given their substantially enhanced roadholding. By then, chassis technology was considered sufficiently advanced to safely contain the more powerful engines, which would more properly reflect F1's status. Furthermore, for commercial reasons, there was a desire to encourage American involvement to give the sport a truly global appeal, and a 1.5-litre limit was completely at odds with the motor industry of that country.

Essentially a state-of-the-art 1.5-style monocoque with a bigger engine was the initial blueprint for success. With such chassis parity, the Cosworth DFV engine, designed specifically for the new formula, instantly became a critical element, but soon that, too, was available to all.

Tyres grew in width to handle the extra power, and four-wheel drive seemed the next logical development to overcome the traction limits that were being approached. Yet that development was rendered obsolete by another that hadn't been envisaged by the rule makers at all.

Cars with Wings

At the 1968 Belgian Grand Prix, both Brabham and Ferrari appeared with inverted wings above the engines – an idea copied from the American Chaparral sports racer. These devices addressed their designers' desire to work the new generation of wide tyres even harder without adding significant weight. These 'upside-down wings' worked in such a way as to push the cars more firmly on to the ground giving better turn-in and traction.

Top and right: The most significant development in the late 1960s, following Chapman's introduction of the monocoque chassis in 1962, was the development of wings to generate downforce. By 1969 they had evolved into outrageous devices mounted on high stalks. Though effective, they were also devastatingly fragile, as Graham Hill found to his cost in Barcelona in 1969 (above). One race later high wings were banned.

Ever larger and outrageously high wings, mounted directly on to the suspension, appeared; some were even cockpit-adjustable, allowing the driver to flatten the incidence of the wing for better speed down the straights. Lap times tumbled. When the Lotuses of Graham Hill and Jochen Rindt both crashed heavily after taking flight when their wings broke during the 1969 Spanish Grand Prix, the governing body was forced to act.

From the next race, the wings were banned initially. Then it was decided that they could be used, but could not be movable, and it was forbidden to mount them directly to the suspension (where they were most effective). Nevertheless body-mounted wings were here to stay, and aerodynamics was no longer purely concerned with obtaining a low frontal area and a slippery shape for good straight-line speed. The wedge shape of the 1970 Lotus 72 showed how the two aims of creating downforce and reducing drag could be effectively combined.

Ground Effect

For a few years, F1 race car design remained largely static, then another quantum leap in grip was made through yet another application of aerodynamics. Peter Wright, an aerodynamicist, had been intrigued by the idea of incorporating inverted wing profiles in the side of the car since the late 1960s, but it wasn't until he arrived at Lotus in the mid-1970s, and found Colin Chapman thinking along similar lines, that he finally got to try the idea on a full-scale car, the Lotus 78. This 'wing car' was further developed into the ground-effect Lotus 79 of 1978.

Whereas the wing car would have produced negative lift, regardless of having a surface beneath it, the ground-effect car took the principle further by using the track to suck itself down. Air entering each of the body's sidepods was channelled through a narrow aperture that opened out into a larger area, thus accelerating the air and creating a vacuum between the track and the underside of the body. The sidepods were sealed to the track by sliding skirts, which maintained the vacuum so that the car was sucked down.

Soon these ground-effect cars were cornering so fast that circuits were having to be altered, either to slow the corners or to move the spectators further away. They were generating so much downforce that suspensions had to be made radically stiff to make full use of it, and drivers were beginning to suffer back problems as a result. Furthermore the skirts were gouging deep channels into track surfaces.

After immovable skirts and a minimum ride height had been

Above: A decade later, Chapman's fertile mind brought F1 ground effect, courtesy of his Lotus 78.

specified and found insufficient to prevent design ingenuity from retaining ground effect, a flat-bottom regulation was introduced in 1983. By making the underside of the car between the wheels flat, there could be no venturi shape to create the vacuum. Designers would discover methods of circumventing that rule, too, but not for a while.

RENAULT POWER UP

In the meantime, in an era when the ten-year-old Cosworth DFV was still powering around 90 per cent of the grid, someone other than Ferrari had decided to look seriously at engine power, as a way of gaining an advantage, for the first time since the 1950s. Renault was the company that bravely took up the 1.5-litre forced-induction option, which had been in the 3-litre regulations ever since 1966. Its turbocharged 1.5-litre V6 powered car first appeared in 1977. This also marked the return of the first major car producer with an F1 factory team since Cooper's dominance in the late 1950s had led to a new power base of small, specialist British constructors.

The turbo immediately gave superior peak power figures to the conventional 373kW (500bhp) 3-litre engines, but it was several years before this advantage could be combined with reasonable reliability. By then though, the power being produced by the turbos was immense – anything up to 969kW (1300bhp) in high-boost qualifying form, around 559kW (750bhp) in race trim. By 1983, it was essential to have a turbo engine to compete seriously.

By the mid-1980s, the chassis into which the turbo engines were installed were universally constructed in carbon fibre rather than aluminium. This followed the lead set by the 1981 McLaren MP4/1 and the Lotus 88, the material giving much improved torsional stiffness as well as better impact protection.

Seconds were being sliced off lap times, but not purely because of the straight-line speeds and acceleration of the turbos. Their enormous power also provided the ability to bear huge amounts of downforce from the wings. The critical point at which more wing ceased to equal better lap times, because the straight-line speed penalty was too great, moved steadily upward.

The turbo era brought huge manufacturer investment into F1,

Above left: Chapman's next baby, the twin-chassis Lotus 88, was deemed too innovative. He never got over it being banned.

Above: *As Chico Serra spins his Fittipaldi, John Watson relishes the strength and performance of his carbon-fibre chassised McLaren MP4/1.*

inspired by Renault's success. This time around, it tended to be in partnership with the small specialist teams, and it made for exponentially bigger budgets for research, investment in wind tunnels and other technology, which continues to this day, long after the turbo was outlawed.

AERODYNAMICS AGAIN

Towards the end of the turbo days – boost was progressively limited until a 3.5-litre normally aspirated formula took over completely in 1989 – teams such as Williams and Benetton were clawing back some of the ground effect denied them since the 1983 flat-bottom regulation.

The 1986 Williams FW11 featured 'diffusers' at the rear, beneath the gearbox and behind the rear axle line. An upswept panel, and the individual channels it contained, accelerated the air beneath it to create venturis and, hence, aerodynamic grip. Then Benetton adapted this, combining it with a high nose that was shaped to make the front wing very efficient, and to accentuate and enhance the under-car airflow. This allowed the diffuser to work more effectively.

Tyrrell's 1990 019 model fed air beneath its sharply upturned nose to a raised middle section (a plate beneath this kept it within the flat-

floor regs) with leading 'splitters' – edges that passed the air to each side of the mid-section, thereby creating a low-pressure area and extra grip.

THE RISE OF 'IT'

Such effects were sensitive to the car's pitch and roll, so active suspension – tried as long ago as 1982 by Lotus and later Williams – which eliminated such characteristics, became highly desirable and was

Opposite top: Turbocharged 1987 Williams FW11B boasted more than 1200bhp in qualifying trim.

Opposite left: Anhedral nose of 1990 Tyrrell heralded a whole new look for F1 cars.

Above: 1992 Williams FW14B was swoopy and devastatingly effective with its active suspension.

much more beneficial than first time around. Microprocessor controlled hydraulic pumps raised and lowered the wheels as necessary, reacting to input from sensors so quickly that weight distribution was optimized at all times. Thus equipped, the 1992 Williams FW14B was virtually unbeatable, as even the best-funded rivals took a season to develop their own similar suspensions.

Traction control, pre-programmed gear changing, and even power steering and anti-lock braking were all either in use or being developed by 1993. Together with active ride and pits-to-car telemetry, they were banned for 1994.

A reduction in tyre size came about in mid-1994 as a reaction to the deaths of Ayrton Senna and Roland Ratzenberger at Imola that year. For

1998, in an ongoing programme to curb speeds, front and rear track dimensions have been reduced, while grooved tyres will replace the slicks that have been universal since the early 1970s.

It can be appreciated, therefore, that the F1 car we have today is a very different beast from that which would have evolved without the constant legislative reaction to design ingenuity. Left to its own devices, F1 probably would have given us a car with enclosed bodywork, retracting wings, active ride and a sliding-skirt, ground-effect chassis. It would have had turbo power – possibly transmitted by four small rear wheels – with traction control, fully automatic pre-programmed gear changing and anti-lock braking.

CHAPTER **15**

Horses for Courses
THE QUEST FOR POWER

In the early days racing car performance was traditionally a component of engine power. When cars slid around on narrow tyres their horsepower was everything. Now handling and grip are at least as important, but sheer grunt remains important. How did today's super-efficient, high-output power units evolve?

In the final season of Grand Prix racing before World War Two, cars raced with engines that developed around 559kW (750bhp). In 1997, the last year in which they could race with slick tyres, their engines also produced about 559kW.

Statistically, that may seem to suggest that not much progress had been made in the search for horsepower during the intervening six decades, but as is the case with so many aspects of F1, appearances can be extremely deceptive. Over the years, speeds have always risen, and there are very good reasons why today's engines have developed as they have.

A NEW FORMULA
In February 1946, the Paris-based Fédération Internationale de l'Automobile (FIA) officially superseded the old Association Internationale des Automobile Clubs Reconnus (AIACR) as the governing body of motor racing, delegating the

government of the sport to its subsidiary, the Commission Sportive Internationale (CSI). It faced an urgent task in the programme to reorganize the sport after the war, and this was to establish a new formula for Grand Prix racing. It had to take into account the effect of the war and the state of several national economies, and effectively what the FIA opted for was the formula that would have been introduced for 1940 had the war not intervened.

Normally aspirated engines of 4.5 litres had been permitted under the regulations of 1938 and 1939, but these had not been able to get anywhere close to the supercharged 3-litre cars, so the FIA knew that an equivalency formula with a ratio between supercharged and unsupercharged engines of 1:1.5 did not work. Instead, it chose a ratio of 1:3, so that its new formula would cater for cars with 1.5-litre supercharged engines or 4.5-litre normally aspirated power units.

BLOWN ENGINES
To begin with, the yardstick was Alfa Romeo's pre-war straight-eight supercharged 1.5, which started off with 198kW (265bhp) at 7500rpm in 1947, but eventually was persuaded to develop slightly more than 283kW (380bhp) on high boost at 8500rpm by the time the company returned in 1950 from its 1949 sabbatical. This was more than sufficient to see off the Talbot Lagos with their slow-revving 4.5-litre six-cylinder engines. These were frugal cars that developed 186kW (250bhp), but they were heavy, so their power-to-weight ratio was far inferior to the Alfa's. Maserati experimented with twin superchargers, its 4 CLT/48 developing some 179kW (240bhp) at 7000rpm. Then Ferrari developed its own 1.5-litre V12 for 1949, which was designed by Gioachino Colombo, but it was late appearing. It broke new ground, however, since it was the first Grand Prix engine since the war that featured over-square dimensions: its

bore (55mm) was larger than its stroke (52.5mm). Unusual for its time, this soon became *de rigueur* for all high-speed engines as the designers sought to maximize revs per minute. Initially, though, this avant-garde design developed only 172kW (230bhp) at 7000rpm, but development would take it to 224kW (300bhp) at 7500rpm.

GREAT IN THEORY, HORRIBLE IN PRACTICE

Of significant interest, although the project eventually proved stillborn when Cisitalia went bankrupt, was the Porsche-designed Cisitalia. This had a twin-supercharged flat-12 power unit

with heavily over-square dimensions of 56x51mm that was intended to run at the unheard of speed of 12,000rpm, at which engineers spoke confidently of around 373kW (500bhp).

The hideously complex BRM V16 also promised similarly prodigious power. This was the product of a liaison between designers Peter Berthon and Eric Richter, and numerous British engineering companies. The multi-cylinder engine also had over-square dimensions (49.53x48.26mm) for its 1.5-litre capacity, and its two banks of eight cylinders were aligned at 135 degrees.

Again, very high engine speeds – up to 12,000rpm – were envisaged, and with a Rolls-Royce two-stage centrifugal supercharger operating at 4.8 bar (70lb/sq. in), power in the order of 336–373kW (450–500bhp) was expected. Both car and engine were extremely late in appearing, but to its credit the V16 produced more than 298kW (400bhp) right from its initial bench tests.

Below: BRM's V16 aspired to put Britain on the FI map, but was too complicated to succeed in time. It produced the power it was supposed to, but by then FI had moved on and the engine lost any of the advantage it would have had.

Normal Aspirations

While these activities were going on, however, Enzo Ferrari was initiating the step that would ring the death knell for blown engines. Unhappy with Colombo's 1.5-litre V12, he had commissioned Aurelio Lampredi to create a 60-degree 4.5-litre normally aspirated V12, with a bore and stroke of 80x74.5mm. By the end of 1950, this was the equal of the Alfa 159 engine, producing 283kW (380bhp) at 7500rpm.

While Alfa and Ferrari could rely on similar horsepower by 1951, their engines' fuel economy was to prove crucial. Stretched to its limit, the Alfa ran only 0.5km for every litre (1.5mpg) of fuel it consumed, for much of that was used not only to develop its final 287kW (385bhp), but also to cool internal components. For an elderly unit that still retained its original under-square dimensions of 58x70mm, this was very respectable, but the Ferrari V12 was a much more advanced power unit and, as well as being reliable, it was also much less thirsty. The tide had begun to turn.

Meanwhile, the BRM duly appeared in sporadic races, developing well over 336kW (450bhp) and eventually getting close to 436kW (585bhp), but by then it had missed the boat. Alfa withdrew after winning a second World Championship in 1951, frightened by Ferrari's writing on the wall. The regulations had been due to be changed that year, although in the absence of any lead from the FIA, most had assumed that they would continue unchanged. Now, however, faced with the collapse of F1 due to a lack of competition, the FIA suddenly downgraded Grand Prix racing to F2 regulations for 1952 and 1953, which meant running 2-litre normally aspirated engines. For 1954, there would be an entirely new formula.

Lampredi had been developing just such a 2-litre F2 unit in tandem with

Above: *1955 Mercedes W196 had almost 300bhp.*

his 4.5 V12, so Ferrari was very nicely placed, and Alberto Ascari went on to clean up the World Championship for the next two seasons. This engine was a neat four-cylinder of 90x78mm, which employed two spark plugs per cylinder to coax out a conservatively estimated 130kW (175bhp) at 7200rpm.

Maserati, meanwhile, created a new twin-overhead-camshaft straight-six engine, courtesy of Ferrari refugee Colombo. At 76.2x72mm, this initially delivered 134kW (180bhp) at 7000rpm, but was developed to 147kW (197bhp) at 8000rpm. The French Gordini company also produced an engine, a 75x75mm evolution of its existing straight-six, which developed 116kW (155bhp) at 6000rpm.

THE SILVER ARROWS

The new F1 of 1954 catered for 2.5-litre normally aspirated engines, or supercharged units of 750cc, and initially most teams simply opted for upgraded versions of their existing 2-litre engines. Maserati's 84x75mm six now produced 194kW (260bhp), while Ferrari's 100x79.5mm four pumped out between 179 and 186kW (240 and 250bhp). At first, these proved the class of the field, but later that year Mercedes-Benz finally returned to F1 after the war-induced ban on German companies competing in international events had been lifted. When the Silver Arrows came back, they brought with them technological advances that would put them in a realm of their own.

The heart of the Mercedes-Benz W196 was its 76x68.8mm straight-eight engine, which featured twin overhead camshafts and two plugs per cylinder. The power take-off was positioned at the centre of the crankshaft, effectively splitting the engine into two blocks of four and preventing the torsional problems normally associated with such a long crankshaft. The camshafts were also gear-driven, Mercedes' engineers deeming this method more efficient than the time-honoured use of chains.

It was in the valve gear and carburation – traditionally areas that restrict ultimate performance – that the engine really broke new ground, however. The higher an engine revs, the greater the tendency for the springs that hold its valves closed to flutter and reach their peak elasticity. Beyond that point, they can no longer

function properly, and the engine loses efficiency. Mercedes had perfected what it described as its 'desmodromic' valve system which, instead of relying on a spring to close each valve, incorporated a mechanical system to do the job. At a stroke, this alleviated the problem of valve bounce, allowing the engine to rev higher and develop more power without air leakage.

Other engines sucked fuel through carburettors, but Mercedes' engineers had drawn on its wartime aero-engine experience and perfected direct fuel injection. This was more efficient in terms of both power and economy.

The Silver Arrows, with which Juan Manuel Fangio and Stirling Moss would dominate the 1955 season, started with around 194kW (260bhp) at 8500rpm, but were eventually developed to 220kW (295bhp), and hardly anybody ever got near them. But for the disaster at Le Mans that year, when a Mercedes sports car driven by Pierre Levegh scythed into the crowd, killing the veteran French driver and more than 80 spectators, Mercedes would have eliminated the architectural shortcomings of its engine for 1956 by introducing a V8 version. But the Le Mans tragedy obliged the Stuttgart manufacturer to withdraw, and the sport lost the first major innovator of the 1950s.

At this point, the only car that had a design approaching the Mercedes for originality was Vittorio Jano's Lancia D50, which was the first ever to use the engine as a stressed part of the chassis, thus saving weight by doing away with the need for a separate supporting structure. It would not be until the BRM P83 of 1966 and the Lotus 49 of 1967 that anyone else followed this route which, today, is taken completely for granted.

Jano's Lancia featured a 73.6x73.1mm V8 with twin cams per bank of cylinders and four twin-choke carburettors, which initially conferred a similar power output of 194kW (260bhp) at 7000rpm, but sadly the car was never fully developed, even when the design rights eventually passed to Ferrari for 1956.

A British Contender

By the middle of the 1950s, another significant engine had emerged: Vanwall's Norton-based big four. Industrialist Tony Vandervell had been impressed by Norton's single-cylinder engine, which dominated motor cycle racing, and envisaged a four-cylinder version as the basis of an F1 engine. In collaboration with Norton engineers, he had the bike engine multiplied by four and, using a Rolls-Royce crankcase and crankshaft of known strength and reliability, created the engine that was to push Britain to the forefront of Grand Prix racing.

In its early guise, the Vanwall engine ran as a 2-litre, but by 1956 it was a full 2.5 litres based on dimensions of

96x86mm. With Bosch fuel injection, initially it developed a significant 209kW (280bhp) at 7500rpm which, in conjunction with very slippery aerodynamic bodywork and disc brakes, made it a serious threat.

For 1958, the FIA ruled that F1 cars should use normal high-octane pump fuel, rather than the exotic mixes of aviation fuel (Avgas) and additives that had been particularly beneficial to the teams that ran big four-cylinder engines. Maserati produced a 60-degree, 68.5x56mm 2.5-litre V12 in response. Running with twin distributors and high-tension coils to feed its 24 spark plugs, it happily produced 228kW (306bhp) at 10,000rpm on pump fuel, but suffered a weight penalty.

Initially power outputs for the four-cylinder brigade fell, although Ferrari's V8s and later V6s were also happy on the new fuel. Eventually, however, Vanwall regained 209kW (280bhp) from its engine, boosted that to 213kW (285bhp), and had the satisfaction of winning the inaugural

Constructors' World Championship despite the upheaval.

A New Way Forward

Before long, however, the Ferrari-induced belief that ultimate horsepower was the arbiter of speed was to be rudely shattered when the 179kW (240bhp) Coopers, with their rear mounted four-cylinder Climax engines, suddenly turned the tables on the front-engined brigade and pointed a new way forward. In the 1950s, more often than not sheer power had been the deciding factor, but by the end of the decade the emphasis had changed: from now on, the driveability of the car and engine package – based on the flexibility of the engine's power

Right: *Stuart Lewis-Evans's Vanwall illustrates how its aerodynamic bodyshell broke fresh ground, Dutch GP 1958.*

Below: *The hugely innovative Cooper Climax shattered the received wisdom for racing cars, although it would take many, including Ferrari, some years to accept it.*

stabilized around 8500rpm in the 2.5-litre days (barring Maserati's air-pumping V12), now they were back on the increase, with the new-for-1962 V8s from Climax and BRM reaching 9000 and 10,000rpm respectively, Ferrari nudging 10,500rpm with its best units, and Porsche claiming nearly 10,000rpm from its flat-8. Later, when Honda came on to the scene in 1964 with its transversely mounted V12, the figure would start at 11,000rpm and, in common with Ferrari's new flat-12, reach 12,000rpm by the end of the formula. By then, power would have risen to 168kW (225bhp) from the best Climaxes, the Ferrari, the BRM and the Honda.

THE RETURN TO POWER

The Vanwall can be considered representative of the best engines of the 1950s, and it produced 85kW (114bhp) per litre. Now the 1.5-litre units were creating 112kW (150bhp) per litre. As the formula changed again for 1966, to permit normally aspirated units of 3 litres and supercharged engines up to 1.5 litres, it was hailed as the return to power.

and torque curves, and the handling of the chassis – would assume far greater importance in the overall equation.

When the regulations finally changed for the 1961 season – and the British teams, which had refused to believe back in 1958 that they would change, had finally come to their senses – F1 cars could have either 1.5-litre normally aspirated engines or blown 750s. F1 was about to enter the first decade in which the supercharger would be defunct.

If any period proved the point about horsepower in relation to handling, it was the early 1960s, for although the 1.5-litre engines produced far less power than their litre-larger brethren, the lap times soon became far better than they had been under the old regulations. As has been proved so often in F1,

absolutely nothing can stand in the way of progress.

Ferrari got off the grid fastest for 1961, producing Carlo Chiti's flat-12 engine, which boasted between 134 and 142kW (180 and 190bhp) and came in 65- or 120-degree guise. And whereas engine revolutions had largely

Left, above and right: Chapman's highly innovative Lotus 25 with its cigar-tube monocoque chassis completely re-wrote the rule book in 1962, and obliged all of his rivals to reconsider their concepts overnight.

And 112kW (150bhp) was expected to be the norm. Things didn't quite work out that way initially, but eventually they would exceed that by a hitherto undreamed of margin.

The 3-litre FI was beginning to settle in by June 1967, but 112kW (150bhp) per litre was still a dream, apparently beyond the capabilities of engine designers at the time. However, there was no shortage of diversity as teams sought 298kW (400bhp) with varying levels of elegance and success. Ferrari stayed true to its multi-cylinder traditions with a V12, which was dominated by exhausts that nestled within the vee like a bunch of white snakes. Maserati reworked its old sports car engine (first seen in FI guise as a 2.5 way back in 1957) for Cooper, while Dan Gurney's newly formed Eagle team had Harry Weslake's bespoke V12, which was both elegant and powerful, but which ultimately would suffer from production quality problems associated with sheer lack of funding. Honda produced a hefty V12 with

Above: Weslake V12 of 1966 was a beautiful piece of automotive architecture.

Right: Honda's V12 was a less elegant solution to the same problem.

roller bearings, power take-off in the middle of the crank à la Mercedes W196, and a Ferrari-like snakepit exhaust. It weighed 45kg (100lb) more than anything else. Jack Brabham had reasoned impeccably during the previous season that a reliable lightweight engine in a similar sort of car would prove potent early in the formula. He had duly won the 1966 World Championship, marking the only time anyone would achieve such merit in a car bearing their own name, and he was continuing to make hay with the same Repco V8 philosophy as the much vaunted V12

sun shone weakly. At BRM, there was no sun, however, just dark clouds, for the team had taken the amazing gamble of flattening out the vee angle of its very successful V8 and gearing one atop the other, to form an H16.

ENTER THE COSWORTH DFV

As the teams prepared for the Dutch GP that year, the Ferrari was probably developing 283kW (380bhp), the Eagle-Weslake 291kW (390bhp), the Honda a claimed 313kW (420bhp), the Cooper-Maserati a feeble 268kW (360bhp), the BRM up to 291kW (390bhp) – but most of it unreliable – and the Brabham-Repco 268kW (360bhp). And then came the car that would change everything: the Ford Cosworth DFV powered Lotus 49.

The DFV was a simple, straightforward and highly compact 90-degree V8, which was the brainchild of Keith Duckworth. Light in weight and small, it produced a genuine 298kW (400bhp) at 9000rpm, although in its original form it was a cammy beast that demanded skill of the Jim Clark or Graham Hill calibre. It took pole position for the race courtesy of Hill, while Clark used it to win with ease. Hill had said to Cosworth's engineers right from the

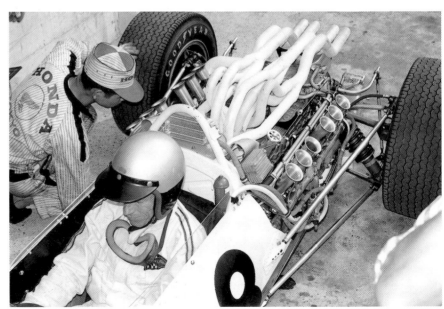

Above: *Chapman
used the brilliant
Cosworth DFV engine
as a stressed chassis
member in his
parameter-redefining
Lotus 49 in 1967.*

Left: *Jim Clark proved
just how good a design
the 49 was by
dominating the Dutch
GP, first time out.*

start, 'That engine of yours doesn't half have some poke.' And according to Ford's head of public affairs, Walter Hayes, who bankrolled the whole thing for £100,000, 'Jimmy always said it was actually like having two engines, one that cut in after the other.' But boy, did it work.

Ken Tyrrell watched the DFV's first race and immediately laid down a deposit to buy them for his own forthcoming F1 team for 1968, even though the units were not for sale at that time. And although his assertion that 'Everything else was rubbish!' may have been harsh, there was a grain of truth in the comment. The Cosworth DFV undoubtedly rewrote the rule book, as did the car it was installed in. Many – with the notable exception of Jack Brabham – had tended to lose sight of the need to minimize weight. Certainly the BRM, the Cooper-Maserati and the Honda, even the 1966 Ferrari to some extent, were guilty on that score.

Above: *Ken Tyrrell built his F1 team on the back of the Cosworth DFV engine.*

Below: *Stewart's 1969 Tyrrell-run Matra MS80 broke fresh ground with its rubber fuel tanks which were housed in its bulbous flanks.*

The Cosworth DFV was a triumph of design that in one imperious stroke redefined F1's parameters and bequeathed a dramatic legacy to British motor sport. All of a sudden, aspiring owners, such as Tyrrell, could put an F1 team together around an engine, which was not just the best, but which, crucially, was available commercially to anyone. It took the situation that had existed in the 1.5-litre formula with Coventry Climax a big step forward, and it paved the way for teams such as Williams to gain their first footholds on the F1 mountain.

'I think we should recognize it as a kind of foundation point in our life when we, in a sense, established this country in an international fashion, not a silly flag-waving fashion, as the place where you go to have motor racing cars and engines made,' Hayes said.

Between that stunning début in 1967 and its effective demise as a world-class front-running power unit in 1983, the Cosworth DFV achieved

attained. There was another big step to come, however, as in 1977 F1 stood on the threshold of a completely new explosion in power output.

When the 3-litre formula had been inaugurated, most minds were on the magic figure of 336kW (450bhp) and the possibility that it would require four-wheel drive to harness such power. And until 1976, when Regie Renault began to investigate returning to Grand Prix racing for the first time since the turn of the century, nobody had given the slightest thought to the clause in the rules that permitted supercharged engines of up to 1.5 litres. But Renault was seeking a boost for its flagging market image and had begun boosting the power of its road cars with add-on turbochargers, which had become all the rage, and was campaigning a turbo sports car in endurance races, particularly Le Mans. Now it sought to exploit the optional configuration, and the first fruits of its thinking were seen at the British GP in 1977.

155 victories and 22 World Championships. Arguably, it stands as the greatest race engine in history.

In those years between 1967 and 1983, the DFV was developed continuously to keep pace with its rivals. Initially the most serious of these was the new-for-1970 Ferrari flat-12, which produced 343kW (460bhp) at 11,500rpm, at a time when the DFV had moved up to 336kW (450bhp) at 10,000rpm. But BRM's V12 enjoyed its days in the sun, thanks to similar power, and Matra's V12 was in the same ballpark, even though it would not win a Grand Prix until 1977.

AND NOW FOR TURBOS . . .

During the mid-1970s, light weight and usable power were the watchwords. Double overhead camshafts per cylinder bank, transistorized ignition and four valves per cylinder had all become established ingredients in the recipe as 112kW (150bhp) per litre was

Above and below: Eight years later after Tyrrell's hugely successful Matra, a new phase arrived in the shape of Renault's 1.5-litre turbo.

The first Renault FI car had been developed by Renault Gordini and used a 90-degree 86x42.8mm version of the 2-litre sports car V6. The exhaust-driven turbocharger was claimed to force 373kW (500bhp) out of the engine at 11,000rpm. Even though the car did not fare well, there were ominous signs for those members of the normally aspirated brigade who chose to seek them out, for the Renault was the fastest car on the quickest parts of the circuit. It had the power; the problem was that the lag between the driver opening the throttle and the turbocharger spooling up fast enough to respond, proved hurtful when nothing less than full throttle was called for. For many years, this throttle 'lag' would prove a major handicap to such engines.

In its first season, the Renault turbo was seen as something of a joke, but by 1979 it had won its first race. And after a dismal 1980 season with its outclassed flat-12, Ferrari began to develop a similar turbo engine for 1981. BMW, too, was going FI with an engine that employed standard used road car cylinder blocks: the better aged the block, the less stressed it was when turned into an FI engine. Soon, everyone would need a turbo.

By 1983, turbo engines were producing 485kW (650bhp) – or a stunning 321kW (430bhp) per litre. Compare that with the Alfa 159's 189kW (253bhp) per litre and you gain a sound definition of the technological progress achieved in the crucible of FI. And that was only the beginning.

Valves Increase Revs

Along the way, Renault's gifted designer, Bernard Dudot, took a leaf from the Mercedes-Benz book when he incorporated a form of desmodromic valve actuation in the Renault V6. However, whereas the German manufacturer's system had been mechanical, the cunning Dudot used engine-generated air pressure to open and close the valves. Thus this pneumatic system revived a forgotten solution and allowed revs to rise once more. Today, no self-respecting FI engine would be seen without a similar system.

Managing Engines

As turbo technology developed, it did so hand in hand with engine management systems. Relying more and more heavily on computer technology, such systems became highly developed as engineers sought precise control of ignition and valve timing, and fuel injection. As engine management became more efficient, power soared. By 1986, the FIA was seeking ways of reducing the burgeoning power of the turbos, and initially it restricted cars to 195 litres (43 gallons) of fuel for a race, instead of the 220 litres (48 gallons) they had been allowed in 1985. But for qualifying, BMW's four-cylinder and Renault's V6 were at their peaks, each pumping out a phenomenal 1007kW (1350bhp) on 4-bar boost, or more than 60lb/sq. in. That's 671kW (900bhp) per litre. Of course, they could not race at such levels, but practice sessions provided truly awesome spectacles.

And that was not the full story, for more than once Renault's V6 went off the dial of the test dynamometer at Viry-Chatillon, which read up to 1044kW (1400bhp).

It had to end, of course, and in 1987 the FIA made pop-off valves mandatory. These were designed to release pressure if the boost

Opposite left: Renault's V6, seen here in its 1983 installation in Lotus's 93T, produced more than 1400bhp by 1986.

Top: Honda's V6 was not quite as powerful, nor was its power delivery as smooth, but by the mid- to late 1980s it was the engine to beat.

Left: McLaren's TAG-funded, Porsche-built V6 was not as powerful in qualifying form as its rivals but possessed great race power and economy and was good for titles in 1984, 1985 and 1986.

exceeded 4 bar (60lb/sq. in), but initially they were unreliable and often opened sooner than that, while there were also suspicions that some engineers had found a legal way to outsmart the valve and prevent it from opening below 4.3 bar (63lb/sq. in).

The FIA took two further steps to curtail turbo power. For 1988, pop-off valves limited boost to 2.5 bar (36lb/sq. in), restricting turbo horsepower to between 470 and 522kW (630 and 700bhp), but this was still far in excess of the normally aspirated 3.5-litre Ford DFV derivative, which struggled to reach 447kW (600bhp), and the turbos continued to reign. However, that was about to change, for the FIA's second step was to ban turbos altogether from 1989, when F1 would

be for normally aspirated cars of 3.5 litres only. Supercharged F1 cars were dead.

Down went the power figures yet again with the new breed of cars, back towards 485kW (650bhp), perhaps a wee bit less to begin with. But the developments in computer control for the engine management systems and throttle systems continued, in conjunction with variable-length injection trumpets on the Honda and Ferrari V12s to enhance torque at the bottom end of the curve, always the failing of the multi-cylinder engine. And gradually the power began to ease back up again, so that by 1990 Honda's V12 was nudging 522kW (700bhp), and Renault's new-for-1989 V10 was running close behind.

TOWARD THE NEW MILLENNIUM
By 1992, when Williams-Renault and Nigel Mansell ran away and hid, it was clear that the V10 was the new yardstick, the optimum packaging solution. Ford's HB V8 lacked sheer power, even if it had the eight's traditionally strong torque, while the Ferrari and Honda V12s were too long and too thirsty.

By 1994, when the compact Ford Zetec R V8 was strong enough to take Michael Schumacher and Benetton to a controversial world title, the Ferrari V12 was the strongest of them all, producing close to 597kW (800bhp) from exotic fuel mixes that included toluene, one of

the constituents of tri-nitro toluene, or TNT. But that, too, was the season in which Roland Ratzenberger and Ayrton Senna were killed at Imola, and Karl Wendlinger left in a coma after a crash at Monaco. It was the year when the FIA felt the opprobrium of national governments and reacted quickly to ward off potential sanctions. By the end of the year, the 3.5s were dead, replaced by 3-litre engines again, which had to run on pump fuel.

Once more, the power levels receded, only to rise with the inevitable application of engineering expertise and technology. Management systems became craftier still; metallurgy was always improving. Designers became ever more adventurous as they sought to save weight and boost power. From 470kW (630bhp), the engines climbed again to over 522kW (700bhp) by 1997, and through that season the Mercedes-Benz Ilmor-designed V10 was thought to produce

more than 559kW (750bhp). Though, because by now details such as the bore and stroke measurements, power and torque levels, revs and other information, once taken for granted, had become top secret. This was the new F1, a minefield of secrets and deceptions. Nearly a decade before, Bernard Dudot had not initially been believed when he described a means of determining a rival's likely power: 'You make a tape recording of your own engine at maximum speed, say past the pits. Then you get a laboratory to work out the frequency to give yourself a datum. Then you record your rivals' engines in similar mode, work out the frequencies, compare them, and you have your answer.'

As F1 approached the Millennium, and the official half-century of the World Championship, it suddenly became all too easy to believe such cloak-and-dagger industrial espionage as the horsepower war showed no sign of abating.

Opposite top: Ford's championship-winning Zetec-R V8 of 1994 lacked outright power but was a very compact package.

Opposite bottom: Mercedes' Ilmor-designed V10 was the class of the field by late 1997, and dominated early in 1998.

Right: The 1997 Renault engine, which won the championship for Jacques Villeneuve and Williams.

THE WEST MCLAREN MERCEDES MP/13

The class car of the early part of the 1998 season, the West McLaren Mercedes MP/13 represented a major achievement for the team. Presented with grooved tyres, the designers at McLaren responded with aerodynamic modifications and a new braking technology to beat the rest.

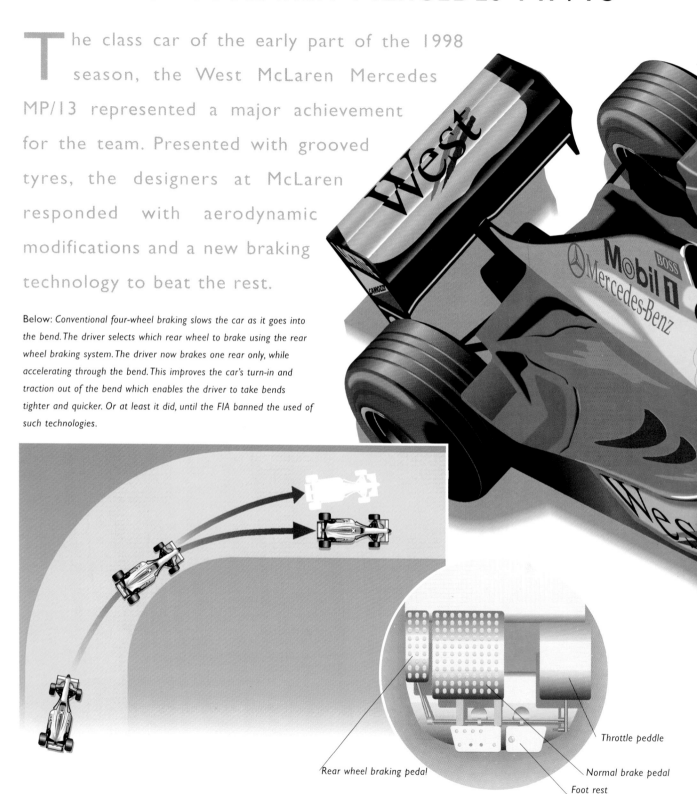

Below: *Conventional four-wheel braking slows the car as it goes into the bend. The driver selects which rear wheel to brake using the rear wheel braking system. The driver now brakes one rear only, while accelerating through the bend. This improves the car's turn-in and traction out of the bend which enables the driver to take bends tighter and quicker. Or at least it did, until the FIA banned the used of such technologies.*

Throttle peddle

Normal brake pedal

Foot rest

Rear wheel braking pedal

Right: *It was widely reported at the time that the new McLaren technology used an adaptation of the pedal lay-out in the cockpit (shown), but others have argued, equally plausibly, that the system was operated from the steering wheel. However the system was controlled by the driver one thing is certain, as with all such innovations it worked too well for the FIA to ignore it.*

Front wing: *The shape of the front wing is designed, not only to maximize downforce, but also to direct airflow towards the rear of the car via inner and outer wing endplates.*

Barge board: *Like the wing endplates, the barge boards behind the front suspension are designed to smooth airflow towards the back of the car, enhancing efficiency and reducing drag.*

Barge Board

Splitter

Air

FI

Front wing: *The shape of the front wing is designed, not only to maximize downforce, but also to direct airflow towards the rear of the car via inner and outer wing endplates.*

Barge board: *Like the wing endplates, the barge boards behind the front suspension are designed to smooth airflow towards the back of the car, enhancing efficiency and reducing drag.*

Barge Board

Splitter

Air

BUSINESS

CHAPTER **16**

Commercial Imperatives
Sport, or a Marketing Excercise?

Without the necessary funding, no motor racing team can survive, let alone maintain itself at a sufficiently competitive pitch to win consistently. No bucks, no Buck Rogers, as the saying goes. Today the multi-coloured racing car is a familiar sight, and advertising at the heart of the action is the norm. But it was not always the case!

Motor racing has never been cheap, and more often than not the team with the biggest – or almost the biggest – budget has been able to wield the biggest stick. There have been exceptional 'giant killing' acts, of course, but generally one can say with a fairly high degree of accuracy that it takes money to win.

Looking back from the perspective of the 1990s, it is frequently difficult to appreciate that, in days gone by, drivers raced because they loved it, and not because strong financial inducements helped to keep them focused. In the 1950s, the leading stars received reasonable rewards, but even at its highest level, motor racing was fundamentally still a sport. It is perhaps ironic that, at a time when it was at its most dangerous, its proponents received the least for their efforts.

Two stories demonstrate the disparity between the old days and today. One concerns Cliff Allison, the promising British driver who was

Opposite: Back in the 1950s the advertising was round the edges of the track rather than at the centre of the action.

Right: Right up until the early 1960s the predominant colour of F1 cars was the lacklustre British Racing Green.

Below: Having worked through Gold Leaf colours, Colin Chapman painted his cars in John Player black and gold from 1972.

Below: The F1 car of 1997 betrayed its funding with a garish livery that reflected the input of a number of sponsors. This is World Champion Jacques Villeneuve's Rothmans Williams-Renault.

invited to test for Ferrari in 1959. Not for him the private jet or club class scheduled flight. He lived in Brough, in Cumbria, and went to Modena by a circuitous route: 'I went by car from home to Darlington, then by train to London, coach to Heathrow, Heathrow to Malpensa, then Malpensa to the Grande Stazione Centrale and off to Modena.' On one occasion, he got there, only to be told that his car wasn't ready: 'They said thanks for coming, you can go home now!'

The other story is about Stirling Moss, arguably one of the top three greatest drivers of all time, and the man who should have won several World Championships. He did win 16 of his 66 Grands Prix. In 1961, the season in which he trounced the markedly more powerful Ferrari V6s with his Rob Walker Lotus-Climax at both Monaco and the Nürburgring, he earned £32,750. This was, of course, reasonable money for the time, but by today's standards it places him a long way behind. The writer Richard Williams once expressed the disparity most effectively in his book *Racers* by measuring drivers' remuneration in terms of the number of Rolls-Royces they could have purchased in their best seasons, an automotive means of tracing inflation. In 1961, Moss could have purchased six; in 1976, World Champion James Hunt could have treated himself to seven; by 1996, Michael Schumacher could have spoiled himself with no fewer than 170.

In 1993, his last season, Ayrton Senna received $1,000,000 for every race, regardless of whether he won or retired on the first lap. Schumacher's Ferrari deal, three years

Opposite right: By the mid-1970s even the Ferraris betrayed some allegiance to sponsors.

Below: In contrast to modern F1 cars, the Lotus 49B which was the first to carry a sponsor's colours – those of Gold Leaf – looks almost modest.

later, was said to be worth £1,000,000 per race, with sufficient endorsements to raise the overall figure to more than £25,000,000 annually.

But what brought about such dramatic change between the eras?

Branding the Racing Car

The pivotal moment came in late 1967 when the RAC, which controlled British motor sport, and the FIA in France relaxed their previously strict rules on advertising on racing cars. Until then, the RAC allowed only tightly regulated stickers to be placed on cars, and these were policed carefully by race stewards to ensure that nobody transgressed the prescribed sizing.

In the 1950s, racing cars in Europe had been unadorned, and teams were required to run them in traditional

national colours – British Racing Green, Italian red, French blue, German silver. But in America, sponsorship had been a factor right from the days when daredevil barnstormer Barney Oldfield drove a Christie emblazoned with the message, 'My only life insurance is Firestone tyres'. Cars at Indianapolis for the 500-mile (805km) classic had long eschewed the names of their manufacturers in favour of title allegiance to a sponsor, hence exotic sounding names such as the Belond Special, the Bowes Seal Fast Special, the Fageol Twin Coach Special and the American Red Ball Special.

By the 1960s, commercial enterprises, such as finance companies Bowmaker and UDT-Laystall, were backing F1 teams that bore their names, but there was very

little visible branding on the cars, which would, of course, be at the centre of the action. Otherwise financial support came from the trade, from the tyre and oil companies such as Dunlop, Englebert, Shell and BP. Even then, racing was expensive, and there was increasing pressure on the governing bodies, from those who actually had to fund it all, for the rules to be relaxed. Finally they were, for the 1968 season, and at last the door was open for the commercial sponsorship of motor racing.

COMMERCIAL ENTERPRISES

Initially commercial sponsorship meant little more than a change of hue and some different, more long-winded names, but gradually the sport began

to evolve in the 1970s, when the first corporate motor homes began to arrive in the paddock, along with the first wave of marketing men. Instead of recognising a sport with traditions and a heritage, they saw only a new weapon in their marketing armoury, a new sales tool to be exploited. It was inevitable that the character of F1 should begin slowly to change.

With sponsorship came a fresh demand for television coverage of the races. John Hogan is vice president of marketing for the Philip Morris Group and the man tasked, since 1974, with making the Marlboro sponsorship work. As he points out, 'Way back in the early 1970s, when we were a fairly small company and Formula One was seen as a promotional opportunity, there were only ten or eleven Grands

Prix, and it was fairly small beer.' The British Grand Prix, Le Mans and Monaco tended to be the only real television staples.

In 1971, however, Bernie Ecclestone took over the Brabham team and the running of FOCA, the teams' association. Gradually, as Ecclestone's own unique brand of marketing developed, the sport began to grow. Expectations became higher, just as budget requirements grew annually. But at the same time, Ecclestone's exploits made his fellow team owners wealthier. And he began not only to promote races, but also to organize for them to be televized, selling the rights world-wide. By the 1980s, it was not just one or two races that were broadcast, but all 16. The sponsors lapped it up.

MARKETING MACHINES

Early in the 1970s, Marlboro had only a small niche in Europe, and the red and white house logo had yet to become famous, but under Hogan's guidance the brand rose to become the clear leader in the 1990s. Hogan likes to stress, though, that the success has not been due solely to involvement in F1. Perhaps this is just because he is conscious of the tightrope tobacco sponsors walk these days and does not want to spell out racing's true value to Marlboro. Perhaps not.

'I agree the parallel is there, but there are far too many other contributory factors to say that there is any one thing. It's just part of the mix, if you like, that has contributed to the size and the shape of the company now.' Nevertheless motor racing is a powerful marketing tool that has been used well, but he counsels, 'The trouble with talking

Above: *Marlboro was never backwards in putting across its message on the McLarens in the 1980s.*

Below: *Nor in identifying itself with event sponsorship. This is John Watson celebrating his 1981 British GP victory.*

about things like that is that it's a bit like talking about the ingredients in a blancmange. If you don't put the sugar in, is it going to taste the same? It goes back to every part of the mix having a role to play, and within that context, yes, it has an important effect.'

Renault Sport's boss, Patrick Faure, once said that if Renault wins rallies, sales can literally go up the next day, but that things are much less clearly defined when a Renault engine wins a Grand Prix. However he had no doubt that in the long term, the overall image enhancement of F1 success was not only crucial, but more important, when it came to ultimate sales.

'I think it provides us, as a company, with something to focus on every second weekend,' says Hogan when asked to quantify the value of Marlboro's F1 activities. 'It's a sort of internal bonding device, if you like, quite a strong one. But you can't quantify direct marketing benefits from winning. I think that's probably correct that you can as far as a car company is concerned, but I think what it does for us is make our brand a bit more well-known.'

Marlboro has long been regarded as an extremely benign sponsor, a sort of corporate father figure. It has never tried to dictate the course of events, although from time to time Philip Morris Group president Walter Thoma has spoken out when he has felt the need. In Monaco, he would often take an annual opportunity to make a point. 'Our concern is that FI essentially must remain a sport,' Hogan says, 'and it shouldn't become like some of the wrestling federations, or anything like that. Or it shouldn't become a junk sport. I think we like to feel that we have played a role in the development of it. Now and then, we see a few signs of things going off

Above: *High earners: Alain Prost and Ayrton Senna commanded massive salaries in the late 1980s.*

Below: *Benetton's initial involvement with Tyrrell eventually led to the clothing company buying the Toleman team.*

the rails, so sometimes we just want to remind everybody that it is a sport, and just like any sport you have good times and bad times. But you have to keep saying that, at the end of the day, it's just a sport.'

Not everyone agrees. Although Ecclestone is a racer at heart, he certainly sees it as a lucrative business and devoted much time in 1997 to his digital television and pay-per-view projects, and his ultimate plan to float FI on the London Stock Exchange.

THE BUSINESS OF RACING?

When Graham Hill won the World Championship in 1968, the first year with Gold Leaf backing, it provided complete endorsement of motor racing as a commercial medium. From that point, a whole new vista opened up far beyond the limited munificence of the tyre and oil companies.

But this all slowly brought about a material change in the perception of the sport's purpose. Was it, indeed, a sport at all any longer? Or, as its entrants grew richer by the year and its sponsors poured in money for purely commercial purposes, had it become little more than a fast moving marketing platform?

Flavio Briatore, who was the chief executive of the Benetton FI team between 1989 and 1997, had his own view: 'Ken Tyrrell, Frank Williams and Ron Dennis, all these people, started in this racing business,' he said. 'I arrived very late, but I like very much this kind of business, and I like very much the people. It is very competitive, very strong and very difficult, because you have always the big challenge. It is a fantastic business.'

With a background in commerce rather than starting as a racer and becoming a businessman, he tended to view things in a different light and spoke more openly about matters his fellows preferred to avoid. He continued, 'Formula One, now, is a big

event. In our structure of the company, we think in the business way, because we are talking about a big organisation, a lot of people working, and we need to pay the salaries and we need to develop the technology. For that you need to set up the marketing side to make sure you have enough finance to do the job. It's not like other sport. To play tennis, you have a racquet and you play tennis. Formula One is much more complex.

'For me, the crucial part is to make sure the team is well financed, because without that it's not going to work and for sure you are going nowhere. Maybe you start the season well, but if you don't develop the car, you arrive at the last Grand Prix and

Left: *One of the architects of Schumacher's Benetton years was the colourful Flavio Briatore.*

Below: *Even Ferraris bore greater and greater allegiance to sponsors come the 1990s.*

the difference is enormous. It costs a lot of money.'

He revealed that Benetton's budget for 1997 was 'about £33,000,000'. McLaren probably spent more, and that is without calculating the contribution of engine supplier Mercedes-Benz. Ferrari's annual budget has long been said to exceed £100,000,000, although its president, Luca di Montezemolo, periodically likes to plead poverty. The need to invest heavily in technology continually drives up the budgets, and F1 operates on the high-water-mark syndrome. As designer Frank Dernie once memorably said, 'The cost of F1 is what you've got. It has nothing to do, whatsoever, with the technical regulations. If you had $150,000,000 and you were racing orange carts, then orange carts would

cost $150,000,000 a year to run.

'And back in 1994, the money that was not spent on active suspension wasn't handed back to the sponsors on the basis of, "Thanks, chaps, we didn't really need this cash." It was spent on something else.'

Frank Williams provided perhaps the most perceptive comment of all when he said, 'This is a highly competitive business that becomes a sport for two hours every other Sunday afternoon during the season.'

Sadly the stakes are simply too high for it to be anything else.

Above: Tartan predominated on Stewart's first contender, which bore subtle allegiance to 'Blue chip' sponsors.

Right: Ferrari president, Luca di Montezemolo.

CHAPTER 17

The Best Sponsorship Liaisons

What sticks in your mind when you watch Grand Prix cars in action? That is the question that the marketing men are asking themselves when they initiate the design of a sponsorship livery. What image will create the most impact, and be the most likely to remain in the customers mind next time he makes a purchase?

Benetton

Where John Player failed in its bid to rename the Lotuses, the Benetton clothing company from Italy managed to do just that – by the simple expedient of buying the Toleman team at the end of the 1985 season!

Benetton's name was first seen in F1 in 1983 with the Tyrrell team, and like all good relationships it was quickly rewarding. Michele Alboreto swept to victory in the US Grand Prix East in Detroit in June, an auspicious occasion that marked the last win for the Ford Cosworth DFV engine.

Benetton switched allegiance to Alfa Romeo for 1984 and '85, without success, and when the opportunity to purchase Toleman arose, Luciano Benetton snapped it up. The renamed team stayed essentially the same, and Gerhard Berger provided the first victory in the Benetton name when he won in Mexico.

When Flavio Briatore assumed control of the team in 1989, he brought a flamboyance of character that was matched by Benetton's avant-garde marketing, a mix of provocative advertising spiced with use of attractive models at races to capture maximum publicity. At one press launch for a new car, the team even resorted to clothing journalists in overalls and letting them throw paint at canvas to reflect the lively new colour scheme for the cars. Benettons have always had outstanding liveries and represent the ultimate combination of brand name with sporting endeavour. Michael Schumacher's World Championship successes in 1994 and 1995 elevated the name even further, helping to sustain the company's rapid global growth.

Top and opposite: From modest beginnings in 1986, Benetton's own identification grew dramatically by the 1990s.

Brabham and Parmalat

The Italian Dairy Association moved into F1 with the Brabham team in 1978 as the replacement for Martini, using the Parmalat name to promote its many products. This was another classic case of an unknown product gradually acquiring world-wide interest, exposure and recognition, for in F1 everyone is curious to know the identity of a company or product behind a logo emblazoned upon a racing car.

Parmalat continued with Brabham until 1985, reaping 17 victories and two Drivers' World Championships with Nelson Piquet. Perhaps even more importantly, its relationship with the sport continues today, as the famous red Parmalat cap continues to adorn Niki Lauda's distinctive head. This is one of the longest lasting personal sponsorship deals in history.

Above: Parmalat's link with Niki Lauda at Brabham was worth 17 race victories.

BRM, McLaren and Yardley

The Yardley male toiletries concern had a staid middle-class, middle-age image when, in March 1970, it stepped into the F1 arena as the title sponsor of the BRM team. Like Gold Leaf with Team Lotus, this would prove a happy and successful alliance that wrought immediate benefits in terms of the appearance of the hitherto drab BRMs. Now, instead of dark British Racing Green with trademark dayglo orange nose bands, the cars were white with brown, ochre and gold 'Y's along their flanks to denote Yardley's involvement.

Jack Oliver drove a Yardley BRM to lead the team's first event in its new colours, the Race of Champions at Brands Hatch, and in June Pedro Rodriguez took his BRM to a fairy-tale victory in the Belgian Grand Prix at Spa Francorchamps. Overnight Yardley's image had become younger and trendier, to the benefit of its

sales. The following season, Rodriguez won the non-championship Spring Cup race at Oulton Park, while Jo Siffert won the Austrian Grand Prix and Peter Gethin the Italian, and later the non-championship race at Brands Hatch.

Ultimately the relationship soured when BRM took on Marlboro, obliging Yardley to switch to McLaren for 1972. Again this was a successful liaison, with Denny Hulme winning the South African Grand Prix, only the second race of the year. In 1973, Hulme won in Sweden, while teammate Peter Revson took the British and Canadian races.

When Marlboro switched to McLaren for 1974, Yardley was less than delighted, and a compromize had to be reached to run a third car in its colours. It withdrew at the end of the season, then reappeared briefly as a sponsor on the Tyrrells in 1984, this time promoting the new Yardley Gold brand.

Above: *Yardley's involvement with BRM brought victory in Austria in 1971 thanks to Jo Siffert's efforts at the wheel.*

Top: *Two years later, Peter Revson won the British GP for Yardley McLaren.*

Jordan and Seven-Up

Colour is a vital part of any racing car livery. When Eddie Jordan's team graduated to F1 for the 1991 season, it did so with an attractive car, the sleek lines and Irish background of which were perfectly complemented by its two-tone emerald green paintwork.

For once, a title sponsor was not a tobacco company, but the Seven-Up drinks conglomerate, whose logos adorned the car without swamping it. The effect was subtle, and besides earning Jordan much kudos during the season, it also pushed the Seven-Up brand very hard in global markets. In addition, the cartoon character Fido Dido, an intrinsic part of the Seven-Up marketing strategy, appeared on the cars and the team trucks, bestowing a light-hearted touch.

The entire package produced one of those liveries that stayed firmly in the memory, even though the alliance did not persist beyond that single season.

Top: Jordan's emerald green proved sharp background for the classic 7Up livery.

Ligier and Gitanes

When Guy Ligier returned to F1 in 1975 as a constructor, having left it in 1967 as a rather unsuccessful driver, his French Blue cars bore clear allegiance to the State-owned SEITA tobacco company and its Gitanes brand. Even during the Talbot period of the early 1980s, when the car manufacturer began supporting Ligier, Gitanes remained a most steadfast sponsor, partly through Ligier's own political connections and adroit handling of an occasionally tricky situation when governments changed.

When Alain Prost assumed control of the team for 1997, taking over

from Benetton's Flavio Briatore, who had acquired a controlling interest in the previous year, Gitanes stayed aboard and enjoyed the benefits of its revival. There haven't been an awful lot of wins, but since Jacques Laffite's breakthrough in Sweden in 1977, Ligier Gitanes crossed nine finish lines ahead of any others. The most recent occasion was the 1996 Monaco Grand Prix courtesy of Olivier Panis, but in 1997 the impressive newcomer Jarno Trulli came close to making it a tenth in the Austrian Grand Prix on the A-1 Ring.

Below: Ligier and Gitanes took French Blue to the fore on several occasions in the 1970s and 1980s.

Lotus and Gold Leaf

Because it was the first big sponsorship seen in Europe, Colin Chapman's deal to turn his Lotus cars into 'mobile cigarette packets' in late January 1968 made a huge impact. Gone overnight were the traditional colours not just of Team Lotus – the dark green with yellow striping – but also of British racing cars in general. Rob Walker's privately owned Coopers and Lotuses had already appeared in his dark blue colours, but that was quite a sombre bypass of British Racing Green and therefore permissible. However the sight of Lotuses painted red and white with gold striping was a shock that rocked some purists on their heels.

The Gold Leaf Team Lotus alliance was immediately successful: Jim Clark won the Wigram Trophy race in the Tasman series in New Zealand and Australia, and went on to win the

Above: *Lotus was the first European team to enjoy commercial sponsorship, and Graham Hill's 49 appeared in the red, white and gold livery at the Brands Hatch Race of Champions in March 1968 and again, here, in 1969.*

Championship. That season, Graham Hill won the World Championship for the team, a feat that Jochen Rindt repeated in 1970. Altogether it yielded 11 Grand Prix wins, and blazed the trail for tobacco sponsorship of F1.

Lotus and JPS

For 1972, Imperial Tobacco wanted to promote a fresh image. Thus Gold Leaf was replaced on the Lotuses with a stunning black livery, pinstriped in gold, to market the John Player Special cigarette brand.

The Lotus 72 was a wedge-shaped car that lent itself particularly well to this remarkable colour scheme, which helped JPS to promote a very strong brand image and loyalty.

Again success was immediate. Emerson Fittipaldi won the 1972 World Championship, and Lotus the Constructors' title. It repeated the latter feat in 1973 when Fittipaldi and team-mate Ronnie Peterson were beaten to the drivers' title by Jackie Stewart. Mario Andretti added Drivers' and Constructors' titles in 1978, when John Player Team Lotus swept the board. The relationship lasted right through until the end of that season, when John Player withdrew, and was restored again when it returned from 1982 until 1986. It stood as one of those that

made maximum impact: visually, mentally and in terms of marketing link. Altogether the black and gold cars won 35 Grands Prix in the hands of Fittipaldi, Peterson, Andretti, Gunnar Nilsson, Elio de Angelis and Ayrton Senna.

The only fly in the ointment served as a reminder to sponsors that there was a limit to how much purists would stand. When the new Lotus 76 was introduced for F1 in 1974, the tobacco company attempted to

delete the Lotus name and type number, simply calling the car the John Player Special Mk III, but the media was having none of that and eventually Imperial Tobacco yielded and dropped the idea. Some things, such as the Lotus name, were held to be beyond price!

Above and below: *The black and gold livery of the John Player Special Lotuses superseded the Gold Leaf colours, and was similarly classic.*

McLaren and Marlboro

Marlboro first came into F1 in 1970, on a tentative basis with the Swiss driver Jo Siffert. At that stage, it was just a subtle exercise, with decals on car and overalls. In 1972, however, Louis Stanley introduced the Philip Morris tobacco brand as the title sponsor of the BRM team, which entered as many as five cars in some races that season. The alliance was difficult and yielded only two victories: the Frenchman Jean-Pierre Beltoise won the Monaco Grand Prix in May 1972 in torrential rain, and later that year he won a non-championship F1 race at Brands Hatch. The partnership lasted only until the end of 1973, but by then Marlboro's red and white logo was already a well-established marketing image.

For 1974, Marlboro switched to the McLaren team, with immediate result. Denny Hulme won the team's first race, in Argentina. Then, as he had done for Lotus, Emerson Fittipaldi delivered the World Championship in the first year of the alliance. James Hunt did the same two years later.

Marlboro proved an understanding and benign sponsor, and it was instrumental in bringing about the merger between the ailing Team McLaren and Ron Dennis' Project Four team, in 1980, to form McLaren International. This was the team that would prove one of the greatest of the 1980s. Niki Lauda won his third title in a Marlboro McLaren in 1984, while Alain Prost was champion for the next two seasons. In 1988 and 1990, Ayrton Senna was champion, with Prost taking a third title in between. Senna gained his third title in 1991. When Senna left at the end of 1993, McLaren's fortunes waned and, after some poor results, the team and Marlboro finally parted company in 1996, after 23 seasons together. It had been the longest running of all sponsorship relationships and the most successful. In that time, Marlboro McLarens won 95 Grands Prix, including the fabulous 1988 season, when only Senna's collision with a back-marker late in the Italian GP prevented the red and white steamroller from achieving a clean sweep of all 16 races. Even then, Gerhard Berger won for Ferrari, whom Marlboro also supported.

Left: The shape of things to come when tobacco sponsorship is banned? Surtees and Durex, 1976.

Surtees and Durex

If the sailor's head on the Gold Leaf Team Lotus cars gave television moguls apoplexy in 1968, the arrival of The London Rubber Company in motor racing in 1975 did not sit well either. Back in those pre-AIDS days, condoms were under-the-counter products that were not mentioned in polite company.

That year, however, racing driver Richard Scott persuaded the manufacturers of Durex prophylactics to sponsor his activities in Formula 5000, a single-seater category just below F1 level, but with similar power. A year later, buoyed by the experience, Durex succumbed to a proposal by John Surtees, the former motor cycle and F1 World Champion, to back his F1 team.

This was a brilliantly conceived sponsorship that brought the product out into the open and presented it maturely to a broad audience, and it was done with admirable subtlety and style. Advertisements for Durex made much of its F1 involvement, depicting the Surtees racer in its colours with the smart and catchy ad line, 'The Small Family Car'. An excellent example of how marketing can be made to work at its very best.

Opposite: Marlboro and McLaren were synonymous for 23 seasons.

Tyrrell and Elf

Most commercial artists will tell you that the most outstanding livery is a white logo on a dark background. Thus Elf's identification in the days of its liaison with Ken Tyrrell's team stood out brilliantly, the fuel giant's lower-case white logo being highlighted against the cars' dark blue paint. It was simple, and it put the message across perfectly at a time when Elf was expanding its global reach.

In Jackie Stewart, Elf-Acquitaine had the perfect ambassador and spokesman, and the title sponsorship relationship with Ken Tyrrell remained one of the sport's most subtle yet successful, from his team's entry into F1 in 1968 with Matra chassis until he secured backing from First National City Travellers' Checks for 1977. In that span, Matra, March and Tyrrell chassis entered by Tyrrell won 30 Grands Prix and three World Championships in the hands of Stewart, François Cevert and Jody Scheckter.

Below: Dark blue bodywork, big white letters. Tyrrell's livery could scarcely have made a bigger impact as Elf sought to establish itself outside its native France.

STATISTICS 1950–1999

The World Champion Drivers

1950	Giuseppe Farina	(I)
1951	Juan Manuel Fangio	(ARG)
1952	Alberto Ascari	(I)
1953	Alberto Ascari	(I)
1954	Juan Manuel Fangio	(ARG)
1955	Juan Manuel Fangio	(ARG)
1956	Juan Manuel Fangio	(ARG)
1957	Juan Manuel Fangio	(ARG)
1958	Mike Hawthorn	(GB)
1959	Jack Brabham	(AUS)
1960	Jack Brabham	(AUS)
1961	Phil Hill	(US)
1962	Graham Hill	(GB)
1963	Jim Clark	(GB)
1964	John Surtees	(GB)
1965	Jim Clark	(GB)
1966	Jack Brabham	(AUS)
1967	Denny Hulme	(NZ)
1968	Graham Hill	(GB)
1969	Jackie Stewart	(GB)
1970	Jochen Rindt	(A)
1971	Jackie Stewart	(GB)
1972	Emerson Fittipaldi	(BR)
1973	Jackie Stewart	(GB)
1974	Emerson Fittipaldi	(BR)
1975	Niki Lauda	(A)
1976	James Hunt	(GB)
1977	Niki Lauda	(A)
1978	Mario Andretti	(US)
1979	Jody Scheckter	(SA)
1980	Alan Jones	(AUS)
1981	Nelson Piquet	(BR)
1982	Keke Rosberg	(SF)
1983	Nelson Piquet	(BR)
1984	Niki Lauda	(A)
1985	Alain Prost	(F)
1986	Alain Prost	(F)
1987	Nelson Piquet	(BR)
1988	Ayrton Senna	(BR)
1989	Alain Prost	(F)
1990	Ayrton Senna	(BR)
1991	Ayrton Senna	(BR)
1992	Nigel Mansell	(GB)
1993	Alain Prost	(F)
1994	Michael Schumacher	(D)
1995	Michael Schumacher	(D)
1996	Damon Hill	(GB)
1997	Jacques Villeneuve	(CAN)
1998	Mika Hakkinen	(FIN)
1999	Mika Hakkinen	(FIN)

The World Champion Constructors

1958	Vanwall	(GB)
1959	Cooper	(GB)
1960	Cooper	(GB)
1961	Ferrari	(I)
1962	BRM	(GB)
1963	Lotus	(GB)
1964	Ferrari	(I)
1965	Lotus	(GB)
1966	Brabham	(GB)

The World Champion Constructors (cont.)

1967	Brabham	(GB)
1968	Lotus	(GB)
1969	Matra	(F)
1970	Lotus	(GB)
1971	Tyrrell	(GB)
1972	Lotus	(GB)
1973	Lotus	(GB)
1974	McLaren	(GB)
1975	Ferrari	(I)
1976	Ferrari	(I)
1977	Ferrari	(I)
1978	Lotus	(GB)
1979	Ferrari	(I)
1980	Williams	(GB)
1981	Williams	(GB)
1982	Ferrari	(I)
1983	Ferrari	(I)
1984	McLaren	(GB)
1985	McLaren	(GB)
1986	Williams	(GB)
1987	Williams	(GB)
1988	McLaren	(GB)
1989	McLaren	(GB)
1990	McLaren	(GB)
1991	McLaren	(GB)
1992	Williams	(GB)
1993	Williams	(GB)
1994	Williams	(GB)
1995	Benetton	(GB)
1996	Williams	(GB)
1997	Williams	(GB)
1998	McLaren	(GB)
1999	Ferrari	(I)

Greatest number of wins – drivers

1	Alain Prost	(F)	51
2	Ayrton Senna	(BR)	41
3	Michael Schumacher	(D)	35
4	Nigel Mansell	(GB)	31
5	Jackie Stewart	(GB)	27
6	Jim Clark	(GB)	25
	Niki Lauda	(A)	25
8	Juan Manuel Fangio	(ARG)	24
9	Nelson Piquet	(BR)	23
10	Damon Hill	(GB)	22

Greatest number of wins – teams

1	Ferrari	(I)	124
2	McLaren	(GB)	122
3	Williams	(GB)	103
4	Lotus	(GB)	79
5	Brabham	(GB)	35
6	Benetton	(GB)	27
7	Tyrrell	(GB)	23
8	BRM	(GB)	17
9	Cooper	(GB)	16
10	Renault	(F)	15

Greatest number of wins – engines

1	Ford	(GB)	175
2	Ferrari	(I)	125
3	Renault	(F)	95
4	Honda	(J)	75
5	Coventry Climax	(GB)	40
6	Mercedes	(D)	28
7	Porsche	(D)	26
8	BRM	(GB)	18
9	Alfa Romeo	(I)	12
10	Maserati	(I)	11

Greatest number of wins – tyres

1	Goodyear	(US)	361
2	Dunlop	(GB)	83
3	Michelin	(F)	59
4	Firestone	(US)	49
5	Pirelli	(I)	42
6	Bridgestone	(GB)	16
7	Continental	(D)	10
	Englebert	(I)	10

Greatest number of wins per season – drivers

1	Nigel Mansell	(GB)	9	1992
	Michael Schumacher	(D)	9	1995
	Mika Hakkinen	(FIN)	9	1998
4	Ayrton Senna	(BR)	8	1988
	Michael Schumacher	(D)	8	1994
	Damon Hill	(GB)	8	1996
7	Jim Clark	(GB)	7	1963
	Alain Prost	(F)	7	1984 1988 1993
	Ayrton Senna	(BR)	7	1991
	Jacques Villeneuve	(CAN)	7	1997
11	Alberto Ascari	(I)	6	1952
	Juan Manuel Fangio	(BR)	6	1954
	Jim Clark	(GB)	6	1965
	James Hunt	(GB)	6	1976
	Mario Andretti	(US)	6	1978
	Nigel Mansell	(GB)	6	1987
	Ayrton Senna	(BR)	6	1989 1990
	Damon Hill	(GB)	6	1994

Greatest number of wins per season – teams

1	McLaren	(GB)	15	1988
2	McLaren	(GB)	12	1984
	Williams	(GB)	12	1996
4	Benetton	(GB)	11	1995
5	McLaren	(GB)	10	1989
	Williams	(GB)	10	1992 1993
7	Williams	(GB)	9	1986 1987
	McLaren	(GB)	9	1998
9	Lotus	(GB)	8	1978
	McLaren	(GB)	8	1991
	Benetton	(GB)	8	1994
	Williams	(GB)	8	1997

Engines of World Champions – number of titles

1	• Ford (GB)	1968, '69, '70, '71, '72 '73, '74, '76, '78, '80, '81, '82, '94	13
2	• Ferrari (I)	1952, '53, '56, '58, '61, '64, '75, '77, '79,	9
3	• Honda (J)	1987, '88, '89, '90, '91	5
	• Renault (F)	1992, '93, '95, '96, '97	5
5	• Coventry Climax (GB)	1959, '60, '63, '65	4
6	• Mercedes (D)	1954, '55, '98, '99	4
7	• Porsche (D)	1984, '85, '86	3
8	• Alfa Romeo (I)	1950, '51	2
	• Maserati (I)	1954, '57	2
	• Repco (AUS)	1966, '67	2

Greatest number of pole positions – drivers

1	• Ayrton Senna	(BR)	65
2	• Jim Clark	(GB)	33
	• Alain Prost	(F)	33
4	• Nigel Mansell	(GB)	32
5	• Juan Manuel Fangio	(ARG)	28
6	• Niki Lauda	(A)	24
	• Nelson Piquet	(BR)	24
8	• Michael Schumacher	(D)	22
9	• Damon Hill	(GB)	20
10	• Mario Andretti	.(US)	18

Greatest number of pole positions – teams

1	• Ferrari	(I)	126
2	• Williams	(GB)	108
3	• Lotus	(GB)	107
4	• McLaren	(GB)	104
5	• Brabham	(GB)	39
6	• Renault	(F)	31
7	• Benetton	(GB)	16
8	• Tyrrell	(GB)	14
9	• Alfa Romeo	(I)	12
10	• BRM	(GB)	11

Greatest number of pole positions – engines

1	• Ford	(GB)	139
2	• Renault	(F)	135
3	• Ferrari	(I)	125
4	• Honda	(J)	75
5	• Coventry Climax	(GB)	45
6	• Mercedes	(D)	37
7	• Alfa Romeo	(I)	15
	• BMW	(D)	15
9	• BRM	(GB)	11
	• Maserati	(I)	11

Greatest number of fastest laps – drivers

1	• Alain Prost	(F)	41
2	• Michael Schumacher	(D)	38
3	• Nigel Mansell	(GB)	30
4	• Jim Clark	(GB)	28
5	• Niki Lauda	(A)	25
6	• Juan Manuel Fangio	(ARG)	23
	• Nelson Piquet	(BR)	23
8	• Gerhard Berger	(A)	21
9	• Stirling Moss	(GB)	20
10	• Ayrton Senna	(BR)	19
	• Damon Hill	(GB)	19

Greatest number of fastest laps – teams

1	• Ferrari	(I)	143
2	• Williams	(GB)	111
3	• McLaren	(GB)	91
4	• Lotus	(GB)	71
5	• Brabham	(GB)	41
6	• Benetton	(GB)	37
7	• Tyrrell	(GB)	20
8	• Renault	(F)	18
9	• Maserati	(I)	15
	• BRM	(GB)	15

Greatest number of Grand Prix participations – drivers

1	• Riccardo Patrese	(I)	256
2	• Gerhard Berger	(A)	210
3	• Andrea de Cesaris	(I)	208
4	• Nelson Piquet	(BR)	204
5	• Alain Prost	(F)	199
6	• Michele Alboreto	(I)	194
7	• Nigel Mansell	(GB)	187
8	• Graham Hill	(GB)	176
	• Jacques Laffite	(F)	176
10	• Niki Lauda	(A)	171

Greatest number of Grand Prix participations – teams

1	• Ferrari	(I)	618
2	• McLaren	(GB)	492
3	• Lotus	(GB)	490
4	• Tyrrell	(GB)	411
	• Williams	(GB)	411
6	• Brabham	(GB)	399
7	• Benetton	(GB)	381
8	• Prost (née Ligier)	(F)	366
9	• Arrows	(GB)	329
10	• March	(GB)	231

Greatest number of Grand Prix participations – engines

1	• Ferrari	(I)	619
2	• Ford	(GB)	483
3	• Renault	(F)	286
4	• Alfa Romeo	(I)	212
5	• BRM	(GB)	197
6	• Honda	(J)	186
7	• Hart	(GB)	145
8	• Matra	(F)	125
9	• Maserati	(I)	109
10	• Porsche	(D)	105

Highest points scores – drivers

1	• Alain Prost	(F)	798.5
2	• Ayrton Senna	(BR)	614
3	• Michael Schumacher	(D)	570
4	• Nelson Piquet	(BR)	485.5
5	• Nigel Mansell	(GB)	482
6	• Niki Lauda	(A)	420.5
7	• Gerhard Berger	(A)	385
8	• Jackie Stewart	(GB)	360
	• Damon Hill	(GB)	360
10	• Carlos Reutemann	(ARG)	310

NOTE *Points are net allowable scores. In some seasons, drivers and teams were only allowed to count a certain number of best results. Gross scores are shown in brackets.*

Highest points scores – teams

1	• Ferrari	(I)	2343.5
2	• McLaren	(GB)	2329.5
3	• Williams	(GB)	1982.5
4	• Lotus	(GB)	1317 (1352)
5	• Brabham	(GB)	836 (854)
6	• Benetton	(GB)	846.5
7	• Tyrrell	(GB)	617
8	• BRM	(GB)	386 (439)
9	• Prost (née Ligier)	(F)	419
10	• Cooper	(GB)	281 (333)

NOTE *Points are net allowable scores. In some seasons, drivers and teams were only allowed to count a certain number of best results. Gross scores are shown in brackets.*

Unluckiest driver

Most races led, but lost, by driver who never subsequently won a Grand Prix

Chris Amon	6
Spain '68, Belgium '68, Canada '68; Spain '69; Italy '71; France '72	

The 1999 Season

1999 Winners

• Australia
Eddie Irvine (GB) Ferrari
1 hr 35 mins 01.659 secs
• Austria
Eddie Irvine (GB) Ferrari
1 hr 28 mins 12.438 secs
• Belgium
David Coulthard (GB) McLaren-Mercedes
1 hr 25 mins 43.057 secs
• Brazil
Mika Hakkinen (Fin) McLaren
1 hr 36 mins 03.785 secs
• Canada
Mika Hakkinen (Fin) McLaren
1 hr 41 mins 35.727 secs
• Europe
Johnny Herbert (GB) Stewart-Ford
1 hr 41 mins 54.314 secs
• France
Heinz-Harald Frentzen (Ger) Jordan-Mugen
Honda
1 hr 58 mins 24.343 secs
• Germany
Eddie Irvine (GB) Ferrari
1 hr 21 mins 58.594 secs
• Great Britain
David Coulthard (GB) McLaren
1 hr 32 mins 30.144 secs
• Hungary
Mika Hakkinen (Fin) McLaren-Mercedes
1 hr 46 mins 23.536 secs
• Italy
Heinz-Harald Frentzen (Ger) Jordan
1 hr 17 mins 2.923 secs
• Japan
Mika Hakkinen (Fin) McLaren
1 hr 31 mins 18.785 secs
• Malaysia
Eddie Irvine (GB) Ferrari
1 hr 36 mins 38.494 secs
• Monaco
Michael Schumacher (Ger) Ferrari
1 hr 49 mins 31.812 secs
• San Marino
Michael Schumacher (Ger) Ferrari
1 hr 33 mins 44.792 secs
• Spain
Mika Hakkinen (Fin) McLaren
1 hr 34 mins 13.665 secs

Accidents in 1999

• February: Johnny Herbert escaped unscathed from a crash in Barcelona. After completing 15 laps without incident, Herbert's car veered to the left and struck the wall at 200 mph.
• March: Luca Badoer was injured at Ferrari's private track, Fiorano, while testing for Minardi. After being rushed to hospital, Badoer underwent hand surgery.
• April: Ricardo Zonta was injured during the Brazilian Grand Prix. Initial media reports claimed the Brazilian had broken his foot, but doctors later confirmed there were no fractures only a badly cut leg.
• July: Michael Schumacher broke his right leg in a spectacular 100-mph crash at Silverstone. He recuperated at his home in Switzerland vowing to return to racing as soon as possible.
• August: Jacques Villeneuve and Ricardo Zonta were both injured at Eau Rouge, during the Belgian Grand Prix qualifying races, within a day of one another. Villeneuve hit the crash barrier at 180 mph and rolled his car; Zonta miraculously walked unaided from his trashed vehicle – neither were seriously injured.

The End of the Road for Hill

In June 1999, Damon Hill announced his intention to retire at the end of the season. During a career that spanned seven seasons Hill drove for Williams, Arrows and Jordan. He won 22 Grands Prix and claimed the World Championship title in 1996.

Drivers Debuting in 2000

• Jenson Button (Williams)
• Nick Heidfield (Prost)
• Gaston Mazzacane (Minardi)

2000 Teams

• Arrows
Drivers = Pedro de la Rosa & Jos Verstappen
Car = Arrows Supertec A21
Engine = Engine Supertec FB02
Tyres = Bridgestone

• BAR
Drivers = Jacques Villeneuve & Ricardo Zonta
Test Driver: Darren Manning
Car = BAR Honda 002
Engine = V10 RA000E
Tyres = Bridgestone

• Benetton
Drivers = Giancarlo Fisichello & Alexander Wurz
Car = Benetton Playlife B200
Engine = Playlife FB02
Tyres = Bridgestone

• Ferrari
Drivers = Michael Schumacher & Rubens Barrichello
Car = Ferrari F1-2000
Engine = Ferrari 049 V10
Tyres = Bridgestone

• Jaguar
Drivers = Eddie Irvine & Johnny Herbert
Car = Jaguar R1
Engine = Ford Zetec-R V10
Tyres = Bridgestone

• Jordan
Drivers = Jarno Trulli & Heinz-Harald Frentzen
Car = EJ10
Engine = Mugen-Honda MF301HE V10
Tyres = Bridgestone

• McLaren
Drivers = Mika Hakkinen & David Coulthard
Car = McLaren MP4-15
Engine = Mercedes F0110J V10
Tyres = Bridgestone

• Minardi
Drivers = Marc Gene & Gaston Mazzacane
Car = Minardi-M02
Engine = Ford Zetec-R V10
Tyres = Bridgestone

• Prost
Drivers = Jean Alesi & Nick Heidfeld
Test Driver = Stéphane Sarrazin
Car = Prost Peugeot AP03
Engine = Peugeot A20 V10
Tyres = Bridgestone

• Sauber
Drivers = Pedro Diniz & Mika Salo
Car = Sauber C19
Engine = Petronas V10-SPE 04A
Tyres = Bridgestone

• Williams
Drivers = Jenson Button & Ralf Schumacher
Car = Williams FW22
Engine = BMW V10
Tyres = Bridgestone

Index